WHAT WENT WRONG?

To all those who are struggling
to keep faith with the
labour movement

WHAT WENT WRONG?

Why Hasn't Having More
Made People Happier?

by

JEREMY SEABROOK

With a foreword by
Studs Terkel

Pantheon Books
New York

Library of Congress Cataloging in Publication Data

Seabrook, Jeremy, 1939–
    What went wrong?

    1. Great Britain—Social conditions—1945–
2. Great Britain—Economic conditions—1945–
3. Social problems. 4. Cost and standard of
living—Great Britain.   I. Title.
HN390.S38 1978   309.1'42'085   78-20424
ISBN 0-394-50598-0
ISBN 0-394-73773-3 pbk.

CONTENTS

Foreword by Studs Terkel   5

Preface   9

PROLOGUE: 'My grandfather was a craftsman...'   11

Part One: THE EXPERIENCE OF OLDER PEOPLE
  1 'Jessie Stevens is eighty-four'   17
  2 'Wigan is a place...'   27
  3 'On a warm October afternoon in Somerset...'   42
  4 'The Rhondda is part of the folklore...'   50
  5 'Alfred Hedley, sixty-three...'   63

Part Two: PEOPLE UNDER SIEGE
  1 'Wherever people meet by chance...'   71
  2 'On the edge of the Black Country, Walsall...'   77
  3 'The effect of growing up in our world...'   95
  4 'Steve Wilson is seventeen'   106
  5 'Parts of Bradford look...'   115

Part Three: CITIES, OLD AND NEW
  1 Nottingham   129
  2 Blackburn   153
  3 Coventry   167
  4 London and Beyond   201

Part Four: WHAT CAN STILL BE DONE
  1 'A Comprehensive school in a northern city...'   243
  2 'The Combine Committee at Lucas Aerospace...'   246
  3 'In recent years, much of the dissent...'   254
  4 'A generation of people who came from the working
    class...'   260
  5 'Some radical dissenting groups...'   264

EPILOGUE: Going Home   271

FOREWORD

THIS BOOK IS, ostensibly, a reflection on the trauma of the English working class. It is more than that. It offers a mirror image of American working people: their hurts, hidden and revealed; their bewilderment and bitterness; their lost vision and a hope of reclaiming it, distant though that be. The parallel is astonishing.

Jeremy Seabrook, who like his grandfather before him worked with leather, has produced a classic, as lasting as a hand-made shoe. It is not an ersatz piece of material, manufactured out of statistics and opinion polls. It is the genuine article, conceived out of familial conversations with survivors of hard times and with their children of no such felt experience.

His companions, old people in new towns and young people in old towns, tell us, with simple eloquence, of a society that has diminished poverty and, along with it, the vision of a better place. Bread without any semblance of roses. 'Nobody can imagine what a better life would be like,' he observes, 'because we're always told this is the best possible life.' If this isn't true-bloodedly American, what is?

Seabrook's people are neither nostalgic nor romantic. In no instance do they long for 'the good old days.' They are no strangers to the degrading experience of poverty and the brutish toll of long hours in the mines and mills. Lost values are what it's all about; a broken sense of belonging; an abandoned sense of place; a mutilated sense of self.

There is a flailing about and a blind striking out at targets closest at hand. Thus, the young English working man becomes more and more furious at the blacks 'who are getting everything.' Writes Seabrook: 'As the marketplace renders redundant the old values of family and neighbourhood, there is nothing left but the appalling nudity of one's whiteness. We have been robbed of everything else.' Hard-working parents are bewildered as their seventeen-year-old son joins the mercenaries in Rhodesia, not so much out of racism as for something interesting to do. Where have we gone wrong? they ask of nobody in particular. We gave him everything.

It is as though their plaint were lifted out of a song by the Beatles.

In the loss of sense of personal worth, there is a transmutation of human gold into dross. A foundry shop steward put it to Seabrook: 'There has been a softening up of working people as far as their own selves are concerned; a hardening up towards others.' On this side of the Atlantic, among intellectuals, it is called New Conservatism. English working people are much less given to euphemism. 'I'm all right, Jack' is their succinct way of putting it.

The same man has more to say of himself and his fellows: 'The people don't realize what their power is. They're always being told how powerless they are . . . They've been told it so long, they believe it . . . They've lost the means of communicating with each other. It's as if they had their ears blocked and their tongues cut out. We don't know what to say to each other any more.'

Rarely has any contemporary observer so caught the deeply felt human needs that cannot be served by the marketplace. On this side of the waters, too, we are told — how many times a day? — via television commercials that things can offer us what people no longer can. We are, like a punch-drunk heavyweight, reduced to grudging obeisance, muscle-bound to the home screen and spirit-bound to the shoddy things we buy but do not create. Occasionally, we awaken to a scream in the night.

At a shopping centre in Nottingham, Seabrook's compassionate eye captures a stunning metaphor for our society as well as for his:

Saturday morning in the Victoria Centre. A crowd gathers where a woman's voice is heard above the subdued murmur of the people shopping. She is crying. This already sounds incongruous; as though someone were laughing in church. A man is with her, coaxing and anxious. They are perhaps in their early forties. He wears a raincoat and grey flannels; her face is distraught and pained; beneath her eyes there are dark bruised-looking patches. The sound of their conflict is magnified by the hush of the shopping area. 'Come on duck,' he says to her, 'you've got your new shoes.' Her cries become louder; a sustained howl. Some security men appear, and look

at her. The crowd keeps its distance. The man is embarrassed.
He explains to those people nearest to him, as though he
owed them an account of the disturbance, 'She's not well.'
He turns back to her, and tries to urge her away. 'Come on,
we're going home now, we'll have us dinners. We got your
nice new shoes.' His voice is protective and reassuring. She is
wearing a pair of high-heeled cork and plastic sandals, bright
yellow and at odds with the shabbiness of the rest of her dress:
they gleam in the subdued shadowless light. The howl rises
higher; a desolate cry of pain. 'She's been in hospital,' he explains to the crowd, as though to dissociate himself from any
accusation of ill treatment. Her cries echo round the precinct,
but she refuses to move. The girls serving in the open-fronted
boutiques come to the edge of their stage; the older women
with blue rinses and mortuary chapel smiles. A moment of
deep unease. Perhaps we recognize that her cry is not gratuitous. It is the cry of a human being in the process of mutilation to fit a pair of plastic sandals.

STUDS TERKEL

PREFACE

IN THIS BOOK I have tried to explore a feeling of pain and resentment which remains in working-class communities, in spite of the considerable material improvements of the past thirty years or so. Some things elude even the most careful research, the most vigilant scrutiny of social scientists, those who have looked at working-class life over the years, redefining poverty, assessing deprivation, measuring the effects of attempts at redistribution of wealth. When it comes to the working class, the need to avoid value judgments in social science seems to join somehow with an uncritical reverence on the Left for the working class; with the result that nobody feels able to say anything of substance at all. What has been lacking is any attempt to evaluate the improvements which welfare capitalism has bestowed on the working class: an obsessive anxiety about being objective means that a moral dimension has been absent from descriptions of working-class life, as well as an account of what it actually feels like to live in those gutted and transformed industrial towns and cities.

I wanted to report on the persisting sense of bitterness and disappointment, which are denied any real outlet but the belief that it can all be cured only by more money. Through the paradox of great material improvement combined with a sense of the desolation of ruined communities and broken human associations, certain questions define themselves. How far have the early ideals of the labour movement been realized beyond the dreams of those who struggled for them; and how far is what has been achieved a caricature, a subtle deformation of them? How far has working-class identity been eroded; does it matter; and what is to take its place? Are what an individual does and where he is born simply incidental details of biography, or are they crucial components of identity? How far do the altered, and in many cases dwindling, employment structures of the old working-class towns and cities affect people's sense of belonging?

For the most part, in preparing this book I have spent time in places: cities, streets, places where people work and live. There is nothing like simply being in places, rather than visiting them, talking to people in the diminishing territory of public contact – pubs and bus queues, supermarkets and streets. The area I have been to is not exhaustive, geographically or socially, but it does cover a fairly wide range of working-class communities: older industrial areas like Rhondda and Wigan, newer industrial cities like Coventry, the new towns of Milton Keynes and Northampton, as well as inner city areas such as Hackney in London, Bradford and Nottingham.

The structure of the book reflects this approach: essentially, I talked to some of the oldest surviving members of the labour movement about the hopes and ideals they cherished, and then compared what they say with the way we live now.

Because I started off from the sense of hurt, the bewilderment and the violence in working-class areas, I have tended to talk to those who are critical of what has happened in these communities; but at the same time I have tried to remain aware that it is a wider feeling that I am attempting to reach: a sense that something has gone wrong, promises have been spoiled, improvements soured. I have sought a flow of feeling that goes deeper than simple opinions, and seldom expresses itself, at least for the present, in electoral terms. For this reason I have had little recourse to tape-recorders. I prefer to report what people say as a result of conversation, a shared meeting, rather than an interview.

In some ways, what emerges from this book is all glaringly obvious; but much of it has become the subject of curious taboos and reticences in recent years: I have tried to articulate a feeling of what it is like to live in working-class areas in this last quarter of the twentieth century.

I am grateful to all those people who showed me much kindness and hospitality, and shared their experience with me. This book is for them, and for all those who have worked and continued to work for real, and not illusory improvements in the way we live.

LONDON   J. S.
MAY 1978

PROLOGUE

MY GRANDFATHER WAS a craftsman, a hand-sewer of shoes with awl and thread. During his early years as a skilled man he earned a living wage; but as his family grew and trade varied, his skill failed to provide enough to feed and shelter them. Later, his fingers became arthritic; he did more casual and unskilled work. He drank, and his family sank deeper into poverty.

All his children started their working life in boot-and-shoe factories. They became rivetters, lasters, closers, eyeletters; mostly skilled or semi-skilled work. But during their lifetime they became increasingly displaced, not only by the spread of mechanization, but by imports of cheaper and inferior products; and of my grandfather's twelve children, only three finished their working life as boot-and-shoe operatives.

My grandmother used to sing:

> Dimes and dollars, dollars and dimes,
> Don't be poor, it's the worst of crimes.
> You can be rogue or knave or fool,
> But don't be poor, it's against the rule.

She recognized that they were held responsible for their poverty, and that this responsibility was falsely attributed. She felt an intense resentment that her husband's skills, laboriously acquired, could not lift them above a level of bare subsistence.

When we were poor, we knew it wasn't our fault. But what shall we say, two generations later, in the face of our apparent plenty? That we are responsible for that? That we deserve it after so many years denied the things we needed to live? Is it to be considered a reward for past privations, or would my grandmother sing now of an oppression even in our abundance?

This abundance is seen as something absolute, like life itself, self-evidently desirable; and as such, is a sacred taboo. But what if it has been achieved in a way that is corrupting and damaging to our human associations and relationships? Under the pretext of being released from a rigid and oppressive system of work we have also been robbed of our skills and the satisfaction in what we did. When those in the boot-and-shoe industry could know which tannery a piece of leather came from simply by smelling it; when they could inspect leather and at once know the use for bright morocco, Levant morocco, bronze kid, glacé kid, russet grain, wax calf, satin calf; when they could tell instantly whether it had been damaged by goad pricks on draught animals or parasites or faults from flaying; when they visited the houses of the rich with their lasts to do bespoke work, they did not despise the work they did, nor the product that they created. They were justly proud of the skills expended each day, even though they knew they were not to be adequately rewarded for them.

Most of us now do not want for basic comforts; and this has been achieved, not for the most part by exercising our skills, but by forfeiting them. Many of us resent the work we do now. We grudge the use of our time, and are often indifferent to the things we make or the services we provide. We feel bored and functionless. We see work seldom as something worthwhile in itself but as a means to something else; it is an unhappy intrusion into the real business of our lives. We measure ourselves not by what we do, but by what we can acquire. Our function is no longer a primary determinant of our identity.

The experience of my family is paralleled by that of millions of others, in all industrial communities, whether based on textiles or mining or metal, manufacture or agriculture.

Because the working class is still haunted by memories of degrading work conditions and domestic poverty, anything that mitigates these things must represent an improvement on the past. That past has been fixed, not only by the experience of our old people, but, in order that it shall be kept constantly before us, also by the media, writers, trades unionists: the past is a fixed tableau, against which our present alternative can be seen only as better. But one of the questions this book asks is whether capitalism, which brought to so many of us poverty, suffering and degradation, can now really bring its promise of happiness, satisfaction and fulfilment; or whether there are not perhaps hidden factors, as damaging to our humanity, as brutalizing as poverty once was. How far has the antique secular dream of abolishing poverty, how has the better life striven for by the socialist and trade union pioneers anything to do with the way we live now?

Despite spectacular material improvements there persist in working-class communities a malaise, an anger, a bitterness; and it is these that I have tried to locate. Clearly, there is nothing wrong with material sufficiency; only the kind of materialism that capital has achieved hurts. Not in its most immediate feature, as poverty (which is absence) does, but in some of its consequences. We are robbed of our skills, and instead of being offered the opportunity to acquire new ones, we are invited to define ourselves by what we can buy rather than by what we can create. Work is to be thought of as a means of gaining access to all the things that capitalism provides – the extended display of perfection, beauty and wholeness in the vast temples of commodities which dominate every town and city in the country. But it is in these things, which are supposed to be our consolations for our fundamental loss of function, that the new mechanisms of social control lie. The competition for all this plenitude and beauty leads to great cruelty; and everywhere the talk is of violence, loneliness, family breakdown, mental illness, racism, the spoiling of human relationships. Everything speaks, not of the boundless joy that should have come with the release from the old poverty, but of great human pain. The anger, frustration and discord are not seen as being part of the material improvements, which are sacrosanct. Things are beyond blame; but people are not, all sorts of people: spongers, scroungers, immigrants, Asians, thugs, vandals, muggers, child-molesters, extremists, wreckers, even trade unionists. Our improvements have been achieved on the terms of capitalism, and the profit still has to come from somewhere. Formerly it was squeezed out of our labour; now, in addition, it is squeezed from the damage done to our human relationships.

This book is an attempt to describe the feeling of that pain in working-class life, in the wake of all the much-monitored changes. The rather threadbare view that all we need is more, much more of all we have now to eliminate our problems, seems pitifully inadequate to account for the increased brutality and cruelty that have flowed from the assault on working-class identity. The removal of traditional communal values leads to a search for a replacement, even in the face of the most relentless pressure to individualism; and when class determinants have apparently been weakened, what else remains but the discovery of an identity of race?

What I am nowhere saying is that materialism in itself is
harmful – only when it is allied to an exploitative and
dehumanizing scheme of values, as has happened with us. I am
not saying that poverty is more virtuous than plenty or that a
return to it would be necessary or desirable. But there are vast
areas of human need untouched by the economics of the
market-place: you don't have to look as far as the thousands of
old people who die each year of hypothermia, or those who are
allowed to die for want of a kidney machine: everywhere people
express the same pain of their broken sense of belonging. The
chance to abolish poverty, one of the great scourges of mankind,
should have given rise to a spontaneous and sustained cry of joy;
but instead, there is nothing but discord and violence, ruined
human relationships, the contamination, not only of work, but
of neighbourhood, kinship and comradeliness, division
between the generations, distrust within families. The price is
too high: humanity is not liberated, but subordinated by this
capitalist plenty, which is sold to us as though it were life itself. It
is joyless and destructive: it cannot be without significance that
when you talk to the old about their poverty, the great
consolation in all that suffering was the quality of human
relationships; now that things have been so well perfected, the
only thing wrong is seen to be people. That is not a gain for
humanity.

Part One

THE EXPERIENCE OF OLDER PEOPLE

JESSIE STEVENS IS eighty-four. Her terraced house in Bristol is plain and unencumbered, reflecting not only her traditionally frugal life-style, but the fact that for the past three years she has been blind. Her voice is deep and rich; trained at street corners, in Mechanics' Institutes and church halls, it is a voice for oratory, for passion and persuasion.

'My father was one of a family of sixteen, employed mainly in the herring-fishing industry. He told us how he used to go down to the quay at dawn, and they could get free herrings, as many as they could string on their fingers for nothing. He was born in 1864 and was eight when he left school. As a young man he left Wick, travelled to London by boat from Grangemouth – journey of thirty-six hours – and he eventually became a tailor, a craftsman. He embroidered waistcoats for the then Prince of Wales, later Edward VII. When he married, he returned to Scotland, and finally settled in Glasgow, where I grew up.

'As a child he used to talk to me about the Highland clearances. Some of his family had come back from the Crimea to find their land cleared and their kinfolk dispersed. The men came back and found they had no crofts, no family, nobody to greet them, and no one to tell them where they'd gone to. Some of them had perhaps emigrated, gone to Canada, and many of them never did find their relatives again. They found sheep where their crofts had been.

'My father was staunchly republican and an early member of the Independent Labour Party. He always demonstrated his socialism to us practically. Once a tramp came to the door while we were having our Sunday dinner. He brought him in and sat him down, got a clean plate and took something off each of our plates; and when he went he gave him a penny towards a night's lodging. And when he'd gone, he said to us, "Now you know what I mean when I say, One cannot help many, but many can help one." It was from him I got my feeling for humanity. His example taught me that human suffering is wide and deep enough to give us all a purpose in life if we lack one.

'I went to the Socialist Sunday School. We were taught the

Ten Socialist Commandments. I can remember a few of them: "Honour all men, and bow down to none"; "Love learning, which is the food of the mind, and be as grateful to your teachers as to your parents". They all emphasized the value of man for himself, not his rank or position.

'My mother was the daughter of a farm labourer, and she was in service in London when she met my father. She used to say, "You know, Jessie, the first time I saw your father, I said Oh, that's the man for me." He always used to pass her as she was scrubbing the doorstep, and he always raised his hat to her in homage to the person behind the servitude. One day she was in Hyde Park, listening to a meeting of domestic servants airing their grievances, and he came up and introduced himself. And from then on there was no doubt in the minds of either of them.

'They came back to Glasgow. There was always plenty of work, quality work, for tailors; but quite often, if the employers found out you were a socialist or a member of a trade union, you were out on your neck. Although we always lived decently, there were some terrible tenements in Glasgow. You'd see figures chalked on the doorpost, $3\frac{1}{2}$ or $4\frac{1}{2}$, the half being a child; and this was the number of people who were authorized to be living in one of these tenements at a time. A policeman could knock on the door at any time to make sure you weren't breaking the regulations. You'd go in there and find the sole furniture was an onion box and a table, sacks on the floor for bedding, filled with straw. That has remained with me all my life, and confirmed me in what my dad stood for.

'We became poorer with an increasing family. My brother and I used to go to the West End of Glasgow, where all the high-class provision merchants were. If you were first in the queue, you could get a pillowslip filled with bread and buns, because they never sold stale stuff to their high-class customers you see. But you had to be there at four o'clock in the morning to take your place. My dad always got up and gave us a cup of tea before we went out. However early we got there, we were never the first, there were some boys from an Irish family who always beat us – they used to arrive at three o'clock. At six-thirty, when the shop opened, you'd get the pillowslip full of bread from the previous day's baking, what they would call stale buns and cakes, although they were only a day old. All for 3d. . . . And Cooper's, the grocers. I'd go there after school: if you were lucky, they used to cut all the first slices off the bacon before they cut any for their customers. And that accumulated over the day, and we could get as much as three-quarters of a pound of bacon for a few coppers. It was the same with the fishmonger – there was no proper refrigeration, only blocks of ice, and they always sold off the fish the same day; so if you went there at six o'clock, they were getting rid of what was left on the slab. You had to know the right time to be in each place. I'd get a basket full of fish for 3d, slices of salmon among it. And the fruiterers would never sell chipped apples or pears or specked oranges, so all that came our way. We really did well.

'Oh I loved school and I loved my teachers. One of them used to say to me "Oh my dear, you've such lovely eyes." Well she ought to see me now. In those days I had nice dark eyes and I was full of energy. But my father was the biggest influence on me. Very often he'd take the children out to let Mother get on with her work. People used to think a man who did things like that must be a bit of a Jessie, but he was proud of us, and always introduced us to anybody he met. He dressed very smartly, and made frocks for us out of pretty well nothing. We never went looking ragged anywhere, in spite of our poverty. He used to say "Always keep your shoe-heels well mended, don't show any frayed cuffs or collars. Don't ever plead poverty." Very proud. That was the legacy he left me, to take pride, to be resourceful.

'I was training to be a teacher. I was doing pupil-teaching. You're actually doing the work by practising at the same time as learning, very good training. I would have loved to be a teacher, but I never did because Father fell out of work. I was the eldest, I could see it was no good to him if I stayed on being a schoolteacher. And if you went into a factory you'd only get 2/6 a week. I said to Mother, "Oh I must go and get some work in domestic service, because at least the money would be clear, it could all go straight home." When I told my dad, he said, "I don't want you to do that, lass," and he actually had tears in his eyes. But I went to my Sunday School teacher and she got me placed. She bought me my uniform. You had to have a black dress, full length, down to your heels, a pair of house shoes, two morning aprons, at least two collars, three or four caps, two pairs of cuffs, and two muslin aprons for afternoon wear and

serving at table. They paid me better than average. The wage was
10/- a week. I insisted that I wouldn't work for less than 16/- a
week; and I got it.

'Conditions were terrible for domestic servants then. They
used to take girls from the industrial schools and reformatories
and orphanages. Sometimes they didn't give them any money at
all, and they were treated like little slaves. I'd not been working
long when a girl wrote a letter to the *Glasgow Herald* complaining
about the conditions of employment in service, and this brought
a lot of replies. So I arranged for a meeting to be held in the
Christian Institute, and invited all those interested in forming a
union. Not only was the hall packed, but they were out in the
corridors as well. Of course a lot of employers were there too,
the mistresses, and they heckled me hot and strong. They said we
should recognize that we had superiors and should obey them
and be guided by them and all that sort of nonsense. I replied as
politely as I could that we had rights too, and I asked them if
they thought it was right to keep girls in every night of the week,
if it was right to pay a pitiful wage and then take most of it back
to pay for the uniforms.

'Well, a hundred girls joined the union that night. I don't
know what they thought of me, a girl of sixteen and a half, full of
life, wanting to get things done. When my employer discovered I
was forming a union, she called me to her and said, "You're
only creating trouble for the girls and their mistresses. We can't
have you working here." She was the wife of a consultant. Her
daughter was a poetess. Not a very good one. She said, "People
would wonder what we were doing if we continued to employ
you." I said, "Is my work not satisfactory?" I knew it was.
Anyway, I stayed on for a bit. I could never find enough time to
do all the things I wanted to. I wanted to study. I used to buy
candles so I could do my reading after I went to bed, because
they used to turn off the gas at ten o'clock. I was in a cold
basement room, stone floor, a bed, chest of drawers and a
mirror. We had a hard fight, but we got what we asked for for
our members: two hours off every day, half day every Sunday if
you were on your own, a proper afternoon once a week and
uniform supplied. Very modest demands they seem now. We
even got into the Earl of Mar's place and recruited all the girls
there.

'I had a good singing voice. As well as all this I won a talent competition at the Metropole Theatre in Glasgow when I was sixteen. I was applauded and encored. The same day I was offered a fifty-three-week engagement with Moss Empires. Of course my father wouldn't let me. He said I was too young to go off alone. I won't say I regret not having had a stage career. I did fill theatres with my voice anyway; only it was for speaking. A lot of people gave up careers for the labour movement in those days. What a contrast now: there are people who actually make a career out of the movement.

'I went to my first socialist meeting when I was five years old: I went to hear Ramsay MacDonald. He should have been a poet rather than a politician. I heard Jimmy Maxton, oh he was full of passion. So many of them were. People made such sacrifices for what they believed in. I've been speaking myself when the snow was coming down on the street corners and you've longed for the crowd to go away, but they wouldn't. We had something to say and I loved it. I spent my holidays working for the ILP. I could raise money from a crowd just by talking. In fact a Salvation Army captain once said he wished I'd join them – I was known as the champion beggar.

'I joined the ILP at sixteen. At the same time they had formed a branch of the Women's Social and Political Union, the suffrage movement, in Glasgow, and of course I joined that with great enthusiasm. They asked me if I was interested in the more militant side. I didn't think I could, being in service. They said, "Well, you can drop these things in pillar boxes" (bottles of acid). And so it was that I used to walk down the street in my servant's uniform at the appointed time, I'd take the cork from the bottle and put it in the pillar box, and then after a time it would begin to smoulder and burn. I'd walk demurely back to my place of employment and take a peep out of the basement window to see what was happening. They'd never suspect a domestic servant of doing anything so outrageous. Then of course they smashed windows – I never did that. They always went for property though, never never to hurt people.

'The family I was working with went down to the coast in summer, and we had more time off. Mary was the name of the other maid; and we used to go out dancing on the pier. You met fellows, obviously. There was this Irishman, and he took a fancy to Mary, and they chummed up together, and they fell for each other. Well, he was only up there working for a few weeks, and

the time came for him to go back to Glasgow. The night before
he went he came to me and said, "Jessie, I'd like you to do
something for me. I've got to go home, but I'd like to write
letters to Mary. I know you've had a good education and you
speak well. Could you draft me three letters?" That was one for
each week till we were due to go back to Glasgow. I says, "Do
you want some lovey-dovey stuff in it?" He said, "I know you
read a lot of books, put some of that in it if you can." So I wrote
these letters and gave them to him. And after a few days Mary
came to me and her eyes were shining. She said, "Oh, I've had
such a lovely letter from Michael. Would you like to see it?" I
said, "Oh no, that's private to you." She said, "Well, I'd like you
to see it, because I want you to help me to answer it." So that was
my next job. I wrote all the letters and answered them, and of
course neither of them ever knew I'd helped the other. At the
bottom of the third letter Michael had asked her to marry him,
and of course I had to answer that as well. They did marry and
were very happy.

'I changed my place then. I went to be table-maid; and one of
my jobs there was to make delicate pats of butter for the family
table. Now they served the servants with a cheap margarine
which they called "servants' butter", trying to disguise the fact
that it was really horrible. So one night, when they had
important guests, I said to the other servants, "I'm going to
make pats of butter for their table from servants' butter." "Oh,"
they said, "don't do that." But it was robbing us of our wages.
We were supposed to have board and lodging as a supplement
to the pittance we were paid; we were supposed to have proper
food, not offal. Anyway, I came back downstairs, and
immediately the bell rang. I went up. "What's this in the butter
dish? It tastes dreadful." I said, "I'm sure it does. That's what
we eat downstairs. I thought you'd like to know what it tasted
like." I never got the sack; and after that we had the same butter
as they did. I think they quite liked me. The mistress used to have
an At Home afternoon once a week, and I served tea. One day as
I took the tea in, they started talking in French. They were
talking about me, something not uncomplimentary. Well, I'd
always been rather good at French and I understood. I said to
the mistress, "I can understand what you're saying, I do speak
French." You should have seen their faces. But she turned to me
very graciously and said, "Thank you, Jessie."

'When I was a girl of twelve I remember one night I was selling the *Labour Woman* outside St Andrew's Hall, and Keir Hardie was speaking. When he came out, he saw me selling the paper and he said, "That's right, my lassie, you'll be a credit to the movement yet." I was so proud; I could hardly wait to get home to tell my dad he'd actually spoken to me. Eventually I worked for the ILP. We went on different missions each week round the country. Every meeting would be crowded, and when we spoke, we spoke to make converts. The speakers were dedicated. Now they speak as though they were lecturing a class. You must show that you care. Whenever I've raised this issue in recent years, they've said, "Oh well, people are more educated now, you can't talk to them like you used to." But that can't be the reason. I've had even university audiences on their feet. You had that rapport with the audience. I loved the heckling, it created a wonderful atmosphere. I still sometimes hear my jokes from fifty years ago on the radio today. I remember at Cambridge once, there were some students determined to wreck the meeting. The minute I stood up, somebody shouted out, "Why aren't you at home minding the baby?" I shouted back, "Because you're here." I loved turning the repartee against them. In Sheffield there was one man who was getting more and more incensed. In the end he stood up and said, "If you were my wife I'd poison you." I said, "If I were your wife I'd take it."* Once at a meeting in Hyde Park a man said contemptuously, "Why do you Scots always roll your r's?" I said, "I'll get somebody to come down and kick yours in a minute."

'I worked for the Women's Social and Political Union in London and Glasgow. I got 30 bob a week – it cost me that for digs. I had to go and have meetings and make a collection to pay for my lodgings. I'd make clothes out of nothing – a remnant of voile for 6d would make a Magyar blouse. You had to have a lot of different skills, turn your hand to anything. I think one reason why there aren't people like me now is that technology does everything for people. It robs them of their skill and inventiveness. Something is lost.

'There was once a huge meeting that we'd arranged in St Andrew's Hall in Glasgow. Mrs Pankhurst was booked to be the main speaker. Well, that was illegal, because at the time she was

* Some of these stories are folklore. This exchange is also attributed to Winston Churchill and Lady Astor.

officially still serving a jail sentence; she was out under what came to be called the Cat and Mouse Act, you know, the hunger strikers, when for some reason or other they couldn't forcibly feed them, they had to let them out or risk them dying. They didn't want that, obviously. They released Mrs Pankhurst for a month at a time, then when she'd recovered some of her strength take her back to jail. Well, the authorities couldn't allow her to go and speak at meetings. The police had men posted all over to prevent her going in; they were even on the roof of the building, all round outside as well as inside, plain-clothes men as well as those in uniform. Well, at seven o'clock the hall was packed. We had decorated the platform with a lot of flower pots and bunting beneath which we'd concealed a lot of barbed wire. At seven o'clock the chairman rose. She said, "Now we are going to have a real treat. We are going to hear our beloved and respected leader, Mrs Emmeline Pankhurst." And she called "Mrs Pankhurst". And Mrs Pankhurst came slowly from the back of the platform, and she started to speak. She didn't get many words out before all these policemen were rushing on to the platform, because this was shameful as far as they were concerned, that she should appear when they'd been trying to keep her out. So there were flower pots flying, and they were catching hold of the barbed wire and getting their hands scratched, and one woman had a pistol with blank shots which she was firing everywhere. Of course she was arrested. But what puzzled everybody was, however did that woman get in there with all those dozens of police guarding the building? The secret was that she'd come in a Corporation laundry basket. They'd brought the linen for some function or other. She was in the hamper with the clean linen, and she'd been there all the afternoon.

'There was once a WSPU delegation of working women going to lobby MPs at the House of Commons. I was one of the twelve delegates from Glasgow; I was seventeen at the time. We were given accommodation in the house of a Mrs Hawkins in one of the nicer parts of London. It turned out that her husband was Chief Superintendent Detective Hawkins, one of the Big Five in London. He said, "Now be careful, I can't bail you out if you get arrested." There was to be a peaceful procession of working women over Westminster Bridge to the House of Commons. As we went past, there were rows of policemen, and behind them all these thugs who'd been incited by the yellow press, the *Daily Mail* and *Daily Express*; and as we passed by, these brutes came and started mauling us, tearing our clothes and punching us; and the police just stood by. A lot of us got badly mauled, I had hair pulled out by the handful.

'The suffrage movement was militant, but we never raised a hand to harm one man or woman. We could defend ourselves, mind. A lot of us learned ju-jitsu. I had a friend in Liverpool who was caught in some militant act or other. She was only small, five foot nothing, and she was arrested by this policeman who was over six foot. Well, she threw him; she laid him flat on his back. When it came to court, the magistrate didn't believe it. He needed a demonstration. They cleared a place in the centre of the courtroom, and the policeman was fetched in, and she was told to do what she had done. So she did it again. She got a month in jail.

'The old ILP finally ceased to exist only about three years ago. That was a sad day. It gave us substance and background in our fight. I think a lot of people now prefer slogans to doing hard work. We worked, we went on marches, we knocked on doors, we spoke on street corners. We'd get a hundred thousand people marching on May Day in Glasgow. Mind you, we've some good things today. The women's movement is a delight to me.

'My work has been my life. I still carry on. For twenty years I've been on the Appeals Tribunal for Social Security, and when I went blind I wrote a letter of resignation. The regional controller rang me up and said, "Miss Stevens, do you really want to resign from the panel?" I said, "Well, you know why, don't you?" He said, "Oh, I know your reasons, but if you want to carry on, we'd be very pleased." So I still do that. I'm on the district committee of the Co-op. I'm on the area council of my union, APEX, I'm one of the three general trustees nationally. I have the Labour Women's Section here once a week. I'm a trustee for the hostel for battered wives in Bristol. I shall carry on as long as I can. Only I sometimes wish there was some of the generosity, the self-sacrifice there was when I was young.'

To talk with Jessie Stevens is like gazing down long clear corridors into the past. She is at the end of a tradition in which the experience of older people was still of use to those who came after: the continuity of poverty. But wherever dissent may go in future, there will be no more radicals like Jessie Stevens. The passion that animates her is that of direct experience of the Poor Law, subsistence poverty, inadequately rewarded skills; and this has been muted for later generations by the substitution of a different kind of experience, in which capitalism is seen, not as a denying and repressive force, but as offering a promise of plenitude.

For most people, the rod of iron has given way to the indulgent tit. Poverty and discipline are no longer the principal means of control; instead a growing dependency has been fostered on goods and services, which are in some measure a consolation for losses of skill, function and working-class identity. We are invited to see ourselves, not as what we do, make or create, but as what we can get, have or consume.

Not far from where Jessie Stevens lives, the church of St Mary Redcliffe still dominates the skyline; a great golden lantern of glass and stone, it is now partly marooned by the brutal swirl of a ring road. It is full of ironic comment on the city around it. It was a shrine for the merchants and sailors who made Bristol rich, but the city dock has now been turned into a marina and floating restaurant. The parish it served has been almost obliterated. The crafts and skills that went into its construction, the lierne vaulting, the gilded bosses, the ornament and carving, like those which later went into the elegant structures of the eighteenth century and into the Victorian city of docks and railways, have disappeared. And the promise of paradise, of which this church was a lasting affirmation, has been relocated in the great shopping complexes of the twentieth century, about half a mile away.

In the Broadmead shopping precinct, almost obscured by a department store of sandstone and concrete, is an inconspicuous building. It stands behind some railings: John Wesley's first chapel, built in 1739. There is a paved courtyard, and beyond, the chapel, perfectly preserved. Plain pews of red wood glow in the dark autumn afternoon, severe and upright as the backs they supported. There is an octagonal skylight, and a sky of torn indigo cloud admits a stormy and diminished day. The pulpit is raised, an unadorned panelled box framed against some eighteenth-century wooden banisters. A plain clock ticks loudly in the stillness. Everything is functional, austerely beautiful. Only the place is empty. The people are lacking, the stubbornness of Wesley's followers attacked by the mob in the 1740s, and the hope which they gave to the poor and despairing, who have forfeited even that comfort now: the shops that obscure the chapel have made all human yearning palpable, and fill men's hands and minds to the exclusion of everything else, in a more total and inescapable way than any materialist philosophy ever conceived.

These two buildings, St Mary Redcliffe and Wesley's chapel, are like monuments to the most significant things that have been denied us in the way we live now: our will to create something of worth and beauty, and our power to feel deeply about the values by which we live; things that have been sacrificed in our unquiet dependency on the flow of transient disposable goods.

2

WIGAN IS A place of ruined Victorian splendour, half-effaced reminders of poverty and clumsy refurbishing. Even the shop windows seem only two-dimensional, pasted over a more lasting décor; and if you walk through the alleys between the pubs and stores of Wallgate, there is the crumbling red mass of the nineteenth-century town. On a clear October morning after days of rain, the streets are suddenly full of a glassy radiance from the sun on steaming wet surfaces; and the ornate civic buildings, the carved gables and the cupolas of the Mining and Technical College, the pinnacles of the tower of the parish church shine red and gold like a celestial city.

There are gaps in the town — not only the rubble-filled hollows where the earth has been turned under demolished houses, but areas of semi-moor, formless fields of withered grass, tracks of hazardous land unreclaimed from vanished pits. On the Manchester Road, beyond the tripe shop where Orwell stayed in 1936, the road is flanked by empty shops advertising surgical trusses and Uncle Luke's tablets and Potter's Balm of Gilead, redundant items of self-medication for the poor. Off this road, the abbreviated terraces and derelict sites, railway sidings and glittering stretches of canal make up some of the most decayed landscape in the area, subsiding cavities in the road filled with water which make some streets almost impassable on foot, broken-down outhouses, gaping doors and windows, smashed glass and rotting wood, heaps of fallen brick. The sunshine streams through the lattice of a roof without tiles; a chapel is bricked up like a sepulchre.

In a pub – a cavernous depleted place, once full of miners – an old man sits down to eat a steak pie. The woman serving tells him that it has gone up to 19 pence, but he is deaf and can't hear. He nods at her and offers 16. He says, 'I like my pie with a bit of gravy. I look forward to it.' He wears baggy flannels and a muffler, and his eyes are crying from the windy street. His voice is plaintive, a timbre of childhood, begging to be cared for. The woman accepts his 16 pence and squeezes his hand. 'I shall have to tell him,' she says. 'It breaks my heart, but he comes in here every day.'

The boundaries of the town are not clearly defined: it meanders along a road for a few miles, incorporates some eighteenth-century farm buildings and an even earlier pub, declines into Ince where the cemetery is ('The dead from Wigan and the living from Ince, nothing to choose between them'). Parts of the town look as if they had worn out and simply been abandoned, as indeed many of the old mineworkings were. Some of them are located now by accident – a boy bird's-nesting in a disused shaft falls 1,500 feet and the body is irrecoverable. A few years ago a railway engine and some goods waggons shunting over some old workings were swallowed up in the earth. Dead sorrel and bleached grass conceal the excavations of old quarries, overflowing with water and rippled by the wind, and in this waste the new building of the Great Universal Stores appears inaccessible as a fortress. Beyond, the austere symmetry of the council estates; displays in every front window of pampas grass, dyed meadow grasses in russet and blue or a colour-flecked glass fish; and further still, the Heinz works, the largest food-processing factory in Europe, with its white boiler-suited workers coming and going like ghosts. In the grass in front of the buildings, the wet autumn has produced patches of dazzling white mushrooms, and dazzling fungus in red and biscuit colour. A Corporation bus stands in the concrete forecourt. A woman is arguing with the conductor. 'You can't get on the bus while it's on company property. The stop's up the road.' 'It's a public bus i'n't it, they don't bloody own that do they?'

Successive waves of consumer sophistication reach the town, but do not obliterate all traces of the past. Side by side with the new denim bazaar and the delicatessen, there is the shopping arcade, with its peacock-tail stained-glass window, and the Market Hall, 1877, with a fretted iron entrance arch, delicate as lace. Inside, you can still buy Invalid Toffee and specifics against croup; a stall advertises Whist and Domino Prizes and goods lent out on hire; while another offers toys made in Taiwan, a make-up and hairset model, a doll with hair that grows for you to style – the exciting way to learn hair and beauty secrets. On white enamel trays honeycomb tripe, neatsfoot and cow-heel, while the stall on the opposite side of the gangway sells Ardennes pâté and Emmental cheese.

Change here seems sour and recalcitrant. Thirty years ago there were 12,000 miners in the area; now perhaps 200 or 300 travel out to the few remaining pits. The shopping arcades, full of consolations for the convulsive changes that have occurred, fail in some obscure way to compensate. Wigan has the atmosphere of a place in which a terrible catastrophe has happened. At first, it feels like some momentous industrial accident; and in a way, perhaps that is what it was.

It was a town built on physical strength, manual labour; and a whole culture evolved around this basic fact. It still strikes as a traditional male-dominated community, although the reasons for its existence – coal and textiles – have vanished. Many women accept their subservience to their men's strength and earning power; many do not know how much their husbands earn; there are still rooms in the pubs where women, by habit if no longer by prohibition, don't go.

But suddenly, in the middle of this century, most of that force and strength became redundant; and the sense of loss is still overwhelming. I don't think I have heard the word 'virility' for a long time. I was to hear it several times in Wigan; not only in relation to the miners themselves, but to describe the resilience of the old family, neighbourhood and work relationships, the stoicism in the face of suffering. Every working-class community can – and does – dwell elegiacally on its past, and celebrate its memory of the communal values of poverty; but most accept the need to yield to change. Improved material conditions are felt to be their own self-evident justification; but in some places they cannot quite console for the loss of identity, the abolition of the

sense of place and function in the productive process. Most
towns have by now radically modified their nineteenth-century
industrial structure; but as long as a high level of employment
has been maintained, no one has questioned what work, or how
it affects people; or even whether it matters.

Here in Wigan, the transition isn't easy. The closure of the pits
struck at something very deep; hit at something vulnerable in
individuals – the point at which social and personal identity
interlock at the most inextricable level. The changed economy
of a town – even when that change involves the abolition of
categories of work considered dirty and dangerous, and even
when accompanied by rapidly rising living standards – can
impose itself as an act of cruel destruction, even though it may
alleviate what seemed an ancient and changeless poverty. The
loss of function and of distinctive place that Wigan, on the
Lancashire coalfield, conferred on those who lived there, leaves
an appalled and disbelieving sense of shock. It has involved an
assault upon the sense of involvement in the primary purposes
of the old industrial structure that is almost wholly absent from
the new Wigan. One man said, 'If your job is to operate an
electronic eye inspecting every baked bean or pea that goes into
a tin, it isn't easy to feel that food production depends on you.
But you go into a mine and, by Christ, you see the machine cut
the coal in the same way that the plough cuts the earth, like a
wave on the sea, and you know how necessary you are.'

I visited the Tupperware factory, which has been in Wigan
since the early '60s. The personnel manager said that nobody
pretended that the work was interesting; the product is made by
injection moulding, and the human labour is simple and
repetitive. Even with an unemployment rate in Wigan close to 10
per cent, the turnover in staff in 1975 was 61 per cent. 'But the
people who work here are the salt of the earth. When one of our
workers had a fire, and his house was burnt out, we were up
there every day for a fortnight with something or other donated
by the work people.'

Coalmining is one of the few industries that still retain a
strong heroic dimension, and the industrial tradition of the
mining communities has not decayed to the same degree as
many others. When the pits were being closed throughout the
'50s and '60s – and many of them were exhausted, or involved
long journeys to the coal face, and would have needed large

infusions of capital to be made workable – this process was accompanied by much public rhetoric about lifting people out of degrading and high-risk working conditions. Many miners I spoke to denied that if the industry is run with a proper regard for the people who work in it, there is anything degrading about it; and some felt that the sympathy expressed by politicians for miners' working conditions simply masked decisions that had already been taken to shift to dependency on Middle East oil. 'But as early as 1954, in conference at Blackpool, the miners had warned that the oil producers wouldn't be content to go on living in tents for ever.'

With the diversification of industry – which often means work that denies rather than enhances the humanity of people – the consciousness of the work place has been eroded, in favour of a domestic or leisure consciousness. I asked a retired miner if he thought things were getting better. He said, 'Oh ah, things are getting better, it's only people as get bloody worse.'

Somewhere, detached from the romantic nostalgia that has accumulated around past working-class experience, there is a sense of something of real worth having been forfeited. 'What we've got now, it's nothing to do with socialism. It's a mockery of all the things we fought for; just because it looks better than what we had then, we fell for it, lock stock and barrel.' There has been a major dislocation in working-class tradition, and with it a sense of bitterness. 'I started work at thirteen. I worked on a milk-cart for twenty-four years. I drove it, horse and cart. Up at five o'clock in the morning, all the milk frozen in winter. In bed eight o'clock at night. I don't know what's happened to folk. They've all got greedy-grabbing, that's the trouble. When I was a kid, my parents always knew where I was. There was nowhere else to be except where you were supposed to be. But now they want to be out enjoying themselves all the time, they give their kids three quid to get lost. You're not put here just to enjoy yourself.' – Woman in her sixties.

People feel they have no power over the changes that affect them. 'My mother brought five of us up on her own. I was the youngest. All of them, all my brothers went down the pit. We're not really close now. Yesterday it was my little nephew's birthday and I forgot all about it. I know somebody who teaches another of my nephews, and this teacher said to him, "I know your Uncle Mark"; and the kid said, "Oh yes, I believe I have got an Uncle

Mark." Well, part of me thinks that is terrible; but everybody seems to have gone their own ways.' – Man, thirties.

With older people, never far from the surface is a torrent of remembering.

'My father was a puddler, and he was out of work for eight years while I was growing up. I remember when I was ever such a kid, my mother had a relief ticket to go and buy some food. My father sat at home in the armchair, I can see him now, not a penny in his pocket, choking for a cigarette. He said to Mother, "See if you can get him to let you have five Woodbines." Twopence that would have been. So she went to the grocer's, and I went with her. She got some bread and tea and sugar, I don't know what, but all together it came to 9/9. And then she said to him, "Do you think I could have five Woodbines?" And he looked at her as though she'd asked for the moon. He said, "This is a voucher for food." So she bought a tin of condensed milk instead. I'll never forget the humiliation of my mother. I hated him. And you know, thirty years later, I read in the paper that he'd died, and I can honestly say that I exulted. I did, I exulted.

'I worked in a rubber factory in Manchester when I left school, and stayed there till war broke out. The train used to leave Wigan at ten past six and it got in at twenty to seven at night. I had to get up at five o'clock and walk the three miles to the station. The tram fare was 2d, but I couldn't afford that out of my wages as well as the train fare.' – Man, sixties.

'Well, I worked at Heinz till I retired. They're still very good to me. They send me a birthday card, a parcel at Christmas. They had a big do when I retired. I worked on the magnetic belt, you know, for getting pieces of metal out. . . . My wife died six years ago; but you don't have to let yourself go, you keep busy. I wake up sometimes in the night and I imagine I can still feel her there, laying next to me. . . . I was brought up on a farm. In Wigan, yes. Gone now, of course. At the next farm I met this lad who was learning to be a jockey. His name was George Formby. . . . We had a bad time with the Means Test, they used to knock on our door at nine o'clock at night, because they said they had reason to believe my sister was living there. She was working, and if she lived there, they would've docked it from my mother's allowance. She was in lodgings, but she came to see us, like. Only she didn't dare stay after nine at night.' – Man, seventies.

I visited a retired miner and his wife in a new bungalow outside the town. The road climbs up to Aspull; the terraced houses open on to an expanse of windswept moor; the hedges of hawthorn, hung with crimson berries, bend to the prevailing wind. Mr Simms is over seventy, but he still gives an impression of strength, power, self-contained dignity. He wishes me to know that he is not my intellectual inferior. He has taught himself French, German and Russian. He sees me look at two white wooden carved plates on the wall. 'That's not Stalin you know,' he says sharply. 'It's Gorki. And the other one's Turgenev.' He asks me what I want. 'What are you doing, studying Orwell? What do you think I can tell you? You're a bit late. We had a professor here three weeks ago, do you know him? He looked like a parson.'

He talks about his first day at work. 'Fourteen I was. Straight after school. My first day I just went down the pit. I was given an oil lamp – no helmet then – and told to get on with it, on my own. I'd no idea what to do. No training. It was about a mile to the coal face. You have to sort of snake your way along, twisting and turning, no room to stand up. I'd gone about two hundred yards and I fell. My lamp went out. Complete darkness. It was the blackest dark I've ever been in. I managed to crawl back, and then they did send a young fellow along with me. That was my first day at work.'

Friday is market day. A woman in her late fifties comes into the pub, laden with shopping. She buys a Guinness, undoes her coat, smiles and talks as though it were the most natural thing in the world that I should be sitting there, waiting to hear her story.

'My mother was a wrong 'un. You don't hear that very often. She ran away and left us, six of us, when I was four. One morning she'd just gone, left a note. My dad had us all in the kitchen and told us what had happened. I was scared to death. I can remember sitting on this wooden chair and looking up at the kitchen sink and bawling my eyes out. My dad went out to the next street and fetched a woman he knew, the widow of a man who'd been killed in a pit accident. By dinner time she was in our house, moved all her things in, and my dad went back to work. She had the front room downstairs to sleep in. Oh, he was strict, our dad. You hadn't to say a word out of place. He expected us to wait on him. But he was good to us. There's not a day goes by but what I think on him with love, and he's been dead twenty years. He never slept with Madge, that was her name, owt like that. He always treated her polite and decent.'

The authoritarianism of the men, who ruled their families in the same way that they themselves were ruled by the industrial discipline, does not die easily; and it jars against the seductive messages from the media and the shop windows, which invite to a self-indulgence which seems to them an affront to their frugality and self-denial. The ubiquitous sexuality disturbs them also. They saw sex-partner as a rôle, not as fulfilling personal fantasies. 'If I went into a room, up to the age of about thirty, and my mother was talking to one of her sisters about sex, she'd say "Shh", and stop the conversation. I wasn't supposed to hear.'

A woman on the bus turns to her companion: 'Did you see that couple on television last night, doing it like, you know, in a boat? I didn't know where to put myself, and I was on my own. If he'd been there, I would have had to turn it off.' 'Well, they're sex-mad if you ask me. All these kids at mixed schools, they're down the park every dinner time. How can they expect to learn anything? Sex is eating their brains away.'

In the pub two women in early middle age watch a woman some twenty years older as she goes down the steps into the street. 'Look at her, she's walking all right now. I know what she does. She makes out she can't get on and off the bus, just so's the conductors'll lift her up.' They lean closer. 'She likes to feel their hands round her bosoms.' 'Dirty old bugger.'

The recurring theme is that something has gone wrong. People talk of having fought and struggled; but what they had been offered doesn't quite correspond to what they aimed for. The disappointment doesn't know where to go: like all that energy formerly used up by work, it isn't wholly absorbed by the new consumer freedoms, and falls back on Pakistanis (although there are no more than a few hundred immigrants in Wigan, Bolton is only ten miles away, and in that distance the horror stories have space to dilate even further. 'They say it's like walking in the streets of Karachi'), on people getting Social Security by post 'so it doesn't interfere with watching telly'; on the man 'who drew £1,000 redundancy money last Friday – he's starting a new job on Monday, 100 quid a week'; on the alcoholics, vagrants, the young, vandals. What is principally wrong is other people.

'I was a prisoner in North Africa. I was behind the wire three years. We had time for thinking and talking in those years like we've never had since. When we got home, 1945, we really thought the revolution was here. But instead – well, look what's happened. We've been let down – I know I shan't live to see socialism now.'

'The first full week I worked, I got 30 shillings. A pound and a 10 bob note. Oh, I ran all the way home to my mother. She gave me a shilling spending money, and I thought I was well off. I wouldn't have dreamed of keeping it for myself. I didn't think of it as mine at all. It belonged to them. . . . But how many kids would think like that now? They don't know they're born.'

'They never used to indulge kids like they do now. It was your father who always had the egg. You might get the top if you were lucky. He was the breadwinner, he was more important than you were. But now, it's the other way round. . . . We used to get clogs from the Chief Constable's Clog and Stocking Fund, we might get a Well-Wisher parcel at Christmas. . . .'

'When I hear on the television that we're in the middle of a crisis, I don't believe it. I've lived through crises enough, when we wanted for bread and couldn't pay the rent. It's not my crisis, it's theirs. You hear them say, "The pound has had a good day, the pound rallied, fell back." It sounds like the bulletins they used to put out about dying royalty. It makes me laugh. It shows their worship of money. Whatever else they might try to tell us, that's what it's all about.'

Wigan has fourteen Labour Clubs, all modern well-equipped buildings, constructed with the help of cheap loans from the brewery companies. Most have a membership of 1,000 or more, and they dominate the social life of the town.

Streaming wet evening in mid-October. People run from their cars into the club, but still get soaked by the time they reach the porch. In the entrance hall there is a notice board announcing a meeting of the unemployed, and a plastic panel advertising the entertainment for the month – unmemorable performers for the most part, who sing or play the accordion. There is a large rectangular hall, with a herringbone woodblock floor and a stage at one end. The wall is flanked all the way round with turquoise leatherette benches, and tables run the whole length of the hall, like a great refectory. People at the tables are playing Bingo; the amplified voice of the Bingo caller

can be heard well beyond the limits of the building. While Bingo
is in progress there is total silence in the hall. The Labour
councillor, who is always at the club on Friday for surgery, says
that he has more than once been told to keep quiet while Bingo
is in progress. The bar is slack while the caller stands in front of a
sort of aquarium full of numbered disks, kept in perpetual
movement by a stream of air. Bingo cards are issued, six for 10p;
nearly everyone takes part. At the top of each card is a motto:
'Marriage is a covered dish', 'If youth is a fault, one soon gets rid
of it.'

When the Labour councillor arrives, he goes to the bar. A
woman approaches him.

'Can you do something about a bus shelter on this estate?
There's only three shelters between here and the town centre.
I've got wet through today.'

'Well, it's a bit difficult. I'll see what I can do. I can't promise.
You see, transport comes under Greater Manchester since re-
organization.'

The woman is incredulous. 'Manchester?' Pause. 'You're the
councillor for this area, aren't you?'

'Yes, only we don't look after transport now.'

'It's terrible. We have to wait twenty minutes for a bus.'

'I'll see if I can get it brought up.'

'There's nowhere you can shelter. Old people and all,
everybody gets soaked.'

Having delivered her complaint, she goes back to her Bingo
card. The councillor despairs of communicating to the people
how complex the structure is.

In the hall one old man is not playing. He sits alone. I ask
him, 'Not playing?'

'No.'

Pause

'I never do.'

Pause.

'Only at Christmas.'

Pause.

'It's free then.' Pause. 'They give us a treat then. Why do they
give us a treat? 'Cause we're old? Bit late in the day. I could've
done with a few treats fifty years ago. Only nobody offered 'em
then.'

When the game finishes, conversation erupts, and the space round the bar fills up at once.

'Hello, how you doing?'

'Not so bad. Considering.'

'Considering what?'

'Old age and poverty.'

The people in the clubs are predominantly middle-aged and elderly. In the lounge there are a few younger people, chiefly couples who are engaged or courting. The lounges are comfortable, warm and safe. There is no fighting. Anyone who causes trouble is likely to be excluded by the committee. The atmosphere is relaxed; people don't stop their own conversations even for the entertainment. 'Well, look at us. We never had our first child till we'd been married ten years. Must've been the way we held our mouths when we kissed.'

'We were happy when we were young. My boy says he's all the while bored. We never were. We had a tandem on tick, went out riding. Had our dinner in a field. Never cost much.'

'My kids never talk to me. I could tell my mother anything. I never had any secrets from her. I don't know where my kids are from one week to the next.'

'I started work tailoring. Six shillings a week. The employers in those days only taught you the job slowly, bit by bit. They wouldn't let you learn fast, because they'd've had to pay you more.'

'My mother didn't want me to go into the factory, so she got me on learning confectionery. Five shillings a week.'

'I don't know why people are so miserable these days. Bloke next door to us he's got some fancy woman. Everybody knows but his wife. You can't tell them. I did say to her, "Overtime, he does that much overtime the company'd be broke trying to pay him."'

'On my wedding night, I'm not kidding, I was that scared, I didn't dare take my clothes off. He kept saying, "Are you tired?" I said, "Oh no, not a bit." I said, "Let's have a game of cards." We were still sat there and it was getting light.'

At 11.30 an announcement comes over the Tannoy. 'Now come on, ladies and gentlemen, it's getting late. We hope you've had a pleasant evening. Good night now and God bless.'

Many of the older trade unionists and Labour Party workers

are not happy about the clubs and the function they fulfil. 'Beer and Bingo, that's not what they were set up for. Originally they were built by the members themselves, bricklayers, plumbers, some of the unemployed got together and started from scratch. They weren't palaces like they are now; but what you did get is something that's gone by the board here – and that's ideas.'

'The trouble is the lack of any attempt at education by the Labour Party. They haven't made the running, they've left it all to Bingo and tenth-rate entertainment. That's all right, in its place. Only we never saw that as the aim of the labour movement. I was down in Nuneaton recently. There's a Labour club with a neon sign that says "Labour Club". Underneath, still in neon, "non-political".'

Few young people visit the Labour clubs. There has been a dramatic break in the transmission of the working-class tradition. Of the young, some said, 'Oh, they'll learn when they get a bit older.' One man said, 'They don't want to listen to us. All we've got to tell them about is Wigan and poverty.'

Because the old have seen the values of the old working-class culture displaced, they can talk about their past with some objectivity. They are evocative and passionate about Wigan as it was. But there is something elusive about the young, something that escapes the scrutiny of the media and the social scientists. They simply live their cultural values, they don't articulate them. They are products of a given world, just as their parents were, when mine, mill and neighbourhood determined their lives; only now it is image and fashion, the endless spool of excitement and novelty that has been unwound before their eyes since they were born. It isn't surprising if they say they are bored. Nothing ever happens in Wigan. They feel passive and purposeless. They have, as their parents say, been given everything. Nothing has ever been demanded of them. They are anchored in a culture of commodities, helpless dependants on the fantasies it engenders.

At night the young dominate the town-centre pubs. In the Merchants' Hotel, behind a door with 'News Room' marked in the frosted glass, the high-backed benches form a semi-circle around the gas fire. The benches are worn, and horsehair is escaping from the cracked and broken leather. The walls are a dirty yellow, and some indestructible lino covers the floor. I am talking to a young man who lives in London but comes home to sign on for the dole in Wigan once a week. He hitches up, and travels back by train on the 'theatre-goers' excursion ticket, which costs only £3. As you are not allowed to take any luggage, his friend buys a platform ticket and then passes his bag to him through the window when he is on the train. He is talking to me about Sufism; how difficult it is to describe to anyone else because of the imprisoning nature of words. A young man of about nineteen turns to us from a group on the other side of the fire. He is unsteady, and finds it hard to focus his eyes upon us. He says, 'Got any drugs?' Only this, and we indicate the glasses we are drinking from. 'Why not? You must have.' He is shaken by violent rage and disappointment. He turns to the mirror above the fireplace, leans close to it and starts beating his own image in the glass. The glass breaks and a stream of blood covers his forearm. He falls backwards, and his fall is broken by some friends. They sit him in a chair, where he slumps, stupefied. No one pays any attention.

In another pub, well known for under-age drinking, a group of boys are playing darts. Their hands open and close like flowers, and the dart leaves them with no sign of propulsion. One of them scribbles on the blackboard with a piece of chalk, walking between the flights of darts. 'Watch it. We pinned his bloody ear to the board twice yesterday.' They concentrate on the game, but at the same time keep up a fragmented conversation. 'My old man, he used to say "Quickest way out of Wigan is through the pub door. Only one thing wrong with it – you have to come back." To me the Tech. is my way out. Get a skill, go anywhere. I shan't need to come back.'

There is another way out for most people now – through their own front door. George Orwell's descriptions of the interiors he visited in the '30s belong to the past. There may perhaps be a few, among the very old, the defeated; some still shocking in their dirt and lack of comfort. It is the enclaves of public decay that are so horrifying. I visited a woman in a terraced house in Ince, one of a short terrace that looked as if it had been chopped in half: it ended abruptly in a heap of rubble. Outside her front door, the road dipped, and there was a crater filled with pieces of brick that the children had flung into it, and which had splashed her door and windows with muddy stains. On the other side, the houses look on to a short slope of grass, a derelict workshop and then the railway. She said, 'You know the slag-heap that Milhench bought for £150,000, there was a lot of fuss about it in the election of '74. You know what they say? Why buy a slag-heap, he could have had the whole of Ince for that. . . . I don't mind it, I'm used to it.' The interior of the house is very clean. There are two moquette armchairs in the parlour, and on a table at the window there is a brass pot with some pampas grass; she did away with her lace curtain a few years ago. There are wedding photographs on the sideboard, some pictures of grandchildren in colour against an impossibly blue background. The open fire has gone, and there is a gas fire in a metal casket.

The back room is more homely. She has kept the open fire, and says she'll keep it until the work gets too much for her. There is a TV and a patchwork rug, a radio, lots of glass animals, a table with a chenille cloth, a dresser with plates standing up like ornaments. The outside lavatory has been covered in, and has a Perspex roof. In the back garden there are some splendid but rain-soaked red dahlias. Beyond, the back way is cobbled, uneven and muddy; glittering with broken glass. 'I never have occasion to go out there. I don't think about it.' I asked her about her sons. 'Oh, I wouldn't let my boys go down the pits. I've seen too much of it. One of them works for the Inland Revenue and one of them is a teacher down Nottingham.' She shows me a picture of her younger son on degree day, and the older one with his wife, children and dog. When they started work, the pits were closing anyway; but their mother insists it was her doing which prevented them from both having to go underground like their father. In this way, she feels she has a profound personal stake in the way things have changed; and she is puzzled by the apparent ingratitude of her children. 'Why don't they come to see me more often?' she asks. 'Why do they leave me here, they both have lovely homes. Why did they have to go so far away? We used to be such a family together.'

Perhaps the most significant building in Wigan is not the 'Olympic-standard' swimming pool, but the new Technical College. Until late in the evening its lights gleam out into the wet darkness: it is the most ample escape route of all. Throughout the day, the Golden Chick receives those who are between lessons; they crowd in after each hour, drink a brew, play the jukebox, read the *Sun*.

JS: 'What do you want to do?'
   'Me? Get out of Wigan.'
   'It's a pit.'
JS: 'What do you most want from life?'
   'Happiness.'
JS: 'What's that then?'
   'Don't know yet. I know what it's not. Being like your parents.'
   'They're jealous of us, because we've had things they've never had.'
   'They try and tell you what to do.'
JS: 'Isn't that their job?'
   'Piss off.'
JS: 'What is their job then?'
   'Give us what we want.'
   'Look after you.'
JS: 'A lot of them say they always teach you right from wrong. Is that true?'
   'Depends what you mean by right and wrong.'
   'There's no such thing. There's only doing what you want to do.'
JS: 'What if that conflicts with other people?'
   'It's the law of the jungle. Kill or be killed.'
   'You've got to fight for what you want. Nobody's going to give you anything are they?'
JS: 'What do you think is the worst social injustice in this country?'
   'Rod Stewart. He can't even live in this country because of tax. Having to live abroad.'

At the next table two girls are drinking Coke. One of them is colouring her nails with a liquid called Wild Pear. It is her boyfriend's birthday next week, and she has just been to buy him a card. It is about a foot square, with a raised satin heart in the middle.
   'Oh, it's lovely. How much did you give for it?'
   'Eighty pence.'
   'God. You must love him.'
   'Yes, I do.'

The changed function of this town is slightly shaming to the old male-dominated values. The traditional strength and energy

haven't gone away simply because they are no longer required
by industry. The sense of rejection remains. Release from
poverty and coercion is one thing, but a real and irreversible loss
of purpose is something else, and strikes very deeply at the roots
of working-class identity. If the energy cannot be harnessed by
society, if new purposes cannot be found, these things will find
their own outlet; and in the social and moral vacuum in which
we live, who can say what ugly crusades and deformed purposes
may evolve?

3

ON A WARM October afternoon in Somerset, when the ripe cider
apples shine like globes of light on top of the thinning trees and
the sun shines through the curdled cloud, you look in vain for
some trace of the way in which the old agricultural workers
lived. At Culverton even their cottages have gone, replaced by
council bungalows; and those that remain have been restored to
something they never were. Perhaps it is in the gardens of the
red council houses that the care for the land is still to be seen: the
dahlias blaze, Michaelmas daisies and golden rod grow wild,
and the summer flowers have all begun to bloom again; the old
men are lifting the potatoes, women gather runner beans in
their faded aprons, pears and apples are being harvested in zinc
tubs and wicker baskets. You can smell the leaves as they fall in
the calm afternoon, crisp golden furls that are caught in the
cobwebs. Dead elms and birches look brittle and wintry,
reminders of another season in all the autumn ripeness, where
you cannot walk two steps in the fields without treading on the
spindly ghost-mushrooms, the agaric and fungus which the
warm wet earth seems to exude like a breath.

The door of Mr and Mrs Ruffard's bungalow stands open to
the sunshine. The house is still full of things that suggest old
cottages – some fire bellows, the rag rug, the neglected fire
barely smouldering in the sunny afternoon. The clock ticks
slowly, a late wasp circles around a basket of sweet fruit.

Mr and Mrs Ruffard are eighty. They talk together, not
competitively, but to complement each other, and each recalls
events in the other's life, as though over the years their

experience had merged and it no longer mattered that it should have been the private property of one or the other.

MRS RUFFARD: 'I went out to service when I was twelve. I went to a place called Kingston, the other side of Taunton. And I used to have £9 a year. I used to have to be up at five o'clock to clean out all the flues, real little tot I was. They had a couple of cows, I used to have to make all the cream and butter. He was a Captain Saunders and he'd lost his wife. She'd left him with a little baby; and we had an old housekeeper who used to drink terrible. The lady of the big house in the village got me all my uniform when I went to service, me caps and aprons and a tin box. I had to pay back so much a month on the amount I'd had for me clothes, and that was out of £9 a year. . . . We was a long family, ten of us altogether. I was the second oldest. Once a month I used to walk home to where we lived, Hillcommon, and my father'd come to meet me, fourteen mile each way it was. Oh, we had to live hard. You can't really believe that you lived through such times really. . . . You had to go where you were sent. I stayed there just over a year, then I went to a place in Weston and stayed there seven year. We had nine servants living in, and others that came in to serve at table. I was in the kitchen there at first. You can think people's being kind to you when you're young, when all the time they're not. We used to do the vegetables, and when the War was on, we used to have to do stinging nettles for greens, and we was all pricked, you know, with the nettles, where you had to strip the leaves off. I used to think it was all what you were supposed to do. I didn't know no difference in they days. You never used to hear of anything different, did you? Boys went to work in the fields, and the girls went to service and that was that.'
MR RUFFARD: 'Well, my father was an agricultural labourer, wages 10/- a week back in they days. We had no choice but to go on the farm to work. There was nothing else. We would have to walk miles in the pouring wet rain to go to school, sit in wet clothes all day, and get a good hiding if we were a minute or two late. . . . Buy broken biscuits for dinner. And when we got home at night, well if Father caught a rabbit, that was a real treat, swedes and a rabbit was a feast. We had tied cottages, sometimes half a mile from each other, a room and a kitchen downstairs, two bedrooms. Galvanized tin in front of the fire if you wanted a bath.'

'The old house we lived in when we were married, he had a kitchen, you could say he had a kitchen, then there was a back place you could go out and have a wash in, but it was pebble stones and a roof slanted down; only one bedroom, four sleeping in there.'

'The kids used to go off in the fields and pick up acorns and sell them to the farmers for the pigs, and that money used to have to be put by to get a pair of shoes.'

'I used to go picking primroses to take to the shops to get a few buns or a loaf of bread.'

'What you know as you went through. You know it's all true. We never had nothing.'

'On Friday afternoons at school, we used to do sewing. The kids all took some bits of embroidery. I had to take all the family's stockings and mend them. That was my embroidery lesson. . . . We were made to work hard. I used to go and do washing up for families, go off and pick blackberries and sell 'em to earn a few coppers.'

'When I worked on the farm, it was straight on all the week, no Saturday afternoon off. On Sunday mornings we had to do all the milking, all done by hand, then I had to go through all the muck and feed over a hundred sheep. I'd go home, have my dinner, and then back to milk the cows, and for that Sunday I'd get a shilling for all I'd done. No holidays. No such thing as holidays then. You worked all the week, Monday morning till Sunday night. . . . We had to concentrate on our gardens for growing food, we grew as much as ever we could, otherwise we couldn't have had a dinner half the time, could us?'

'When I was a girl going to school, I used to go and pick up potatoes for a gentleman at Hillcommon; and he used to give me a piece of bread and jam for that, and I thought I was well paid.'

'You all worked near where you lived. Families didn't go far afield for work.'

'Only if you went away to service. I never even got the time off to go to Taunton. You were shut up in the house, either jam-making or cleaning. They cleaned everything, all the time. It was all work. We weren't allowed to meet a boy-friend. Of course I did.'

'I was England's last hope.'

'You weren't allowed to meet anybody. It was the same as slavery. You had your pittance of wages, and when I'd paid for my clothes, the rest went to my mother. I never had any money for myself. . . . Me and him met through Culverton church. I used to go to church and he used to potter up behind me like they do, don't they?' (*Laughs.*) 'Then he used to meet me down the road. There used to be two or three of them, and in the finish I picked up with him. . . . Then of course I went to Weston, and I only got home once a year. . . . What kept me going was the thought I was helping they at home.'

'She weren't allowed to keep it.'

'What did I want money for?'

'All of our children have got on.'

'One of the girls works at school dinners, the other lives in Northampton. One of the boys is a supervisor at the hospital, another is the maintenance chap up the hospital, and the other one's a builder. . . . The way we were brought up, they didn't have it easy either, but they were determined their children should have a better going on than they had.'

'They've got good jobs. When I worked, no fixed hours, you never knew when you were going to get home. You'd go away to work in the dark of the morning and you wouldn't see your wife till in the night. People thought of us as country bunkums, but, really speaking, all the labour on the farms was really skilled labour. When you had to plough with horses you'd be ploughing all day, not stop for dinner, and each day you'd walk twenty miles at the plough. You'd leave off in the middle of the afternoon after you'd ploughed one acre of ground with a nine-inch furrow as we called it. Twenty-one mile each day. . . . Then making ricks was skilled, it was all done by hand. Making hedges, that was a craft on its own. It's all machinery today. I wouldn't want to work on a farm today. . . . It wouldn't be classed as skilled; and if you put a man today to make a hedge or cut corn with a scythe, I think they wouldn't be able to do it. . . . We had more mates to work with, the fields were full of workers. Today you only get one or two on a farm. We had more comradeship.'

'We had some fine times, harvesting. We used to go round following the reapers, waiting for the rabbits to come out. . . .'

'We had a good old free-for-all for about a fortnight at

harvest. And then, at the end of harvest, the old farmer used to give us all harvest supper where we'd all be together in a big barn. Have a lovely evening.'

'The old farmer used to bring out the cider when you were working, in a jar, for the men, and a piece of bread and cheese. You'd have your tea in the fields.'

'Nearly every farm worker used to rear two pigs a year and then bring them in the house. A special slaughterman used to come round and kill them. And he'd be hung up in the front room, the old pig. And the next day he'd come and cut en down in pieces and salt en in what we called trinnels, great wooden things; and then they'd buy another young pig and bring en up with the waste, potato parings, acorns. Two a year. 'Twas very nice. It was a big day when the pig was killed. You had a lot then, the liver, the hearts, especially the chitterlings. Then they used to go to the rivers, take the chitterlings, get them washed out in the river. . . . Or the well. . . . We had a pump before the water came. . . . I pumped for my old granny be the hour while she used to be cleaning the chitterlings. That was high-class dishes. We lived well for weeks after the old pig was killed. Then we had to wait six months for the next one. They used to kill the pig any time when they thought he was ready. "Oh, 'tis fit to kill the pig," they'd say. They liked the cooler weather of course. . . . Many times it would break your heart, because a pig can get quite tame you know. You wouldn't like it, not when the pig was killed. . . . You felt it. . . . But they used to have to go, of course. They wouldn't hang the pig up in the front room now, would em.'

'Ah, we've had a hard old life of it up till now.'

'Now we be happy.'

'We survived two wars.'

'Ah. All the villages like Culverton shrunk so much after the First War. . . . We lost thirty chaps from this village, I knew every one of them. . . . Just before the war ended, we were on the German border, and as the line shortened, we weren't required to go forward. We walked from the German frontier to the coast of France. No transport. We walked so many days. It was terrible. When you've a chap next to you, leaning agen you, shot dead. . . . You lost all your mates.'

JS: 'The second part of your working life, you did gardening, didn't you?'

'That was all stooping, and I wore out the muscles in my back, so I had to give that up at the finish. Then I got to be caretaker at the school.'

'I used to help him. Light the fire at half past five in the morning, six coal fires. I had to clean out all the cupboards in the classrooms. One day a rat come out at me. There was a Union Jack in the cupboard, and this old rat had nearly eat the Union Jack.'

'The schoolmaster said you could hear her shout the other side of the village.'

'He must've lived on that Union Jack.'

'I worked till I was seventy-one, the wife till she was seventy. Then we thought, Now let's have a good time. Only she got nearly blind, and things didn't turn out like we thought they were going to. Time cheats you at the finish.'

'I lost one eye to start with, had en took out and a glass eye put in, and it wasn't long before the other one started. . . . I was lucky, the surgeon saved my light, I've got a little light in this eye. That's all I've got for my hard life. . . . I looked after my mother for ten years when she was bedridden.'

'My mother, in her young days, she used to be a washerwoman. She had to go to people's houses and do their whole washing for them. Then if you came home from school, you'd find this washing all over, drying, all the sheets sweet and fuming be the fire. Then at the end of the week she did all the ironing, and my father took it back in a flask we used to call it, a withy thing, all for a copper or two. You couldn't get in our house, you'd get all hitched up in this washing.'

'When we were young, we had to behave ourselves. There was none of this vandalism. We used to have a bit of mischief sometimes, knock on someone's door and run away, but not ever to hurt anyone or cause fights. Dances were nice and sociable. But now it's different altogether, the way of the world. It's no good to try and compare them, our world and the world today. . . . We can try and tell you a story, but they're like two wedges that won't come together.'

JS: 'Why is it different?'

'Education.'

'Too much greed.'

'Greed – selfishness.'

'Too lazy.'

'There isn't the friendliness.'

'When we were about more, we used to get up parties for the old people. I remember as many as a hundred parcels delivered at Christmas time for the old people, go round house to house with them. . . . The children had parties, all dressed up in different coloured frocks.'

'We been married fifty years. We were married in the village, we had no wedding cake, no reception, no honeymoon. . . . I had to put in an extra stint digging potatoes to raise enough cash to buy a bottle of port for our visitors.'

'Seems a long time ago. We've been happy. Culverton's changed. We used to have a bakery shop and a coalyard, a drapery and everything. We had twenty-six shops here at one time.'

'Now there's hardly anything.'

'Twenty-six shops, and you couldn't ask for anything you couldn't get here. Even down to having a horse's harness mended. Once a week there used to be a old horse and trap would go into Taunton, for about 6d he'd bring you back anything you wanted.'

'Everything's changed. Even the Labour Party is like the rest of the world, it's got so educated that they aren't the same as they used to be. Everybody's so clever, 'tis hard to explain. . . . In the old days there weren't so many Labour people, they couldn't afford to be falling out all the while.'

'Well, I was twelve years old when I thought I was something different to a Conservative or a Liberal. . . . What started me thinking first, we were a long family, and one night when Father came home from the fields with his old basket, Mother said, "Now you children, don't touch your father's basket, because if he's got anything left in it, he's got to take it agen tomorrow because I haven't got anything else for him to take." I thought, Well, I'm not a Conservative, and I'm not a Liberal. Whatever can I be? It went on for a number of years, and it took me a long time before I said to myself, "Well, I must be a Labour man." . . . And seven of us had the nerve to start a Labour Party here in Culverton, out on the road, under a window. We asked later if we could go in a pub room, but when the landlord knew what it was for, he said, "You can come just this once, but I don't want ee afterwards." So we had to hold all our meetings in one of the old cottages. . . . I lost my job over it once or twice. When

Labour started standing down here, they had a rough old time. Some people are afraid, even today.'

'I love Somerset. I'm proud of where I come from. That's what makes you what you are. You'd be lost without it. . . . I feel real proud when I hear the Wurzels sing some of our old songs. Some of them are from ever such a long time ago.

(*Sings*) 'Where be that blackbird be?
I know where he be
He's up yonder turnip field
And I'll be after ee.
Now he sees I, and I sees he
I'm buggered if I don't get en.
I'll take a gun and shoot en down
Blackbird I'll get ee.'

'I could sing you a song. . . . You'll not've heard this one before:

'Now as I strolled down a shady lane
A sweet girl rambled with me
She sat down on a mossy bank
And I sat down on a bee.
Oh where oh where has that bumblebee gone?
Oh where oh where can he be?
I don't know where that bumblebee's gone
But I do know where he stung me.

Now I go to work, I can please myself,
A pound a week is me wage
Last Saturday night, I came home tight
And the wife commenced in a rage:
"Oh where oh where is your wages, John?"
Says I, "I got it in 'ere.
I've brought home a shilling in coppers, love,
And nineteen shillings in beer."'

4

THE RHONDDA IS part of the folklore of the labour movement. The name itself produces the sense of awe that great suffering evokes in us. And yet, there is something prosaic and homely about the valleys, not the substance of an epic somehow. On a summer afternoon with the shadows of the clouds blotting the green forests and the houses on the hills projecting long shadows over the slopes, there is a feeling of calm. Although the houses are small, inside they are cool and airy. The stone is chill grey, and the vestigial grime in its rough cutting is a reminder of the time when the coal dust was everywhere, and the valleys were dominated, first by the mines, and then by the closing of them.

By road, it isn't so different from any other industrial area. Perhaps the natural setting is a little more dramatic. The little towns meander into each other and end abruptly, without suburbs, which shows that all those who had enough money to leave, did so. But by rail, you see something more evocative. From Pontypridd, with its imposing station through which the wealth of the valleys was drained, the railway passes through abandoned collieries, rusty wheels and black metal, charred and twisted props, the symmetrical pyramids of the tips covered with a sheen of grass, the derelict buildings, houses and shops, and especially chapels – Bethel or Ebenezer, where the windows are broken and the buddleia has taken root in the stone, and birds and butterflies wheel in and out of the shattered glass. A chapel graveyard is being dug up, and the fine slate memorials are stacked in rows, stone tables of kinship. The chapels still stand over the other buildings, splashed with mud and dust, commemorative foundation stones defaced; but they have been conspicuously deserted by a new generation. 'I can think of those places only with revulsion,' said a young man who grew up in Porth. 'They taught such an austere and unloving view of life. To me, they are symbols of repression, sexual repression and social control. I'm pleased to see them in a state of ruin. I exult in it. To me this represents a triumph for humanity.'

And yet, there is something compelling there; perhaps it is the passion they engendered, an intensity of feeling that still seems to hover around the wasting stone – not the element of discipline, but the power of human beings to be moved and deeply affected in their lives by what they said to each other in the sombre theatre of these stone caverns.

Loss of belief in the chapels has been rapid and considerable. But it is not only as symbols of social control that they have been rejected. With them have gone the moral force and power which they represented, and in its wake the values which grew out of that morality to fight the social control, and which borrowed from it so much of its rhetoric. The passion of the social alternative has been forfeited as well; the belief in socialism. Belief – all belief – has been the victim. The idea of personal salvation has taken up its dwelling in the promise of material things; but so have the forces of social control. As yet, the opposition to this shift still circles restlessly around the changed conditions, uncertain of where it should locate itself. There is only one place left – the chapels, and that part of them that doesn't represent social control, but belief in morality and human dignity; only they are in ruins or bricked up; and only the butterflies continue to flit around the mauve spindles of buddleia. The chapels mock us now, empty husks of spent belief and exhausted passion.

The man from Porth no longer lives there. He is a Marxist and a revolutionary, a historian. 'The working class, in what we regard as their traditional form, was really only a historical accident, and spanned only a brief moment in time – perhaps from around the 1880s up to the 1950s. It doesn't matter that all that should go, there's certainly no point in being nostalgic about it. Particular forms of struggle, resistance, pass; but others will arise. Circumstances are changing all the time, and the working class is changing with them. . . . The working class has had a distinctive value system, but it has been corporate; it has never been an alternative culture *to* capitalist, but an alternative *within*.'

In 1861 the population of the Rhondda was less than 4,000. By 1921 it was 162,000; and now it is perhaps half that. Throughout the 1930s, it was losing 3,000 or 4,000 people a year. At that time, over half the population was unemployed. It still bears the mark of this convulsion; and the young continue to leave.

Annie Powell is one of the few remaining Communist councillors in South Wales. She was a teacher, whose grandparents were from mining families. Her parents became teachers, and were involved in the first teachers' strike of 1919, as a result of which the Burnham system was evolved. She lives at Llwynypia, a house in a grey stone terrace.

'My mother's brother lived in Barry, and whenever I went to speak in Barry, he always said to me, "You'll live to see socialism, you will"; and he was saying that until he died at the age of ninety-nine. In 1945 we thought all the changes we'd fought for were going to come. But of course, we'd been living on the colonial empire, we had to live through the loss of that, and the repercussions filtered through to the people. This is what makes so many working-class people racist: they've seen all these black people asserting their right to those things which they have been given the fruits of, and they see it as something being taken away from them; although when the expropriation of the colonial empire was at its height they never got any of it.

'We grew up in a world where we argued about every damn thing. People talked to each other then. Now there is an absence of communication between people. The television tells you things. It makes absolute statements; people feel inferior and inadequate in the presence of that. There was such a sense of excitement when we were growing up. Anything seemed possible. It's ironic really, how the Labour Party has been absorbed by capitalism, as many of the leaders of the trades unions were; and now the labour movement is being used as a scapegoat for what is wrong with capitalism. It is an odd quirk of history that the Labour Party, which at one time seemed to represent a threat to the continued existence of capitalism, can now be terrified of being accused of making it fail to function properly. Well, almost within living memory, we've seen the rape and decline of these valleys. It's been a very rapid process.

'Because the mining industry was dangerous and insecure, parents tried their hardest to prevent their children from going down the pits. Education was the only secure outlet; the people of the valleys were always anxious to get the best education for their children. The boys who went to college all became teachers or preachers, the BA/BD mentality. The export from these valleys in human resources, the teachers and preachers, took away a whole generation. A few came back, but the vast majority went away. It was a grievous loss to a community which was being despoiled of its riches in every way. Their sisters went to London, into service. I still feel bitter about it to this day. We used to go down to Cardiff with them to see them off on the train, these children. There was nothing else for them to do. It was heartbreaking. Perhaps only a few days after they'd left school, off they had to go.

'My parents had become teachers. They built their own house; one of the best built houses in Rhondda it was too. It cost them about £800 to build. It's just been sold as a matter of fact for £27,000. And when the time came for me to inherit that house – and it was a lovely house – I had to say no. I felt, Well, I work with miners, that is my life. So I declined it. I don't regret it for a minute. I came to this house, and I've always been happy here.

'I think in politics you have to have a certain element of showmanship in you. When I was a girl, people were always saying to me "Hello, where's your pretty sister?" She was the beauty of the family. She was pretty and she had a beautiful singing voice. I felt I wanted to be noticed. I couldn't sing; I croaked like a frog. And then I discovered I could speak. I made my first public statement in chapel when I was three. I remember it quite distinctly. All the men used to sit on one side, and all the women on the other; and I can remember getting up in my seat and announcing to the congregation, "My grandmother is very ill." People thought it was an omen of death for a child to get up and say that in chapel without being prompted.

'People often say to me "How would things be different under socialism?" I think it is sad, that capitalism has even obscured our capacity for visions. Nobody can imagine what a better life would be like, because we're always being told that this is the best possible life. The things we are promised are so dazzling they blind us to any real alternative. There are so many things that would change in socialist society. People would have the opportunity to develop their personality in a way that doesn't happen now; their whole personality, not just a fragment of it. I know a teacher who would have made a very good electrician, but, because he felt he would have been looked down on as an electrician, he became a teacher, and has been rather unhappy in his career. In our society, we are told that one

of the worst things that can happen to people is to remain in the
working class; if you have any chance at all, you get out. This is
how working-class life is made to appear. It doesn't have to be
so. Work doesn't have to deny the whole personality because it is
a working-class occupation. On the contrary. But that awful
divide is created by capitalism, by the constant erosion of able
people from their background. It may be "bettering yourself",
but it's also worsening somebody else. Society doesn't have to be
like that; it wouldn't be under socialism.

'If you have seen great poverty, as this valley has, the despair,
you are very susceptible to some of the appeal of life today. I
think after the War, in 1945, people were claiming some of the
things they'd had to do without in the '30s; and these demands –
perfectly reasonable – got harnessed by capitalism to the barren
acquisitiveness we see now. Parents wanted to give something
better to their children, which is of course a fine instinct; but like
so many good instincts, it gets misshapen through capitalism.
Everything gets filtered, modified. There's a little boy I know,
not far from here, he got £150 worth of toys at Christmas. He
comes in here sometimes, and I've no toys, so he takes out my
old saucepans and plays with them quite happily for hours. He
pretends he's cooking. His mother comes in and says, "I can't
understand it, he has those lovely things, and yet he prefers to
come and play with all this."

'Most parents wanted their children out of the coal; but at the
same time there was a pride in cutting coal. There were thirty
pits in Rhondda; as they closed, such diversification as we got
was no answer. Even before the war, when the pits were closed,
there was the Treforest Industrial Estate; but firms had to bring
their own key people with them, and then the council houses
were allocated to them. There's been an enormous loss in job
opportunities; the non-productive service industries, where is
the job satisfaction in them? You must have work where people
can give something of themselves. With technology, we're told,
people get released from toilsome jobs; but the monotony, the
repetitive work, the lack of involvement with what one does,
what effect does that have on a person? If work is made tedious,
mechanical, this must be reflected in a man's life, it must take its
toll of people.

'People were educated only for escape from the valleys. And
even then, the education was narrow. For years, English and

Mathematics were all that were needed for the 11-plus; and the 11-plus came to be seen as the avenue of escape even by young children. That is the way we organize society: equality of opportunity to escape from working-class life. It's the basic premise that's wrong – why should working-class life have to be something to be avoided? Why should children grow up to despise the place where they were born and the people they grew up with? That's what damages the community.'

Mrs Powell showed me a copy of a book written by a retired miner, an old friend of hers, now too seriously debilitated by pneumoconiosis to be able to talk to me. It is an autobiography, sensitively written, and illustrated with the kind of photographs that many families used to keep, dog-eared and faded, in shoe-boxes and biscuit tins. Of his life in the pit, he wrote:

I hated being sealed in for the day.
The first shovel of coal seemed to fall into a bottomless pit.
I felt the mice were fellow-prisoners in my tomb.
The walk through the lamp-room was like the prom at Porthcawl.
I hated the thought of giving my all to be exploited.
I hated the long dusty sticky walk to the faces with the smell of fresh horse-shit drifting in the breeze.
I hated the measuring-boys, trained to rob us of pence.
But I followed my mother with shyness, and a love of the countryside.
My greatest walking was always around our mountain tops.
I loved the crunch of coarse grass under my feet.
The brilliance of red ferns on the mountainside in autumn.
I loved my parents for their great fight to feed and clothe us.
I loved it all, including the rows and sing-songs. Love was the basis of our family, through thick and thin.
Even the pits could not alter these things.
My grandfather used to go on the tramp every so often. He used to walk out with his little cloth bag and walking stick. He'd walk into mid-Wales, working on farms for a few months, and then, when he came home, Grannie always accepted him. My father went into the pit when he was twelve. He was an active trade unionist. I will always picture him,

facing a fiery crowd with the spotlight of Llwynypia baths
shining on him, high cheekbones, deep sunken eyes, a typical
Welshman, always a fighter. In winter he never saw daylight
except at weekends. His interests were religion, boxing and
keeping game chickens; he went every Sunday to the Calvary
chapel at Ynyscynon. He bred game chickens for cock fights.
He used to make a special cake to feed the birds in training,
and it was made to a secret recipe. The venues for the cock
fights had to be changed regularly so that they never got
caught. They would be on the mountain tops, sometimes as
early as four-thirty in the morning. My father used to wear a
flannel shirt and drawers tied at the knees, a waistcoat and a
half-hunter watch, dark coat and trousers, a white starched
front or dickey and a good tie. We went out walking in the
country; the fresh air made us feel like fighting cocks.

When I was thirteen, the time came for me to go down the
pit. My father said 'When you go down the pit for the first
time, Johnny, the first drop in the cage will frighten you, but
that will pass. Then hang on to me till we reach the face, and
take no notice of the strong language.' I had a sleepless night
before the Monday I was due to start. I wore cord trousers
tied at the knees, hobnail boots, an old coat and scarf and
dai cap. Tommy box and jack – it was so hot and dusty you
needed five pints of water each day; and a few sharp pick
handles completed my gear. . . . A few words from Mam and
we were on our way. First of all into the lamp-room, and then
plunging through the darkness, my heart seemed to lift out of
my body and float about in the black space. It was one of the
deepest pits in Wales. We came to a black cavern, lit by electric
lamps; trams and men and then the horses and stables,
dozens of horses in a long row of stalls where they lived most
of the time apart from when they were working on the coal
face. A long drift downhill, 200 yards, and we were met by
warm air and dust from the horses. The main haulage engine
was bringing coal from the faces before sending it to the pit
bottom; suddenly, I felt proud to be a fellow worker in this
tough crowd. We followed the road called the main heading,
and we were already sticky with sweat and dust when we came
to our branch heading. We stripped off, wet with sweat, and
there was a wall of coal, five foot six thick, reflecting twinkling
lights at us. My father cut the coal, two foot six thick, and I

carried loads of about twenty pounds of coal to the tram. I got
a lot of bumps and bruises, a dry throat and I was wet
through. Then he saids 'She'll start to boil'; and there were
some cracks, and the place was alive with gases. Large lumps
spewed out in all directions, and the floor was covered with
lumps of coal. There were mice who lived in the mines, eating
the crumbs from the men's food; I was surprised by that. You
have to be very alert while sweating profusely in a confined
space. You could bang your head on the timber that was put
up for safety, you could be hit by falling stones, the scraping
of coal along your naked body, long painful scratches mixed
with sweat and dust.

We carried a big jack of water. My dad would set down his
jack, and sometimes it would be stolen by other people who
had run out of water. One day, we saw a shadowy figure
coming up behind us. My dad said 'Leave him.' And we took
no notice, till suddenly there was a moaning and groaning
behind us. The man who'd taken it didn't know that my dad
suffered from colic and had put cayenne pepper in his water.

After the first day I walked home, and when I got there I
slumped in a chair and I didn't care when I got out of it. But
after a good feed and a bath, I felt better.

All the talk was about the Cambrian miners' strike of 1911.
The men had closed all the pits except Llwynypia. They
marched towards the colliery to picket, and to stop blacklegs
from working. The owners, in the meantime, had asked for
protection from the police and possibly the military. There
were 120 police out in the colliery yard. The first thing the
men wanted was to get the blacklegs out, but they got a severe
rebuff at the first attempt. So they got hold of any implements
they could find and a furious and bloody battle took place.
Men and police went down like ninepins. They were beaten
off and retreated. Police reinforcements came and made
baton charges. The pickets made towards Pandy Square,
being harassed all the way; but fresh implements appeared
for the men and the vicious battle continued, wooden palings,
mandrill shafts. After the fighting, it was like a battlefield.
Experience told them that it was no good trying to dislodge
the police with direct attacks, so they made use of the hills and
terraces around the colliery. The main thing was to keep on
higher ground. There were stones on the mountainsides that

could be used as missiles. When there was a baton charge, the idea was to make a strategic withdrawal, and to keep on higher ground at all costs. The struggle went on for weeks. An appeal was made by the coal-owners to send in troops. Churchill promised Mabon that troops would not be sent; but they were, and were trained on the mountain tops. Keir Hardie made a complaint in Parliament about police brutality and the fact that troops were in the valley. The Lancashire Fusiliers were trained on the mountains. During that time the people suffered. One miner was killed; there were two suicides that I knew of. After ten months, the Cambrian miners were exhausted, and gave in.

One older man had taken part as a child in the Tonypandy riots. I called on Mr Thomas one afternoon, as he was about to start his tea. I said, 'Oh, don't let me interrupt your meal,' but he pushed his plate aside and said, 'I don't want bloody food when I get a chance to talk about the labour movement.'

'During the riots, there were three kids who sat next to me in school, and all that time their lockers were stuffed with sweets and chocolate they'd got from shops where the windows had been broken. The strike started over the price list in the Ely Colliery. The men claimed they couldn't make up the minimum wage on that price list; the Company said they could. The leaders of the other Lodges said it was impossible; so there was a strike. They were out for eleven months. A lot of the rioting was provoked by the police. The police were billeted on Pandy and wandered round in a half-drunken condition, heavy men, they had nothing to do all the time but eat and drink. Men used to go round the streets in gangs, my father-in-law was one of them; one day all the shop windows in Dunraven Street got bust. There was a real battle at the old Llwynypia Colliery entrance. The Company was trying to get the colliery started, and the men were determined it shouldn't. The first clash, the miners were routed; but after that they were ready, they carried mandrill shafts, staves, anything. Us kids used to go along with the men, backing them up. They had a march on the Cambrian Colliery; my mate and I went with them – it was in your blood, you see. You were a miner long before you started work. Anyway, they had to get the army here. It left marks on the minds of people that haven't gone to this day. I was eleven at the time.

'I was born in 1900. As a matter of fact, I was born 50 per cent blind, but it never stopped me going down the pit. I got my first pay from the pit on Christmas Eve 1914. That night, my father came in with a face like the rising sun: he'd just entered me as a member of the union. My father was a militant – he couldn't read or write, he never went to school, but he could talk and do head-work. I've lived for the labour movement. I've always been teetotal and non-smoker. About the time I was born, there had been a tremendous religious revival in the valleys. There was a preacher, Evan Roberts, he could control the people completely. He swept them off their feet with emotion, carried them away. Of course, the coal-owners loved him. He was a lunatic, of course; he died as a lunatic. But for all that, they couldn't stop the march of the working class.

'The amount of talent there is locked up within the working class is enormous. If we had socialism, you'd see all that talent come out, it would be a most wonderful awakening. You don't see it under capitalism, you can hardly imagine it. The Labour Party has always talked about what it will do for you; never what you can do for yourself; and that's where it has made its mistake. The Labour Party expects gratitude. Socialism will come, I know it as I've always known it. In the meantime, the struggle for more wages, less hours, prepares workers for running their own industries when the time comes; and then, at last, they will be involved in the control of and the responsibility for their own lives.'

I had a number of conversations like this; in the cool, wood-panelled interiors of the stone houses, many of them owned now by those who live in them: the Coal Board has sold most of its houses. From Rhondda I have a memory of brilliant summer afternoons, of dark silhouettes, almost black, against sun-filled windowpanes; and scarred hands and voices of reflective melancholy describing the experience of change, and the persistence of hope. 'This was once the richest valley in the world. I survived in the pits, only I never got enough pay for the work I did, ever. . . . I saw the struggle in the pit as a battle against the elements. Extracting coal from two sections of strata was a struggle against nature; and this is perhaps what gives mining communities a sense of a shared epic that they live through each day: this was the root of the working-class struggle, the fight of man for survival, and that is the dimension we've lost, the universality of it.

'I was down the pit at fourteen. We'd always accepted that this was our destiny really. We'd played around the colliery as children. We used to go into the tunnels in the mountainside, where the outcrop of the coal had been worked. We'd go in as far as we dared. There were levels that went straight into the heart of the mountain, and these were our playground. I was thrilled when the time came to go down the pit. You soon lose that, though. The first weeks underground were a real adventure. I shall never forget the first sensation of going down the shaft – you feel you're going up. It all depends on your butties, what sort of men they are. I was lucky, I was with a young fellow who really tried to help me. I've seen other men, no attempt to instruct you, just exploited the boy. I got 14/6 a week. My father was in the First War, and I was the oldest of twelve. I had resentment in me, because I passed for the higher schools, but I couldn't go. I saw the pressures on us as my mother saw them, and I had to go out to work to help her out. You don't realize when you're young – I think I took more out of the household than I put into it.

'There used to be a trainload of coal leave this valley every twenty minutes – 500 or 1,000 tons at a time. From Pontypridd, where the valleys meet, there was a trainload to Cardiff every five minutes. This valley was gutted, its heart was ripped out. The resource and the substance of the people were taken away: a flow of humanity and wealth that went in only one direction. . . . And now it's all over, they pump in a few millions here, a bit extra there. It can never compensate for the people who had to leave, the lives that were blighted and destroyed in the pits, the mutilation, the migration, the sense of loss. . . . People you knew were leaving all the time: it was like a constant bereavement; houses stood empty, people stood around all day; there was 60 per cent unemployment at times in the '30s.

'As a kid I was always forced to go to chapel. When you got to be fourteen and went down the pit you were a man, and I stopped going then. But by the age of sixteen, I started going back again of my own accord. My mother said to me, "Well, if there is such a place as heaven, my mother will be there." And that remark set me thinking. I became very sceptical; and the last time I went to chapel I was upset by the attitude of the minister who named me from the pulpit for sleeping during the sermon. I wasn't the only one, but I felt insulted and publicly humiliated. I never went again. He thought he was disciplining me; but he lost me for ever.

'I used to sit by the oil lamp at nights, reading anything I could lay my hands on. I read *The Ragged-Trousered Philanthropists*. I'd sit laughing at it, and my mother would say, "What are you laughing at, George?" And I'd say, "At myself." He was talking about our lives, I'd never met that before. I had no guidance in my reading.

'I was a bit of an anarchist really. I was a rebel without a cause at that time. I was married, but that didn't last, and I had a life of boredom, not knowing what to do with myself. I decided I'd join the International Brigade in Spain. I wasn't out of work at the time; I was getting reasonable money. I went to learn more about the Left – a drastic way of learning, maybe, but effective. I was in every action the International Brigade was in. If I went for adventure, it was a rough one. But in action, you never notice time; and whenever we weren't fighting, there was political discussion at every opportunity. I've never heard people talk as they did then. And since then my life has been full. I met Jack Jones in Spain; same as me, learning.

'It isn't the same now in the valleys. There isn't the fight in people there used to be: Nothing's changed as far as I can see. But my belief in the future is unbounded. The struggle we'll have may be hard; harder in some ways even than it was in the past; but I'm confident of the future outcome.'

A stone house in Tonypandy; double-fronted, with rustication around the doors and windows. Inside, the house is plain and old-fashioned. A chenille curtain at the door to exclude draughts, a dresser, a plain deal table with an oil-cloth; a high open grate; a runner along the mantelpiece, a square clock, two metal vases. There is an ancient armchair, covered with rugs and cushions; a footstool and a television. Mrs Phillips is eighty-six. She is waiting for her son to come home, as he does for two weeks every summer. He left in 1936, when he was seventeen. He went to London, where his sister was in service. 'I gave him a few pounds I'd put by for an emergency – and that meant funerals – to buy a suit. He got himself a job in a draper's shop in Wood Green. It makes you bitter, to see your family broken up like that. Over the years I've felt I haven't seen my children or my grandchildren grow up. Oh, they've been good to me, but I want them where I can see them and touch their dear faces. I've nothing else in my old years. I can't tell you the tears I've shed, and still do. My children were demeaned by the work they did, and nothing is going to make up for that now.'

David, who went to work in North London, is now fifty-eight. 'I had to ingratiate myself with the customers. It was so different in shops in those days. I even developed a slight stoop, you know, always eager to help them choose their linen or lace. I resented the people I served, because I always thought it was their fault I'd had to leave home. If Mother tells you she cried when I left, believe me, so did I.'

'I've still got all his letters to me.'

'My sister had a boy-friend, and I lodged with his family. I went to evening classes. I always had this in me, I knew I was never going down the pit. I come home every summer, on my own. I leave my wife and spend two weeks here with Mam. I shouldn't think there's half the people I was at school with still here; and those that are have been marked by the pit in some way – lungs or accidents. . . . I love to come home. I look out for every single thing that's changed from year to year. I'm hungry to see it all, the valley, the kids fishing out on the flat stones, the gulls, the houses, the ruined pits, the sunlight on the trees. I always know what to expect, but there's such a feeling of excitement in me. Something about home, a place to come back to. I know everything in this house, but I walk round for a day or two, to make sure everything is still there. I sometimes wonder what my life would have been like, if I had stayed here. It opened up a lot in London; but you lose something tremendous. You can't quite describe it. It's as though I had had two lives – the one here and the other one there. I come back looking for the part of myself that's up there on the hills watching the shadows on the green and the boys fishing and listening to the boots of the miners on the road. . . .'

5

ALFRED HEDLEY, sixty-three, Bradford:

It's been one of my life's interests to preserve the dialect, to capture some of the depth and richness of the working-class tradition in Yorkshire. I think that all the pressures that have been on us have made us lose contact with our own roots; and that doesn't enhance people's lives.

'My parents were both mill workers. I can remember my father telling me about when he worked in Luddenden End mill, along with his brother, father and mother; four members of the same family worked alongside each other – it wasn't unusual in those days. One day, when my father was quite a youngster, the boss of this mill, he said to him, "Hey lad, I want you to run down to the pub and get me a jug of ale." Well, my father went to his dad and told him what the boss had asked him to do. His father said, "Get back to your work, I'll see the boss." And he went to him and said, "No child of mine is going in alehouses. I've never done it, he's never been to fetch ale for me, and he's not doing it for anybody else." Well, that was it. The boss said, "Right, you can get out, all of you, your wife and your kids." He gave them a moment's notice. Not only that, but they had a company house, their things were put out on the pavement right away, and the door was locked against them. They had to pile up all their bits and pieces on a handcart and walk into Bradford. The whole family livelihood was gone.

'When I left school, I walked all the way from Bradford to Halifax, and I called at every office and every mill on the way to see if there was a job going, any sort of job. There wasn't. I got my first job through somebody my father knew in the end. I stayed at school till I was sixteen; our parents had ambitions for us. I got 10/– a week for that job. It was 1931 when I left school; the Depression was at its worst. It wasn't until I went into a mill, preparing the warp cards, that I really felt happy. I met all the workers at the mill that way, and that was when I first got passionately interested in the industry, and the life of the mills and the people in them. There was always such a strong hierarchy of labour; the high- and low-status jobs. Many of the low ones were associated with the smell, because some of the work made the people smell terribly. And in our part of Bradford you could plot where all the people used to live, street by street, according to their position. The managers, of course, lived outside the area, but everybody else lived locally. Those in better jobs had quite superior housing, down to those who did the casual and rough jobs, who would have lived in lodging houses. You know, the women had lovely hands, working with wool, because of the lanolin. Once I went to where my father was working at the hospital, and he showed me the hand of a woman that had been severed by one of the machines. I wrote a poem about it. It was perfect, a beautiful hand. And she was upstairs, being stitched, with her perfect, beautiful hand down there. The hand she would perhaps have clasped a lover with. She never did; as a matter of fact, I took an interest in her life, and she never did marry. I often wondered whether it was because of that. There were so many of them lost fingers or a hand in the machinery.

'I've many happy memories of the warmth of the people, their lives and humour. There was one woman who used to talk and talk and talk; oh dear, nobody could shut her up. One day, two of the directors, directors mind you – they'd never do a thing like that today – they bundled her up and put her in a skep, a big basket they used for the wool, and they took her out into the mill yard, and fetched the lorry. She was yelling and carrying on, banging away inside, but they said to the driver, "Take this yarn up to Keighley, it's needed there urgently." Then they beckoned the driver and whispered, "Just drive her round the mill two or three times, and then come back in here." Well, it changed her. She became a different woman. But that was what they used to do, they'd teach them practical lessons, if there was anybody who was a nuisance or who was unpopular. It was rough maybe, but when you're all working close together, you can't afford to think too much of yourself. There was a sense of common purpose.

'But the best example I saw of people's capacity for sharing was in the war. I was called up in 1939. I wouldn't kill, but I didn't want to be a conscientious objector. I didn't want to fight, but I did go on sick berth duty in the navy. I was on HMS *Pegasus* in the autumn of 1939, when the *Royal Oak* was torpedoed and sunk in Scapa Flow. That was on the night of 13/14 October

1939. I shall never forget it. We picked up 428 men; and we had a crew of only 150. The *Royal Oak* had been torpedoed in her ammunition locker. Some of those who survived told us a great sheet of flame had swept through the mess where they were eating. A lot of the men had no chance at all; others were severely burned or injured; a few were sheltered from it, and they were the ones who at least escaped with their lives. We took on all these casualties, some of them in a terrible state – you couldn't describe the injuries. It was an inferno, the whole ship was swamped with blood and oil; and there was just myself and the ship's doctor. The doctor decided we should just apply First Aid to as many as possible. You had to make decisions that were unbearable. If people were too badly injured, and likely to die within an hour or two, you had to leave them and decide to help those you had a chance of saving. They were crying, some were screaming with the pain, but you had to concentrate on the work you were doing, and try not to be distracted by the noise and the pain all around you. I was attending to one man, and suddenly I felt someone grip me round the throat from behind; and he started banging my head against the post with such violence, and he was screaming, "Help me, why don't you help me?" – once, then twice, and then the third time I was struck so hard I just passed out. Fortunately, the doctor was near by, and saw what was happening, and he came up and forced this poor man's wrists loose. The next thing I knew, the doctor was pouring whisky down my throat and shouting "For God's sake wake up, Hedley." I came to, and the doctor said "There he is", and I looked, and the man who had attacked me was lying on the floor. Dead. He was in his last desperate throes, but his grip had been so strong he almost killed me.

'On that ship, most of the crew were either eighteen-year-olds, just been called up, or pensioners, men who'd retired from the navy; but do you know, the spirit of those people was extraordinary. They rose to what was required of them without any hestitation, without flinching. It was an inspiration. "How can we help?" "What can we do?" We'd no bandages left, so I thought, Now what's to do? and then I said, "Boil up as much strong tea as you can in the urns, and soak all the cloth you can find in it"; the tannic acid, you see, could act as a disinfectant and bind the material together to stanch bleeding. That way, we could at least cover all the wounds. And by the time we'd finished, most of us had given virtually all the clothes we had. I'd no shoes or socks; the men had given their blankets, coats, everything they had. It was a dreadful ordeal. But it was wonderful to see what those eighteen-year-old boys could do in coping with it. But doing something together, when you can see before you what needs to be done, brings out a wealth of resources and courage that you'd never know were there otherwise. I think that is it: if nothing is demanded of you, you give nothing. And that's what is wrong with us now.

'After that, we went back to Portsmouth. The doctor and I had a conversation before we separated. He said "We shan't get any medals for what we've done, but we know that we did what was necessary, we've nothing to be ashamed of, in spite of all that death and destruction all around us." I did actually pick up some medals in the later stages of the war, the Atlantic star and the Mediterranean star, but I wouldn't flaunt them. In fact, *Pegasus* was off to Dunkirk not long afterwards; by that time the men had already had their baptism by fire, they were experienced and had a new confidence. Having survived that, it gave them something which I'm sure has stayed with them for the rest of their lives.

'I've always felt that death and suffering are our real enemies. They happen to us readily enough, without inflicting them on each other. It isn't other people who are foes, it's the things that destroy humanity anyway – disease, loneliness and loss: those are the things we should always be fighting. Only the trouble is with those things you never win; whereas you can vanquish men, you can destroy human beings, and give yourself a sense of victory, triumph. But it's not real; the thing you've inflicted will overtake you in the end as well.

'I think this is one of the reasons why today's world seems so strange to me – people try to deny death. I think that is worse than repressing sex in many ways. A lot of people now, they won't even have the body of their loved ones in the house when they die. They die in hospital; then at the funeral, they just call at the house in the funeral car, like somebody making a visit. When the wife's mother died, they didn't want to have her in the house; so they put her in the chip-shop. "That's where she worked all her life," they said; "she'll be all right till the funeral." I said, "No, you'll have her in the house, that's the least you can do." I had a look at her, and poor lass, her hair was all dishevelled. I put a comb through it, make her look nice. They thought it was stupid. I should hate to think there was no one to perform a last act of kindness for me; it's all we've got after all, our sense of each other's dignity. It's the fear that we might lose that that is the worst nightmare to me. It seems to me that a great sickness has come over a lot of our working-class traditions; something cheap and gaudy is trying to destroy them. It mustn't happen, because in that industrial world of the nineteenth century we did develop dignity in the face of brutalizing processes. . . . And what frightens me, what poverty couldn't do to us, I think greed and money perhaps might.

'I don't think I ever found a real outlet for my talents in work. I always enjoyed work; and I'm not embittered. My great consolation has always been the people I've worked with. I've been very lucky, I've always seemed to attach people to me. I worked for many years in the Mass Radiography Service. And then, in recent years, I was a security guard in the University at Bradford. I talked to everybody, and as I did so, it occurred to me that I might as well have a go at getting a degree, even at this late stage of my life. When I was younger, my wife was very ill for many years. Looking after her and our daughter was a very important part of my life. And so at fifty-nine I went as a mature student to Bradford; and I started doing some work on my neighbourhood. My tutor took an interest and was very helpful and encouraging. I've always written things, especially dialect, dialect poetry. I love the dialect, its richness and vividness of expression. It's a living part of me, the voices of the place where I grew up.

'I had a heart attack last year and I had to interrupt my studies. Not give them up. Now my wife is ill again, in hospital. Even when somebody needs constant attention and you feel they are very difficult to look after, you miss them terribly when they're not there.'

Part Two

PEOPLE UNDER SIEGE

1

WHEREVER PEOPLE MEET by chance in public places – supermarkets, launderettes, bus stops, pubs, libraries, clinics, doctors' surgeries – there is a flow of discourse and exchange, much of it apparently quite trivial. It is commonly regarded as purely incidental, a polite but meaningless ritual that makes easier the random closeness of strangers in crowded urban areas.

But it is far more than this. It has a definable content and a very specific purpose. It is an attempt, clumsy and haphazard perhaps, to reconstitute some sense of communal values that have been lost. In it there is a body of assumptions about shared experience and background, which can act as a defining edge against a chaotic, menacing outside world. And the outside world is indeed hostile and formless. The only thing missing is a tangible shared experience; and in consequence communication between people depends almost entirely on identifying the external threat.

People talk as though they were under siege; victims of some universal and impenetrable conspiracy. A fictive sense of shared values evolve *ad hoc* to fill the vacuum which ought to be occupied by a shared sense of social purpose. These values are reductive and inconsistent; often vengeful and cruel.

It is as though we have never seen such terrible times as those we are living through. The whole world, even the familiar world of the High Street, with its bright luminous posters announcing this week's reductions, is suddenly full, not of neighbours and shoppers, but of threatening creatures with names such as we have never heard – muggers and extremists, vandals and paedophiles. Monsters and aliens are all around us. Just as the medieval Church attracted demons and evil spirits, so the dazzling displays of our abundance call into being hosts of wreckers and malevolents. The analogy is not misplaced: any system which claims for itself perfection, absolute goodness, must attract its opposite in some form; and this is the guise in which capitalism now presents itself. During the last thirty years or so, it has become sanitized, purified, sanctified. It is now the universal provider, the bringer of all richness and diversity; and as such is sacred.

If you talk to old working-class people, however oppressive the poverty and insecurity under which they lived, they will always recall that the greatest consolation was the quality of the human relationships; how comforting it was to share, with kin, neighbours, work companions. But now, in the face of the vast improvements in material conditions, it is the people who are all wrong. Things are better; but all that has been gained has been at the expense of human relationships.

Things are more than better; they are perfect. A colour supplement opened at random in December 1977 offered this flow of superlatives – best loved, most desired, handsome, desirable, excellent, loving care, original, fun, stimulating, exciting, best, sophisticated, creative, important, harmonious, distinguished, convenient, fascinating, classic, impeccable, new, fresh, high quality, satisfying, magnificent, masterpiece, unique, joy, style, trust, happy, finest, most distinguished ever, best, perfect, enjoyable, quality, most distinctive, brilliant, most beautiful in the world, a better start in life, super, sheer pleasure, genius, real, natural, invaluable, countless new possibilities, well-being, goodness. It doesn't matter what any of these words refers to; what does matter is that they all describe inanimate objects, and many of them are borrowed from the kind of experiences that have traditionally been felt to belong to humanity, not to the realm of its artefacts. The transference of human attributes to things, their power to bestow satisfactions which previously only people were thought capable of giving, is a visible part of the process of dehumanizing others, and substituting commodities for the debased humanity. It is not the things themselves that are at fault: it is only when the terms on which they are available adversely affects people. Of course, we are not totally susceptible: people do triumph over circumstances, just as we did when we were brutalized by poverty. We learn more from the reality of our human involvements than from official agencies of instruction, even then these appeal to the most selfish part of us. But at the same time, the very insistence and repetitiveness of these things do have their effect. The malaise does persist in what remains of what we still call, sentimentally, our communities; loneliness, dissatisfaction; the powerlessness of parents over their children, the indifference of the young towards the old, the sense of reluctant acquiescence in values that seem to be beyond our control, the cynicism towards others. It is impossible to exaggerate the depth to which we have been affected. It isn't a question of materialism, it is the whole process of manufacture, the spread and allocation of things, and the money which is the key to access to them. It isn't that the removal of this oppressive power would liberate us in any absolute sense; only the kind of violence, anger, distrust, mental illness, indifference, bitterness that have grown in recent years are directly attributable to the way in which we have no choice but to live. Our terrible human vulnerability, our aloneness, our deepest sense of shame and inadequacy, instead of being protected by our shared values, have been annexed and exploited for gain. We have been told that things can offer us what people no longer can; and we are reduced to compliance.

And in the few fragmented places in which we still meet communally, we echo this barren creed.

In the supermarket, a child of about four is carrying a huge packet of washing powder, almost as large as himself. As he stands beside his mother, his hand works open the perforated aperture in the packet. It becomes too heavy for him to hold, so he turns it round, and a stream of blue powder accumulates at his feet. When his mother sees what has happened, she is furious. She shakes him and screams at him; the powder continues to scatter. The anger bears no relation to the offence. When she gets to the counter, she apologizes exaggeratedly to the girl who says indifferently, 'Oh, that's all right.' The child's crime is against the supermarket. She goes out, saying, 'You wait till I get you home, Gavin.'

Woman, in her late sixties: 'Well, I was coming up the hill with my shopping, and this kid – he couldn't have been above eight or nine – he comes up to me and says, "Carry your bag, Ma?" I thought, Well, that is nice, to see a kid as considerate as that. I says, "Oh, that is kind of you, son." He says, "It'll cost you." I was speechless. I says, "You can bugger off then." They want money even for acts of kindness now.'

'Well, how about this one. My mate works in a garage. This black comes in with his car, you know, American job with leopard-skin upholstery, bunch of plastic tulips in the back. My mate says, "Okay, come back Monday." He comes back. It's a big job, eighty quid. He drives off, winds down the window and says, "Send the bill to Social Security." '

A supermarket queue, at the checkout counter. An old woman stands with her shopping, waiting to reach the till. A much younger woman, wheeling a trolley, stands in an adjacent queue. She talks to the older woman across the aisle. 'Oh, hello love, how are you?' She shakes her head. 'Not good.' 'Oh, I am sorry. What's the trouble?' 'It's my legs. They just give way all the time. I've had one or two nasty falls.' 'Oh dear. What causes that then?' 'Old age, love.' The younger woman sees it is her turn at the checkout. She says goodbye to the other. 'Well, I hope you'll soon be better.' The old woman turns away and says bitterly to the empty air, 'Better. I'm seventy-six. How the hell does she expect me to get better? Only one cure as I know for old age. Silly cow. They're all the same, got no time for anybody but themselves.'

'Well, of course, I know how it's done. I know how they get away with it. You can get a television from Social Security, it's quite true, only it's not as straightforward as that. They buy one with doors, like a cabinet. Then, you see, it's classed as a piece of furniture. And if you've no furniture in your flat, they are obliged to provide you with so much, and one of the items is a cupboard. I know that's right. I've got a friend who works in Social Security, she told me that's how they do it, so I know it's true.'

This kind of communication has little to do with any alleged facts, however solemnly presented. The feeling is everything, and because of this, it is impossible to engage with it on rational terms. You say, in vain, that Social Security won't accept bills from garages in respect of repairs, and that it really doesn't run to television sets. These are not really the issues: it is the overwhelming need for a sense of shared predicament in the face of an identifiable enemy. The prejudices are only a kind of hard outcrop of all the profound needs that are unanswered in the way we live now. Wherever these exchanges take place, they can flow in only one direction. If the ideas and values carried in this flow are harsh, it is because they are a refraction of a real pain; only the true agents that inflict it are taboo.

In a pub some men are talking about the repatriation of immigrants. One of them tries to stem the surge of indignation; but his objection sounds feeble and unconvincing against the irresistible force of the resentment. He subsides, powerless against the belief that there is a conspiracy to do us harm, to deny us our rights, to thwart our merited happiness; one of his companions says something about a strain of venereal disease that is untouched by penicillin, and he concedes that they may be right.[8] This process is like a caricature of that traditional working-class sense of being embattled against an inimical and exploitative world; only the villains are shifting and amorphous: the blacks, muggers, groups of workers, the government; or, more vaguely still, extremists, wreckers; the breakdown of discipline, loss of respect.

This flow of feeling sweeps everything before it. It is cynical and knowing, it expects the worst of everybody. Everybody is out for number one. The whole world is on the make. All politicians are dishonest and self-seeking. Instead of friends, neighbours and kin, there are loonies, fiends and maniacs everywhere. 'My friend, she got mugged, had three fingers broken. She didn't even dare go to court to give evidence, because their friends told her that if she did, they would come and get her. There were ten of them. None of them above seventeen. They got a conditional discharge. My husband said he'd give them an unconditional discharge, straight out of the barrel of a gun. There's one law for the rich and another for the poor, we've always known that; now we can see there's another for the blacks as well.'

The need to share, which is the initial impetus for the fumbling after enemies, soon gets lost in a self-flagellation of resentment and hatred. All positive feeling is falsified, and in the end, is submerged in the torrents of vengeance. The most mild and law-respecting individuals are heard publicly offering themselves to pull the trigger, press the button, tighten the rope around the neck of all the supposed malefactors.

When the funeral workers were on strike, two women were talking in their local library: 'I think it's wicked. People's grief. Not to be able to bury your dead. I think that's the worst thing you could do to anybody.' 'I know what I'd do. I'd shoot the sods down and dig the graves for 'em with my bare hands.'

A bus stop in Hackney. A street of decaying mansion blocks and crumbling villas – rusty palings, flaking red-brown paint, damaged doorsteps, moss-grown basements. An old man stamps his feet against the cold, and his extinguished gaze takes in the cracked pavements and corroded brick. 'It used to be lovely round here. I'm thankful it's Monday. I dread the weekend. I hate Sundays, God forgive me for saying it, that I should hate His day. Sunday used to be our best day when I was a kid. My poor old mum, if she could see me now, it'd break her heart. . . . I've got four kids. I never see them from one month to the next, not till they want something. Money generally – and I'm on supplementary.'

'I don't go out any more than I have to now. Not day or night. They had an outing from the pub. The coach wasn't getting back till it was dark, so I couldn't go. There was one old dear round here, in her seventies, she was raped by some drunk, while a gang of kids stood round and watched.'

The sharing in these brief public situations is, of course, only provisional, and it soon passes, leaving a residue of dissatisfaction. The person standing next to you in the supermarket queue is obviously in the same situation as yourself as long as he or she is standing there. In that situation he has an identifiable rôle, when you can see an open wire basket full of Chum and Cornflakes and sausages with the extra meaty taste. There is something reassuring in people's public recourse to the same basic products as yourself. But as soon as he leaves the supermarket, he is claimed by the anonymous world outside, and his Tesco's bag might as easily contain a bomb or a severed head as tonight's dinner. Waiting for a bus, drinking in a pub before going home after a day's work, sitting in the launderette watching the multi-coloured swirl of other people's underwear – these experiences yield isolated moments of insight into what more continuous sharing would be like. They are precious little pools of light and warmth in the prevailing darkness and mystery of other people; but they are instantly lost as individuals separate with a 'Mind how you go, love', 'Don't do anything I wouldn't do'; and the smile fades as you are again plunged into a world in which evil and malice hold sway. And the next time you meet the person with whom you shared a fragment of yourself, you may not even recognize him.

This thwarted need runs through much of the popular culture of the '70s. It has been used as the basis of many of the most popular films, the paperbacks and comics, the television re-runs of horror movies. They all express the same pain. The preoccupation everywhere is with giant spiders or killers from the deep, the monstrous worm or evil spirits; demonic possession or creatures that have survived from the beginnings of time or have reached us from the furthest confines of space. Everything speaks of the attempt to locate an external evil against which we can all unite and share. But these cultural phenomena are in many ways only a metaphor, suggesting evils that are already among us. 'I believe there are people from other planets actually here on this earth, only we're too stupid to recognize them. There are alien beings who wish us harm. They must have some mark on them somewhere, and I think it should be our purpose to spot them before they do us some terrible evil.' – Girl, eighteen.

Among us walk the alien, the undead; vampires, werewolves and demons. The distance from the metaphor to groups of people we can identify is small. A whole sanguinary scenario is posted in the wings, like the plot of a macabre *commedia dell'arte*, waiting to be summoned, as it were, if needed. It has surfaced a little in recent years in the guise of the National Front; but it is in this direction that the mainstream of the culture has been moving for many years now, through the floating and largely unlocated evils of rapists and terrorists, muggers and extremists, to the undead, the alien and the intruder; above all, the inhuman. And every diminishing exchange in public, every moment of false community fashioned out of the difference of others, is fed into this drift, which becomes a flow, and ultimately, a resistless tide. We risk creating a hideous deformity of communal values out of the pain at our broken sense of belonging.

2

ON THE EDGE of the Black Country, Walsall's industrial base was metal and leather, small foundries, tanneries and ironworks. Caldmore is a characteristic nineteenth-century industrial suburb, half a mile from the centre of the town, just beyond the pillared Georgian houses which speak of substantial entrepreneurs who did not disdain to live close to their works. Caldmore Green is the centre of the area, with its Liberal Club, an old cinema, a gaunt Co-op; the shells of decayed foundries and factories, saddlers and harness makers, and the scars of demolished houses which seem to take so long to heal in these city centre areas, with willow-herb growing everywhere, as though the acres of red brick had seeded another kind of flowering.

The area looks permanently in the process of becoming something else, although whatever it is is never quite achieved. There is a row of half-built shops, begun by a property company that went bankrupt: a row of concrete cells in which windblown litter collects, couples with nowhere to go take shelter, and flowers manage to take root in cracks in the floor. There are some almshouses endowed by a local factory owner, an old bakery which is now the Co-op cleaners. Part of the district is bay-windowed, with rusting ironwork stars on the gables and flaking ornamental railings, which suggest high tea behind lace curtains, parasols and muslin behind a screen of high sooty laurels. The cobbled alleyways between the houses evoke stern and vigilant employers, who warned their people that if they didn't vote Conservative, they would be found out.

Caldmore looks much like any other Victorian working-class community; what distinguishes it is that it has one of the most vigorous community action groups in the country. Barrie Blower has a passionate and direct love for the place; he talks of stability and constancy in a world that believes happiness can be reached through restlessness and novelty. 'Well, it's not much to look at as a place, but it isn't that, you know. It's your feeling for it, what it means to you. We've had a lot of visitors come to see us, the Housing Action Group, the advice centre, and sometimes you you can see them thinking, Why does he want to get all excited about a dump like this. It would be meaningless for me to leave it. Where else would I go? This has happened to a lot of people – they leave the place where they grew up, and then go searching all over the world to try and find it again. They always feel a dull sense of not belonging, an ache for something they can't even remember.'

We walk round the district. 'The working class that lived here is something we shall never see again. They did develop their own culture, their own values, in opposition to the poverty and exploitation; but that's mostly gone now. We've just bought this site for the Housing Association, two streets have been pulled down here. There was some delay, because there was one old lady who wouldn't move; her son, who was still living with her, had died in the house. And she felt that if the house was demolished, it would take away all the memories of the boy who'd died. They had to promise her a flat on the spot where her house had been. You can understand it. Of course people are attached to places through the human bonds that they've shared in them. I think all feeling is looked on now as sentimentality; the only thing that matters is efficiency – except we're not even any good at that. I can respect that old lady. When I see houses coming down in this area, I more or less knew who lived in them, it's a bit like seeing their lives churned up. When they say "unfit for human habitation", it somehow denies that people who lived here in the past were human beings. Our house was pulled down a couple of years ago, and now we live just outside Caldmore. It's a nice house, where we are now, only when you see the places where you spent your childhood disappearing: well, it's a denial of something.

'Look, you can see from the size of the factories they were quite small concerns; up there it says "Saddlery", chocolate brown paint on the brick. Fancy leather goods, metal polishers. Round this area there used to be a lot of skilled jobs; people used to be making things in all these workshops, a lot of creative work, carpentry, metalwork, leather. Nearly all of them required the individual to be involved in what he did. Now the firms that are left employ unskilled or semi-skilled. You might stand eight hours a day at a lathe, simple repetitive actions. The kind of work that's here now is the sort where going to have a piss is a major event in the day. They've time on their hands; no, not time, they're occupied, but not fully, never fully involved with what they're doing. There's a terrible weariness of the body and spirit. A lot of people are severely underemployed; and that's before you get to the issue of unemployment. People are under-used.

'There's a rolling clearance programme here.' Rows of houses with narrow Gothicized porches, dating from the 1870s and '80s, so that even the houses were slightly redolent of ceremonial chapel entrances. 'It's bad property, this, it couldn't be saved. In five years' time there's no doubt that it will be a well-planned environment, but whether it'll be a good community, or even a community at all, is open to question. This area contains about 8,000 people, 2,000 households. The biggest change I've seen here over the years has been an increase in competitiveness, people's rivalry with each other. People don't know each other as they used to. We did know, we used to know everybody. You knew who worked where, what the domestic circumstances were of all the families in your street and the streets around you. That is just about the right number that an individual can encompass – about 8,000 people. When I was a kid, people went to work, they went home to dinner all at the same time, then back again, only a walk or a short bike ride away. The only people you saw around in the daytime were women shopping and old-age pensioners. That's what gave these places their sense of community – everybody was conspicuously in the same situation. It did act as a discipline, not very pleasant. People had to conform. But the reward was that you were looked after. Now all the tragedies take place in secret. You only hear of them when someone is found with her head in the gas oven or some kid runs away from home. There was an Asian girl who was brought over here for an arranged marriage; she could speak no English, she knew no one. In the end, she set fire to herself. There is so much you can't reach in people's lives now. People are ashamed of their own suffering; they believe it's their own fault.

'I know they say I'm a romantic about the old working-class communities. I don't accept that it's romantic. The way things were seems to me common sense. We band together to help people through situations that are painful; however rich we may become, however much we can afford to pay people to simulate caring, whatever sycophancy and service money can buy, there isn't any substitute for a caring that comes organically out of the way you live.

'Now people talk as though they believed they could buy happiness, if only they had enough money. The point is, you can never have enough. People don't admit that money is everything; quite the reverse, in fact. Only they don't behave as though they believed it. There's a poster over the road. It says _Can buy me love_.* Parents buy their kids things instead of relating to them.'

Barrie Blower went to the local grammar school, but was expelled. 'I just couldn't relate to all the things we were expected to do and believe in. Then I went to the high school, that was the

* Salvation Army poster.

technical college. It was seen as being one step down from the grammar school. But by that time, I'd already got my character mapped out for me. I had a reputation of being a troublemaker, a tearaway. So I got slung out of there as well, and finished up at the secondary modern. That was the kind of place that nobody got chucked out of, because there's nowhere else to go. I left there at fifteen. My dad said, "You'd better come and work with me, I'll be able to keep an eye on you there." He was on the railways. So that's where I started my working life. I was there fifteen months; it was a wonder I lasted that long. My father said, "I've worked on the railways thirty-five years, and I've never had a mark against me all that time. You're there five minutes, and the name Blower is mud." So one morning I just decided I wouldn't get up. I stayed in bed, and that was it. I'd given it up. I went down to the Labour Exchange, no idea of what I wanted to do. I saw a poster on the wall, pictures of men in white caps. Join the Royal Navy. I thought, That's what I'll do. I said, "I want to join the navy". He got the book out, blew the dust off – I don't think anybody from Walsall had joined the navy within living memory. He said, "Can you swim?"' I said, "No". He said, "Any relatives in the navy?" I said, "No". Obviously that did it. I was in. I was a stoker, twelve years. Travelling around. I didn't have any fantasies about faraway places – well, if I did, I got them out of my system. Then when I came home, there seemed to be a lot of uneasiness in Caldmore. People were dissatisfied, restless. Nobody knew what was going to happen to the community; a lot of the houses were in bad condition, everybody felt that the place had lost something. I got involved, and the Advice Centre has been here eight years now.'

The Housing Advice Centre is on Caldmore Green, occupying a central conspicuous place. It is open and accessible, where people bring, not so much isolated problems, but their whole lives: as they talk of their fears and anxieties, it is like a tally of the price we have paid, in human terms, for the kind of material improvement we have experienced. Many of those who come here are those who have failed to adapt, or have adapted badly to the altered demands that have been placed on them. Being in Caldmore reminded me, more than anywhere else, of going home, in the richness of the feeling for the details of people's lives, the sense of involvement.

An elderly man, probably in his mid-sixties, comes into the Centre. His eyes are watery and unfocused; their vague dilation suggest wonder and confusion. His speech is slurred; his face corroded by the effects of alcohol. He wants to talk to someone about his wife. When they were married and he still lived in a house – Do you live in a house? he asks – she used to have men in all the time, while he was out at work. 'I know who she went off with. She must be punished. I want you to tell the police.' Suddenly, the flow of his anger at distant wrongs weakens, and something of the sympathy of the girl who is listening to him reaches his pain; he observes that he is heard, and forgets for a moment. He takes her hand. 'You've got a lucky face, you're going to have a lucky life. . . . You'll have everything you want.' He asks if she will let him read her hand, tell her fortune. His aggression and anger fall away, and he responds to her tone, and becomes pliant and eager to please her. His wife left him thirty years ago. He sleeps in derelict houses, or in the daytime in a cubicle in the public lavatory on the Green, with a mangy dog beside him.

In a corner pub, all frosted glass and battered brown furniture, a woman in a herringbone coat sits anxiously waiting and playing with a beer mat. Every time the door opens, she looks up and is disappointed. At last a man of about fifty in a donkey jacket comes in. He is thickset, with thinning hair. There is mud on his boots from a nearby building site. When she sees him, the woman's face, which had been clenched and lined, recomposes itself in a smile of relief that almost transforms her into another person. He doesn't speak, but goes to the bar. He buys her a Guinness and himself a pint of bitter. Their hands meet fumblingly through the ornamental wrought iron of the table. She looks at him inquiringly; and he expresses to her something softly, which he seems to offer as a gift or a concession. She listens to him, and, as she does so, her face slowly contracts again; a look of anger almost. She says, 'How can you leave her if she's as bad as that? Who'll look after her?' He says, 'She won't get any worse, she's been like it for years.' They are silent for a few minutes. Then he says to her, 'That's what you want, isn't it? That's what you said you wanted. It's all because of you, it's for your sake.' She looks at him intently. 'Would you leave me if I was like that?' 'I wouldn't leave you.' He reaches for her hand through the iron again, but she withdraws. 'If you'd leave her, you'd leave me. Anything could happen. I'm not young either. I could be ill.' He looks bewildered. 'But that's what you said you want. You've been saying it for weeks.' 'No, I'd never sleep easy again.' 'Well, what do you want?' She shakes her head. 'I don't know.' They sit in silence for a long time. He indicates the clock over the bar with his head, and rises to leave her. He says, 'I'll see you Saturday. All right?' 'You might,' she says. She sits looking down into her drink. Her eyes appear closed. From beneath the lashes a tear sparks but doesn't fall.

BARRIE BLOWER: 'These communities were a mixture of discipline and charity. You always got a certain number of people who didn't fit in, but a lot of them were accepted. They were part of the landscape, a few subnormals, a few eccentrics who might have been mentally sick. There was one man who wandered these streets for years. His mother died, and his father committed suicide when he was sixteen. His sisters were taken off to a home, and he lost track of them. Being sixteen, he was thought to be old enough to fend for himself. He slept rough for years. I don't think he worked. His back became bent with malnutrition and sleeping in damp places. He was always around. He used to do odd jobs for people, dig a garden, fetch coal in for old people, that was about all he could do. Sometimes they fed him, or he slept in their sheds on their allotment in winter. There was an old widow; he'd done a lot of work for her, and when she died she left him her little house because she felt sorry for him, and she'd got nobody belonging to her. So for the first time since he was a kid he gets a proper home. By this time he must be in his fifties. And he's been living there for about a year, when the council decide it's a slum, they're going to knock it down. How can you expect him to understand that? Here's a man, he's been a vagrant for maybe thirty years, at last he's got a place to live. He loves it. If they chuck him out, he'll be off again, he won't go and live in a council flat. You need places like this, you need some of the old housing, a place for people to hide, who feel that the blank empty glare of new estates only shows up their frailties. There are quite a few people like that: those who've lived through some terrible shame, those who feel inadequate and don't want to be laughed at, there's something enfolding and protective here. It's a haven for them. The only alternative is institutions.

'It's not only the neighbourhood that's been broken down. It goes much deeper than that. Look how relationships inside the family have been contaminated by the values from outside. It really is every man for himself, people inside the same family at each other's throats, rivalries, jealousies; parents buying things for their kids because that's the only way they can express feeling, and then wondering what's gone wrong when they find they've nicked something or beaten somebody up.

'There was a bloke – the street is demolished now – who was stealing stuff from the firm he worked for, oh, for years and years it went on, and he was selling quietly, you know. Metalwork or something, I don't know exactly what it was. Anyway, what he used to do with the money, his parents lived in a little house in one of these streets, dark little place, built-in cupboards, full of nooks and crannies, gaslight, you know. And the old couple were getting on, in their seventies and eighties. They never used this top cupboard where he was hiding all this money, you had to climb to reach it. He visited them every week, and every week he put some more money away. It went on for years, until in the end he'd accumulated quite a sum. The cupboard was chock full of money: pound notes, fivers, ten-shilling notes. Anyway, by a strange coincidence, his parents both died on the same day. The father died, and, when the old lady found him, I think she had a heart attack and died on the spot, more or less. Their son was out of town at the time, on his holidays I think. He'd got a sister, who lived a few doors away from the parents, and she went down and made all the arrangements for the funeral and everything. She was a bit of a drudge, not married, and she'd been helping her parents out with a bit of cash over the years. She didn't get on with her brother – the parents thought he was wonderful, whereas she was the one who did all the work. Well, she went through all the things in the house, naturally, and when she came to turn out the cupboards, of course all this money came floating down. She had no idea there was anything like that in the house. She thought it must have belonged to her parents; and she was furious because they'd always pleaded poverty, and she'd been giving them money for years. So she packed it all up in a big suitcase. She took it all down to the church and said she'd found it in her parents' house, and she'd like it all to go to the church.

Of course they accepted it. When her brother got back and found out what had happened, well, he couldn't believe she had done it without malice. He went mad. He had no claim to the money officially; he couldn't prove it was his. And if he could, he would have had to account for it. He wanted us to help him get it back, but there was nothing we could do. You can imagine the effect it had on him; it really broke him up.

'Then we had the drama of the couple who were living with the woman's parents, in the same area as the other one. The mother died, and the old man was a bit of an encumbrance to them. He just sat around moping after his wife died, getting on their nerves. They wanted him out, but they couldn't because, of course, it was his house. He deteriorated, he just sat there all day; the daughter said he wouldn't do a thing. If the flies settled on his face, he just let them wander all over him, he wouldn't even get up to go to the toilet. They tried to shift him, get him out to the pensioners' club, and in the end they smartened him up and he met a widow at the club and decided to get married again. She had a nice house, a semi on the Sutton Road, and his daughter was really pleased when he decided to go and live there. Only once he'd married her, it wasn't all he'd hoped. He married the muck-heap for the manure and got poisoned by the stink. She was really stuck-up. They didn't get on at all. She wouldn't even give him a key to the front door. She wanted him to go out when she had her friends to tea. So gradually, he started going back to his old house, and he spent more and more time on his allotment. In fact, he wasn't really welcome anywhere. Anyway, one day he died on his way home from the allotment. And his wife, as soon as she knew what had happened, went round to the daughter's house and told them she'd let them have the first week rent-free, then after that they could start paying her £10 a week rent. He hadn't made a will; so she was the next of kin and got the house. There was nothing you could do; the house where the daughter had lived all her life. We couldn't do anything for her.

'I love the work I do here. I wouldn't be a car worker for £500 a week, but I'd do this one for £5 a week. I did it two years for nothing at the beginning. I think the greatest privilege today is to have work that is enjoyable and purposeful. In fact, we are part of the most privileged class – those who have something worthwhile to do. It's funny to think that work should be a privilege, when what everybody is supposed to be striving for is leisure. Just because the system used to screw the last ounce of energy out of a man, it can persuade him that leisure is a release from his slavery; only leisure has already been sewn up in advance, so nobody has time to start thinking about a system in which so few people seem to be doing anything of real value, and all the products we turn out are designed to last about twenty minutes. Dignity of labour. What does it do to a man, to be subservient to a machine making things he despises? A society based on that is bound to be sick.'

Workers talking in the pub at midday. A shop steward in a foundry, a big man with a Mao badge, who fought in Korea, says, 'I have to educate my own children in labour history. They'll get no knowledge of it if I leave it to the schools, and even less if I leave it to television. That's what the working class doesn't get: any official recognition of its worth. No instruction about its past. For one thing, the schools don't know anything about it, and if they did, they wouldn't be allowed to teach it. All this nonsense about keeping politics out of school. That is a political decision. It is politics. Everything they do has a political content, not only the syllabus, the whole curriculum, the decision about what shall be taught and what omitted. The whole thing is one-sided. I talk to my children, I always have done, to try to give them some alternative to what is rammed down their throats at school. My daughter has just started work in a factory where there's no trade union. American-owned company. Well, the first thing she wants to do is to get them organized, even though she's only seventeen.

'I think the working class has become corrupted. They're a bit better off, and that's given them a false sense of security. They're told that the worst thing that can happen would be to lose all the things that have been "given" to them. I think that the level of debate in my union is very high. We get good discussions at branch meetings; the problem is if you say to the blokes on the shop floor, "Would you rather we should fight to have a fume extractor installed or an extra thirty bob a week," they'd ask for the money any time. It's getting that across, that money is only secondary sometimes. The place where you work, you spend so much of your time, conditions count where there is a risk to health. But it's as though they've accepted capitalism's evaluation of themselves – what does it matter about us? It's funny that is. Whereas the bosses used to damage their workers, body and spirit, to get the last scrap of strength, a lot of people now will damage themselves for the sake of the money and the things it will buy. This is the greatest problem to my mind. Private consumption gets in the way of people thinking of any shared experience. It insulates you from each other.'

'I find you can't talk to people about politics. It's become a forbidden subject. Now to my mind, there's something to wonder about. Why is debate about what are, after all, public issues so discredited? People just turn off. The most you can get out of anybody is "They're all the same." It makes you wonder what really is going on. Why is politics the big switch-off?'

'Yes, it's even more strange, because people do feel angry and puzzled. But they don't quite know where to place it, whatever it is that's wrong. There's a lot of racism there, on the shop floor, on the streets. That's a beautifully easy answer, only I think people are a bit ashamed of it, they feel it isn't the real answer.'

'People aren't happy about the way we live. They're afraid of losing what they've got, but it doesn't make them happy. The alternatives they see are both unsatisfactory. There's a family I know, both parents working, two kids. They bring into the house a clear £120 a week. To look at them, they've got everything: two cars, holidays, beautiful house. Everything. Only they're in debt to such a tune, they have to lay £37 on the table every week before they can buy a loaf of bread. They can't afford not to have two incomes. They live in terror of being ill, anything that might upset it.'

'I know a fellow, car worker, Birmingham. He was on strike, and his wife really quarrelled with him over it. She left him in fact. She'd planned a big wedding for their daughter, and of course, the money was right down, so they had to cut back on this big do they were going to have. She walked out; only she had to walk back in the end, because their commitments were so great she couldn't afford to leave him. That's what being trapped really means; it's the way quite a few marriages are held together.'

'We had the opportunity in 1945. They had a thumping majority, they could have done anything with the people then. You've got to force people to change; you'll never get socialism any other way. You can still see how rotten capitalism is, what it

does to people. At work the attitude to anybody who is in
hardship, whether it's accident, illness, old age, "That's his
fucking bad luck." It never used to be like that. It used to be
"Oh yes, what can we do to help, those things could happen to
us any day." Now it's fate. Bad luck. Old age is fate. It's mad.
People's attitude towards each other is ugly. People on the dole
can't go into a pub for a drink because everybody will think
they're scroungers. It's their own fault. It's no use using a
balloon on a stick to fight capitalism, because they've got a
bloody sword.'

'There has been a softening up of working people as far as
their own selves are concerned; a hardening up towards others.'

'I think beneath the surface there is a great giant. Only the
people don't realize what their own power is. They're always
being told how powerless they are, how many times do you hear
people say "What difference will it make, what can I do?" They
shrug and don't want to know. They've been told it for so long,
they believe it. They only see their own individual situation,
they've lost the means of communicating with each other. It's as
if they'd had their tongues cut out; ears blocked and tongues
cut out. We don't know what to say to each other any more.
When everybody was poor, we could see what it did to people.
Now it's in our minds. When nobody has any clothes, there's no
shame in being naked.'

Cold afternoon; dust and waste paper. Some old men, mufflers,
walking sticks, faces pinched with cold, take shelter under the
awning of a shop; framed against the fashion models in the shop
window, their past poverty is a shaming redundancy. But behind
the faces, apologetic for being a spectre at the feast, there is often
an epic of appalling suffering. 'When there was no work, my
father walked to Yorkshire. He was a miner; he did the journey
in a few days. When he got there, he slept out on the stones, got
up at five in the morning, and by five-thirty he was down a pit.
He was killed in a pit accident when I was seven. I started work at
thirteen, half-time at school, half-time at work.'

In her house, in the ward which she represented on the
council for the Labour Party for twenty-three years, Mrs Alice
Taylor, eighty-five, an alert and dignified old lady, asks us to
draw our chairs closer, because her hearing and eyesight are

failing a little now, and she doesn't want to miss a word of what
is said:

'I was in the labour movement, because as far as I was
concerned, we'd got to do it. We weren't forced to, but we had
to. To me, it was a faith. It was something that informed your
whole life. We were Methodists, and I believed that the
inequality of people was an affront to man and God. I can
truthfully say I learned my socialism in Sunday School. It was an
intense moral faith with us. I have been disappointed in later
years, the vision seems to have gone. We used to sing "Lift up the
people's banner, now trailing in the dust." I'm afraid it may be
our own people, not the Tories, who will fetch that banner
down. Better times have made people more selfish, less willing
to give. It's not what you can get that counts, it's what you can
give. I remember when I used to collect for the Labour Party,
there was one man I knew who was dying of consumption, but
every week he wanted me to keep calling; his penny was always
on the table waiting for me. One night I looked in at the kitchen,
and there was his wife, frying a few potatoes for their dinner. I
gave the penny back to her, towards something more
nourishing, but she said, "No, he wants you to take it." Who
would do that now? Can you imagine the faith of a dying man
that would make him think like that? It made you humble, but
proud of a movement that could inspire that devotion. It was
because we couldn't afford it that we did it. And people were
avid to learn from us. They wanted to know, they wanted to
understand why conditions were like they were. Now who wants
to know, who cares whether what he does has any moral basis,
whether what we enjoy is at the expense of others, whether we
have any responsibility towards anyone else?

'Of course I'm proud of what the labour movement has
achieved. I'm proud to think there's no pawnshop and slate
where they write down all the things you can't afford to pay for.
We had a social revolution, there's no doubt about that. Have
the people achieved what they wanted and now lost interest? It
seems now if people don't get their way they just start a row. We
lived for the party. We used to give to it, our time, our money,
our love and faith.

'I came from a Liberal family, but my father was easily
converted to Labour. He said, "If it's good enough for my

daughter, it's good enough for me". I left school at thirteen, I passed the Labour exam to leave. If you were smart, you left school in those days; get you into the factories quickly, as cheap labour where they thought you could do no harm with ideas. I never wanted to leave, but I saved my coppers and went to night school. The first thing I bought was a dictionary, so whenever I went to political meetings and someone used a word I didn't understand, I could look it up.

'I had to fight for my education, but now they get it as a matter of course. But it never used to be. And without the Labour Party it would never have happened. Labour's been good to the unemployed – they're not on the starvation line like they used to be; good to the old people. Even some of the old ones seem to have forgotten what it was like, the way they complain sometimes. When I was a girl, at sixty you sat in a corner and waited for the end.

'The Labour Party was our social life as well. There was nowhere else for young people to go. I was the youngest of six. When I left school, I went to do tailoring for 2/– a week. Oh it was rough. I remember when a woman came organizing the garment workers, I went home to my mother and said, "We had a woman come to the works today, Mother, to see about a union." And she said to me, "Never join a trade union." The reason why she said that was that it had been through a trade union that my father had come to Darlaston from Bristol in the iron trade, and she always missed her home place. She blamed the union. My father would always try to find work, even if it meant uprooting himself, rather than have charity, as he called it. But my eldest brother was out of work for a long time, and they visited him from the Board of Guardians and saw that he had a piano, and they told him to sell it to buy food.

'When I think of what it was like in this town when I was a girl, the back-to-back houses, the courts and tenements. They called them the barracks: there was a toilet block in the middle of the courtyard with pumps for water. With the taps being outside, when it froze in winter you had to thaw them out before you could even get water for a cup of tea. The homes were very cheerless. You had a wooden settle and maybe what they called a squab – a sort of wooden bed. Married women didn't work, but young girls had the choice of going into a factory or service. My oldest sister went as a servant, 5/– a week. She went to a couple who'd just bought a factory and thought they'd gone up in the world, they had to have a maid. Called her Mary although her name was Florence – they often did that. I can see my mother now, washing and ironing her cap and streamers so that she should look nice when she opened the door to visitors. A lot of them went into service, because at least that way they got a good meal once a day, and that was something you couldn't always guarantee at home.

'I wonder how we managed. We all sat round a deal table for our meals. If you'd got a tablecloth you thought you were somebody. We never had one. We had a little house, three bedrooms, six children, the boys had to share a bed. We lived in a row of eight houses; my mother had the letting of them for the landlord. If she let one, she got a week's rent free. But she had to take responsibility for who she let them to. She used to ask them questions when they came to enquire, where have you come from, why are you moving, is your husband in work?

'All the time we were children, we never had a whole apple. We had half a one, half an egg. We were taught to share; we had to share. There was something in those big families which taught you to share, almost despite yourself. You learned a sort of practical unselfishness. It almost predisposed you to accept a more socialist way of life, especially if your parents were fair and just. Now, they don't learn to share; and if there's only one or two children, some of them never have to share anything. We shared, not only our food and our rooms, but we shared our problems, our hopes and dreams, our whole lives. There weren't these barriers between people. We couldn't have imagined not doing it.

'The Labour Party has brought people up to a standard they'll never fall from, and I'm thankful for that. They'll never go back to the life we knew. I lived on the street where the workhouse was; and there was a hill leading up to it. One of the public works schemes was to level it out, so those in receipt of relief could get there. Poverty Knob they called it. They got a shilling a day for working on it, I've seen people go up to the workhouse for their loaf of bread. We shall never see that again, thank God.

'My oldest brother was in tube-making. I remember he got commended by the boss for the way he kept his machine. He idolized it; cleaned and polished and cared for it, although it

never provided him with a living wage. This town was built up
on the foundries, a lot of them small family businesses, and the
worst of the housing was all round the foundries. People were
told they had to vote Tory in elections, and they thought their
employer would know how they voted. You had to work hard to
convince some of them that the ballot was secret. The bosses had
such power, how were they to know he didn't have some
supernatural way of telling how you'd voted?

'The home influence isn't what it was. The parents don't teach
their children right from wrong, because they're not sure
themselves what it is any more. I heard a little child in this street
the other day say to her mother, "Don't go to work, Mummy,"
and the mother turned round and said, "If I don't go to work,
how will you get any pretty clothes?" Now what kind of an
answer is that to give to a child? They go to work to shower all
these things on the children, and that isn't what children need at
all. They need the security of their relationships, a warm and
loving home. Some of the homes around here are lovely, but
cold, emotionally cold.

'I have a neighbour, and she has a little boy. This child had
got a piece of wood with a nail at each end, and he said to his
father, "Daddy, this is a horse." But the child couldn't make up
his mind which end was the head and which the tail. He played
with it for days; and he kept going to his father and saying,
"Daddy, which is the front of the horse and which is the back?"
His father said to me, "I shan't tell him, it's kept him amused for
weeks." Their imagination is caught by something that has
scope for ambiguity and speculation: so many toys are too
perfect, the details crowd out any chance for the child to give it
anything from himself.

'I'm afraid that even some of the ministers of the Church are
afraid to speak their mind about these things. I know one
minister who was in lodgings. The neighbour brought his
landlady some flowers. She said, "Would you like these few
flowers? I've got more than I want." Well, that isn't charity, to
give away things you don't want. To give is to deprive yourself of
something; and that is a spirit you don't find frequently today.

'It sometimes seems to me that when you've done away with
poverty, you've done away with politics. Nobody is going to give
the working class anything; you've got to fight for it. I think we
may be going through a bad patch, but goodness will come of it.

People will come back to the fold – you see I'm speaking like a good Methodist. Some people do describe the Labour Party as a church. There has to be a moral sense there, care and compassion.'

We go to visit a friend of Barrie's, Colin, who is a teacher. He lives with his brother and parents. The family has been re-housed on a small estate just outside Caldmore. The interior is modern and newly furnished; almost nothing remains of the old house. Colin's brother, Vince, comes in from work. He is a tool-setter, an active trade unionist and a member of the National Front. He enjoys the shock effects of his arguments; but he does convey a feeling of the distorted radicalism of the working class. 'Why do I fight for the National Front? Why, because I don't want parts of my country to become no-go areas, where I feel I can't walk without the risk of being knifed or mugged. I don't want to be with black people, I don't want a multi-racial country. Why should I? I've got nothing in common with them, they don't want to mix with me any more than I do with them. Why should I be forced to live with them? I want to be able to go into a pub, I want to be able to go to work without seeing a black face. The National Front is saying the sort of things I want to hear. I wouldn't be cruel. If I ran over a black in my car, I wouldn't just leave him lying in the road; I'd kick him into the gutter. I don't want them here. I want them to leave. I understand that this might be a bit disruptive. If the barricades do go up, it won't be middle class on one side and working class on the other; it'll be white on one side and black on the other, with just a few race traitors on their side. I want to be just with our own. I don't want to live in a system that falls over itself to favour blacks. If there's anything going in this country, I want it for myself. We've suffered enough in the past, and now it's our turn. We've had one flabby government after another saying, "We've got to learn to live together." Well, why? They don't have to live with them, killing goats, wailing at dusk and fasting and being a nuisance.'

COLIN: 'You've got to let people have their freedom for religious beliefs.'
VINCE: 'Why?'
COLIN: 'It's no worse than our religious practices. To an

outsider, at communion, we eat our God, we eat the flesh and blood of God. Now isn't that as barbaric and outlandish as anything you could find among the immigrants?'

VINCE: 'I don't care about any of that. What I do care about is that I don't want the race to degenerate; diseases we've wiped out are coming back, all the drain on our services.'

COLIN: 'It's not true that they are a drain on the services. They give more than they take out.'

VINCE: 'I don't believe it. They get favoured for everything. Poor old women going out and getting mugged, you ask them if they should be all forgiveness.'

COLIN: 'What you're saying now is exactly the same as what the rich used to say about us, the working class. They thought we were rubbish. We were supposed to be violent and dangerous, dirty and disease-ridden – sub-human. Why should we regurgitate all that shit we had heaped on us a hundred years ago? The reason you know what to say is that it's just a replay of what we had said about us. There's always got to be a scapegoat, the most defenceless members of society.'

VINCE: 'Defenceless. If you go down some streets in this town, even if you take a child with you, I bet ten to one you'll be attacked. They expect everything to be given to them. These West Indians, they won't bother with learning anything at school, then when they leave and can't get a job, they say' – he snaps his fingers and imitates the accent – "That ain't cool man," then they knife you because nobody hands them the star off the top of the Christmas tree.'

Their mother comes in; anxious, and always upset by the endless argument in the family. She says, 'There's good and bad in all of us, Vincent.' I say, 'I'm sure he's kinder than his words sound. If he had the chance, he wouldn't really do all those things.' His mother is relieved at this explanation. She smiles, 'Yes, yes, he is. He's a good boy. He wouldn't want to hurt anybody.' She is pleased to be able to go out to Bingo for a couple of hours. The argument abates; but the tension remains.

The values of the National Front find an easy passage in the moral vacuum left by the breakdown of the old communities; a vacuum sometimes represented as a freedom from the repressive morality in which the working class lived for so long. That a different kind of brutalization lies in wait for those previously degraded by work and want, is not perceived by those who see only the liberation from poverty; but when that liberation is into a world in which the only moral imperative is to get and have, the liberation is invaded and spoilt. If Vince says, 'Why should I, I want whatever's going,' he simply reflects the values he has been brought up with: that is to say, not the attenuated influence of the family, not that of the school. He has certainly not been formed by the diluted admonitions that came from those dusty bricked-up chapels, but by the culture of the market-place. If the market-place renders redundant all the determinants of family and kin, neighbourhood and work, there is nothing left but the appalling nudity of one's whiteness. We have been robbed of everything else.

3

THE EFFECT OF growing up in our world of material abundance, in which the stridency of the market-place is the most significant influence, is to become a new and unfamiliar kind of human being in working-class communities, in which for generations children had been formed, like their parents, for work and want. The culture which has supplanted this is that of the great shopping precincts, the spectacle of plenitude behind plate glass, the clamour of competitive superlatives. It has assumed a power over the upbringing of children which has eclipsed all traditional influences. These now look constricting and limiting by contrast. We sense what has happened, but we sometimes shrink from some of the consequences. There is something pervasive and compelling in the values of the great commercial theatre in which we now live, which mould and shape our lives, determine the standards we live by; something which escapes our will or control.

To grow up under the dominion of consumer capitalism is to see that part of us which used to belong to society be colonized, torn away from traditional allegiances, and be hurled, lone and isolated, into the prison of the individual's senses. The child tends to be stripped of all social influences but those of the market-place; all sense of place, function and class is weakened, the characteristics of region or clan, neighbourhood or kindred are attenuated. The individual is denuded of everything but

appetites, desires and tastes, wrenched from any context of
human obligation or commitment. It is a process of mutilation;
and once this has been achieved, we are offered the consolation
of reconstituting the abbreviated humanity out of the things and
the goods around us, and the fantasies and vapours which they
emit. A sense of self has to be sought in the parade of images and
products; and this culture becomes the main determinant
upon morality, beliefs and purpose, usurping more and
more territory that formerly belonged to parents, teachers,
community, priests and politics alike.

First of all, the world of our peculiarly elaborated market-
place is a world of total perfection. There, everything has been
brought to its point of greatest refinement. From the beginning,
we are surrounded by the images of people who are the
embodiment of all grace and beauty. What children first hear
from the television is the desirability of everything, a hymning
of commodities. Life there is intense, passionate and full.
Everything speaks to us of our own inferiority, our own
vulnerability. All we can feel is a humiliating sense of our
inadequacy. No human being could match the models who are
nevertheless proposed to us all the time. They are exempt from
frailty, from human complexity and the constant ambiguity that
assails us. This is the only place in a world in which values have
been overturned, where certainty still reigns. A serene and un-
shakeable sense of abiding truths lies in the claims made for
man's artefacts. It is an absolute and total vision: beatific, eternal.
We can be made worthy of it only by imitation and obedience.
Our posture to it is one of unvarying gratitude. Despite our
feeling of unworthiness, we are astonished from our earliest
years to hear its soft caressing tone, its maternal concern that
hints at its power to heal, to mend, to assuage the pain of being
ourselves, limited, imprisoned within one body, with our own
pitiful resources. And this is where its controlling power lies.
It is as though capitalism had changed from paternalistic
authoritarianism to maternal indulgence: a change of sex.

The maternal power is far more pervasive and unassailable. It
is surrounded by so many taboos – mother as saint, as giver, as
martyr, as an image of idealized selflessness; and it is this
apparent bounty of the giving power which masks what in reality
it takes from us – a sense of the worth of what we do, our ability
to determine our own lives, to be challenged in the use of our

skills and human resources. In such a society, we all become like children, locked in dependency, frozen in attitudes of supplicating and misplaced gratitude.

The oppressive power of capitalism no longer shows itself as poverty. It isn't its materially denying power that crushes people, but the means by which its promised plenty is to be reached. The argument is never about what capitalism offers, because it offers everything. The argument is always about the competitive means of getting the money to acquire what is represented as good, desirable and worthwhile. If the competitive process of achieving these things leads to violence, loneliness, a broken sense of belonging, the destruction of identity and the disintegration of community, these 'social' problems appear to have been separated from any causal connection with the exigencies of capitalism (in a way that poverty could never have been). They are not perceived to be a consequence of it, but seen as a result of people's greed, self-inflicted ills. Capitalism is merely the provider, the purified and benevolent bestower of good things.

We know that we are imperfect; subject to decay and death; and that the culture has the power, the sole power, to make us proof against these things is the lie on which it is built. We learn early in life that it does not disdain our plight. It invites us to collude in the proposition that human beings can be absolutely happy. There need be no secret shame, no concealed blemish, the wound in the consciousness of our mortality can be cicatrized, the great hurt of our aloneness abolished. All we have to do is be ourselves, express our needs and wants through the channels ubiquitously provided.

But of course such perfection must call forth its opposite somewhere. So much goodness must give rise to evil, somewhere. The collusion we enter into with the great bestowing power is a conspiracy, that the secret anguish and the repressed fears do not really belong inside us. They can be exorcised by being transferred to others. And while material things have reached such a high degree of perfection, there is nowhere for evil to go but into people. People embody all that is malicious, perverse, and malevolent. It is they alone who thwart us in our perfect self-expression, by their demands on the display of abundance around us. The tireless smiling parade of all that can satisfy human yearning only emphasizes the inadequacy of other people. If we find that in spite of all the promises a lack of fulfilment persists, the dull ache of our aloneness, it is because there are others who contest our access to the fount of goodness and plenty.

The only thing wrong with the way we live is other people. Through all our discourse runs a fear of rapists and muggers, child-molesters and vandals, thugs and wreckers. And the sharing part of people becomes blocked, denied an outlet by the needs of the machine which regulates our lives. We grow up immured within our own experience.

It is as though we didn't believe that this kind of individualism is socially produced. The horror we have of the idea that children in socialist countries are borne off by the State into great closed mass nurseries is somewhat misplaced, when our own are in fact carried off in the fleshy arms of private consumption, and to an unidentified location (fantasy, actually), to be systematically shaped to the products which it will be their duty to want, to compete for and consume. We project a fear of something we do ourselves on to an alien creed, and then shrink in revulsion from it.

Our children, our children's future, our children's children, are perhaps the most frequently offered reasons for accepting what people describe as the rat-race, the struggle, the jungle, all that are felt to be the most negative aspects of the way we live. If we submit to a lifetime of work that seems functionless, a style of living that is not fulfilling, we do so 'for the sake of the children'. They are our reason for living; the one area of our humanity that we feel is still uncontaminated by the values we are compelled to live by. They will vindicate all our humiliations and disappointments. They represent all that is most altruistic in our lives. They will expunge the past, they promise an endless renewal. 'I worship that child'; into them have gone religious feeling and secular hope. In a world of warring and incomprehensible ideologies, the children seem to represent something simple and lucid: they are the human repositories of our faith.

What then is more likely than that our children should be given over to the intense altruism of the bountiful providers in consumer capitalism, who reach into the family, prising open its grasp on children, interrupting the transmission of traditional ideas, ancient practices, old values, and take upon themselves the responsibility for the development of children?

In their rôle as redeemers, the children belong to the future; and this has important consequences: we can defer the worry about how they will achieve it. All we need to do for the time being is make sure that they get the best of everything from the maternalistic culture whose purpose it is to ensure that the passage of the children to maturity is made secure. The children are institutionalized as our hope for a better life; only it is a better not set against any definable good. The purpose of children becomes part idolatry, part evasion. They represent the only thing that is not already known – the future – and are the only remaining escape route from a present that is over-explained, over-exposed.

They are born into an atmosphere of intense and obsessive expectancy. And the parents, humble self-effacing servitors of their own progeny, can only monitor all their needs and wants; not in gross clumsy ways as mothers used to, dipping their breast into the sugar bag before nursing them, but measuring scientifically. 'He knows what he wants,' says the mother admiringly of infantile recognition of its own needs, as though this were already proof of advanced intelligence. And on this basis, the needs dilate in a climate favourable to them, which sets no limits. Parents soon learn that they are helpless: merely enabling agents for all the beneficent industries and professions devoted solely to the process of coaxing children into their natural growth and development. It is through this that the old transmission of identity has been broken. Parental caring is secondary in providing things indispensable to the child. Instead of learning by imitation and absorption from the past, childhood has become virgin territory. The real human fear about the vulnerability of young children through the early stages of life is exploited by all the industries and manufactures which alone claim the power to guarantee children a safe passage through the conquered domain of childhood: they are the occupying colonizing power, to which parents have no choice but to defer.

In this way, the caring instinct risks contamination by those who know how to do it better. It is not a far step for the child to be turned into a vessel for a bewildering sequence of material symbols which for the adults, especially adults who were themselves deprived as children, may be the tokens of concern. But they remain tokens. It is in this sense that the children are given over to a power superior to that of the parents. They are humbled, de-rôled by the expertise and confidence of the caring agencies outside. And the children soon learn to listen to the seductive voices that reach them above the lullabys, a wheedling message that the parents are simply subordinates of the providing power, mechanisms to manipulate so that they will provide all the stimulus and sweetness in the world; like the voices of good fairies over a christening, endowing the children with virtue and truth. Nothing blocks the communication between the children and the professional caring power. The parents expend themselves in an effort to comply; making sure that only the best is good enough, that they get the right start, enjoy all the advantages, keep up with their friends, want for nothing.

And so the children grow, penetrated with a sense of destiny. But it is a destiny pre-selected by the culture. They are burdened with a rôle which no human being – least of all a child, waiting in vain for the limiting stamp of its own upbringing to show it the boundaries of identity – could ever fulfil. Children are messengers from the beyond, a source of revelation, truth and meaning. It is a conjunction of the limitless development of children and the clamorous perfection of the market-place which claims them, that will create the future in which ugliness and pain will be abolished.

Confronted by this, the traditions of a working-class past look thin and unrewarding. Those traditions grew up to deal with poverty, the kind of poverty that scarcely exists now, and cannot be discarded too quickly. The local accent sounds crude and limiting now: the working-class estate looks mean; the home town seems ugly, with its red terraces and council houses of stippled concrete, its derelict chapels and timbered pubs, the old Roxy cinema, which has been skating rink and supermarket since then, and now invites enquiries to an address in Mayfair; the workmen's buses with their smudge of resigned faces behind the mud splashes; the new cosmetics factory; the incompletely refurbished railway station with its cream-painted crenellations; the concrete swirl of the new motorway; the office block in the town centre and the shopping precinct. The people are uninteresting, by definition, simply because they are there, in that familiar place. And everywhere else seems to beckon: Manchester, London, anywhere. The main industry has disappeared: some motifs incorporated into the mosaic of an underpass remind you of what it was – spinning, brewing, cobbling. Even the cruel dynamism of their reason for being there in the first place has been taken away from them. Everything that has always served people as a social reference point now looks squalid. When those who have grown up to expect something better look round for some sense of social identity, they see nothing. And when they look inside themselves, they see only a cluster of personal tastes and individual preferences – a girl who likes to wear blue, a boy who wants a motorbike. In the search for social purpose, there is nothing, and they reach out to the furthest confines of identity, even if all they can find is the colour of their skin.

As the children grow, the benevolent processes to which they were given over do not produce the kind of people they were thought to. But the influence of their parents has been weakened in a way that cannot be retrieved now. As their rôle decreases, the bewilderment of the parents grows. 'He only sleeps here.' 'I'm the ever-open purse.' 'It's the kids he mixes with'; 'I don't know where they get it from'; 'He's never heard things like that in this house'; 'I've tried to teach him right from wrong.' There has been a progressive relaxation of a grasp they never really had, and they cannot imagine where the values which their own child seems to embody, actually come from. Poverty, for them, had meant control and self-denial; and through their children they now learn the morality of capitalist plenty – getting, having and taking. Their appetites are kindled at the expense of their abilities; and the sense of destiny turns out to be a future of underemployment, idleness and lack of function.

A terraced house in a Midland town. The street was originally in a clearance area, but was saved by a lack of money to demolish. It is a mixture of houses owned by the council, and the old owner-occupiers, mainly former workers in the local factories and tanneries. The council houses are said to be full of problem families. There is bitterness between the old residents who have always kept their houses spotlessly clean, and the houses of those housed by the council. Some immigrants have painted their houses lilac and orange, whereas the old inhabitants prefer traditional cream or green or brush oak. The houses of the council families have pieces of cardboard covering broken windows, the stains of dog-paws on the doors, dingy curtains, pieces of dirty and sagging net, windows smeared, and deteriorating gardens in which an Alsatian on a chain barks all night long.

In one of the more neglected houses lives Mrs Austin. Her husband is in his late fifties. He is her third husband and they have been married only a few months. Her son Gary is now nineteen. Five years ago, he was one of a group of seven boys, aged between thirteen and seventeen, who went into a public lavatory in an old part of the town and beat up an old man who had taken refuge in one of the cubicles. He was badly injured: he lost an eye, and almost died. Gary was one of the youngest, and was given two years probation. Since then he has driven and taken away a car and been convicted of housebreaking. He has not yet worked.

Mrs Austin was shattered by what happened. She is a small nervous woman, who talks very quickly; desperately propitiatory:

'I said at the time they could do what they liked to him. I wouldn't've minded. I did everything for that boy that flesh and blood could do. His father always hated him. He was a funny man. He thought Gary wasn't his, always swore I'd had him by somebody else. I didn't. He always said Gary never looked like him, and he used to punish the kid. He used to tie him to the bed when we went out, all that sort of thing. He once kept him locked up for a week when he nicked some money from my purse. But he couldn't do a thing right in his dad's eyes. That was why I left him in the end. For Gary's sake. I done it for him. And Gary has never wanted for anything. He's had put into his hand anything he wanted. I'd have given him my eyes if he'd asked for them.

'Gary was about seven then. Well, I'd only done factory work, I thought this is no good. I went on the streets for him. Not here, Birmingham. Balsall Heath. I got a room for the two of us. I sold myself to give him the best money could buy. I could easily have walked out on him. My mother left me in care for two years while she went off with a man, came dinxing back when I was fifteen, she thought I might earn her something in her old age. . . . I made up my mind I wasn't going to let that happen to no kid of mine. I saved up some money, came over here and got a council flat. It was very nice, only it was seven floors up. It was terrible. Still, I stuck it. I went out to work, not what I'd done

before, I got a job at the Infirmary, cleaning. I didn't mind what
I did for him. He always had more than the other kids, I didn't
want him to feel left out of things. He had clothes, records, toys,
he always had holidays at the seaside. Anyway, I met my
husband at the Infirmary. I can honestly say it's only since I met
Stanley that I've known what it's like to be cared for. I never was
as a child and I never was by Gary's father. Nor the other one. I
had a whirlwind marriage, it lasted a fortnight. I stuck a knife in
him.

'Gary was about nine when we came here. . . . It was the
funniest thing, the way I met Stan. I'm not ashamed to tell you, it
was on the bus. I was going to Bingo, and I left my shopping bag
on the bus, and he came running after me. And we went for a
drink and that was it. . . . It was the most wonderful thing.
Nobody had ever bought me a present in my life before Stan.
His wife had died; as a matter of fact, I think they were divorced,
but he was on his own, and he offered me and Gary a home. He
had a good job in those days. I mean, his problem is that he
can't stay away from the horses, gambling, greyhounds,
anything. He'll bet on anything. If he's standing at a bus stop,
he'll make a book on how long it'll be before the bloody bus
comes. But he's a good man. He loves me and that's something I
never thought I'd get when I was pushing forty. He's been good
to Gary and stood by him.

'Well, Gary started mixing with the kids at that school, and he
seemed to change. They were rough, some of them. I don't
know what their parents are thinking about, half of them.
Drinking, fighting, effing and blinding. When he was little I
wouldn't let him play with really low kids, you know, only you
can't be behind them all the time, not when they're growing up.
And he was weak. It was never having a father who cared for
him. Still, that sod got his bloody desserts in the end, he finished
up with a woman who wasn't right in the head. She nearly killed
him. I almost wrote to her thanking her for doing my dirty work
for me.

'Well, kids have got to be free. Gary started drinking with
these kids. They all do it. You can't make them feel different,
show them up with their mates. He used to go out at weekends.
Well, weekends you don't mind. He always said he'd be at so-
and-so's house, and I expect they told his parents they were
coming round here. He'd never been in any trouble. They had

one or two fights over football, but all the kids do that. He'd never been a thief. He had no need for that. I said to him, "Don't you pinch anything. If you want it, come and ask me, and by hook or by crook you shall have it." I could leave money lying around, and there's not many can say that. I did my best for him. When he wanted football gear, he had it. You should have seen the things he had. He had a Chopper, he had a car, he had skates, all the clothes he wanted. I've bought him one of them games you plug in the television for Christmas, I bet you think I'm a soft cow. I wasn't going to let him say just because he hadn't had a father he'd had to miss out on anything. I was the one who did that, for years. I was only earning ten quid a week, I don't know how I did manage. I went to work at the Co-op toyshop at one time so as I could get things, cheap. I have lifted things for him before now as a matter of fact.

'So when all this happened, well, I couldn't believe it. I knew something was wrong. He came in that night and said he thought he'd have a night in, which he never did at the weekend. Fortunately, he met a very nice girl, Julie, she's helped him more than anybody these last two years. They're having an engagement party at Christmas, I think she's going to be the making of him.'

Gary sits sideways over the armchair. He has short blond hair and an earring with a cross in silver. He says 'I don't know why they made so much fuss about it.' His mother is shocked. She says, tearfully, 'Don't you ever let me hear you talk like that again,' but her command is unconvincing.

'He was a dirty old bastard anyway. He used to flash at the girls. . . . Everybody knew him. He was filthy and he stank. We only meant to give him a lesson, we didn't mean to hurt him.' 'You shouldn't have had knives,' says his mother. He ignores her. 'Anyway those toilets should've been closed. There's nothing to do in this town for young people.' js: 'What do you want to do then?' GARY: 'I don't know. It's boring. To go anywhere you need a lot of money. There is a club in Birmingham, only you've got to get there, pay to go in, get a taxi back if you want to come home late. You can't afford it. Not that I want to go to fucking clubs anyway.' 'Gary, don't use that word.' 'I like going to disco with Julie, only that costs money. She don't mind paying, only I don't like her to. I should be paying for her.' 'He's ever so generous when he does get a bit of money. When he was sixteen, Stan gave him ten quid, and he went out and bought me this' – she holds up a blue glass fish standing on the sideboard.

'I go to parties sometimes, see my old mates, only we don't go about now so much. I don't go drinking much. I've got a temper, and when it gets going, there's nobody dares get in my way. I once smashed a bottle in this kid's face because he said I talked pooffy. . . . What I'd like to do is go somewhere and be somebody. I'd like to be a footballer or a singer.' 'I bought him a guitar, it still stands there.' 'I'd like to have a really good car, and live in a mansion guarded by my own personal bodyguards, with a lookout tower and my own helicopter fleet. Me and Julie in there. That would be my ideal life. I'd look after my mum though. I'd kill anybody who did anything to her.' 'See, he's a good boy. He only wants the chances in life.'

The mother's commentary, anxious and appeasing, was like an attempt to make everything all right again by talking; as though in this way everything could be restored to the time when he was young and things seemed to be still within her control; start all over again and expunge the sad sequence of events that had led to this first real act of self-definition that was part fantasy of avenger, part the rôle of outlaw, and part deed of distinguishing bravado. The fact that the object of their violence was one of the few eccentrics who still survive in these standardized communities, shows the power of fantasy over reality.

However, at the same time that the parents are robbed of their functions, they too are offered some of the consolations which their children come to regard as part of the necessary sustenance of their life. The messages to the children – the primordial importance of immediate gratification – reach them also; and insofar as this undermines the traditional altruism and self-effacement of parents, they regress. The distinction between adulthood and childhood becomes blurred. As the children hurry towards a beckoning future, imitating adult attitudes, fashions, adult self-consciousness, so the adults become increasingly child-like, dependent on the flow of addictive consolations which have so deeply influenced their own children.

Of course the adult who ultimately emerges from these influences is a long way from the idealized child. The infant

Jesus grows somehow into something quite unrecognizable. The things that have been showered upon them have been bestowed by adults as an apology for their own inability to relate to them in other ways, and the children are left to create their own identity out of a succession of fleeting and dream-like stage-props. Such an identity may well be barren, reductive and cruel. There has been nothing else to guide it. In this way, Gary, however unique his personal circumstances may be, is no less the product of social influences than those people who were crippled and constrained by grinding poverty in the nineteenth century.

4

STEVE WILSON IS seventeen. He lives with his parents in North London. He left school at Easter 1975, and worked as a central heating and ventilation engineer until January 1976. He felt bored and uninvolved in his work. Nothing challenged him, nothing provided an opportunity to express himself in any real way. In January 1976, he read an article in *The People* about the recruitment of mercenaries for the FNLA in the Angola civil war. He rang the recruitment agency, and was told that men were wanted to help with the training of black troops. Although he had had no military experience, he was told that the pay would be £150 a fortnight, and that if he was interested, he could expect a telegram within forty-eight hours. His age, he was assured, was immaterial; there would be no danger.

Steve flew out with the first group of mercenaries in late January 1976. When they arrived in Zaire, they discovered they had been hired to fight. About fifteen of them refused to do so, and of these thirteen were massacred under the orders of a man known as Callan at Maquela. Steve and another seventeen-year-old had been separated from the main group of non-combatants, and this saved their lives. He was reported killed along with the others, but this news was superseded the following day by the news that he was in fact alive, and on his way home. He arrived back in London in mid-February to newspaper headlines, television cameras, interviews, his hurt and bewildered parents, and the resumption of life in a first-floor flat in Edmonton.

His mother and father both agree that if they had considered anything like that when they were Steve's age, their own parents would most certainly have prevented it. But things are different now. Children do not belong to their parents in the way they used to. They listen to more powerful and more seductive voices.

Mr Wilson is a milkman; his wife works in a firm which makes surgical goods.

'They live in a fantasy. They think they know everything. They do things, but it has nothing to do with experience. If you try and tell them anything, they just think you're standing in their way, and they resent it. They think you're jealous because they've got more opportunity than you had to do what they want. He's always saying "Oh, I've got to do my thing, I've got to be myself. I want to do it my way." You say to him "All right, what is your thing?" and he can't answer. It just means following any idea that comes into their head, and they're not going to be stopped by anybody.'

Mr and Mrs Wilson felt vulnerable to criticism that they could not prevent Steve from going. They were made to realize very forcibly the diminished power of parents, the reduced rôle of the family in forming their son's ideas and values. They were far from being unconcerned or indifferent, as appeared from some of the press reports. Mr Wilson spent two days and a night trying to represent to Steve what he was really doing. His mother said she had told him nobody pays £150 a fortnight to anyone just to help train people, when they are not themselves trained. She broke down and pleaded with him not to go. His brother cried ('And you don't see him do that every day'). His boss called him a silly sod. His mother rang up the recruitment office and spoke with a woman who said, 'Of course he won't be fighting, there's no danger at all. Do you think I would let my husband go if there was any risk involved?'

MRS WILSON: 'It was like a nightmare. I kept thinking I would wake up and find it hadn't really happened. I was in a trance. I didn't go out for three weeks. I couldn't face anybody. On the Sunday night, we heard the early news – you know, you listen to every news bulletin, there was no other way of finding out anything – and that was when there was the first report there'd been a massacre. On the Monday afternoon we were told that Steve was among those who had been killed, or so they thought. I couldn't believe it. I hardly knew what I was doing. We were besieged by newspaper and television people. Somebody asked me what I'd do with the money he'd been paid. I said I'd cash it and burn it in public. They said, "Well, wait till the television cameras get here." It wasn't until the next morning at seven o'clock, the 'phone rang, and a man said he'd got Steve on the phone.'

Mr and Mrs Wilson go over their whole life with their son, trying to find the reason for what he did. 'You ask yourself: Where did we go wrong? What could we have done to make things different? Even when you know you've always done everything you could, you know you've nothing to reproach yourself with, but you still feel it must be your fault.'

MR WILSON: 'He's just immature. What he did was stupid. He was just bounty hunting. If they'd watched the television, they'd have known the FNLA were losing eight miles a day, they only had a hundred miles or so left. They should have known it would be all over by the time they got there.'

MRS WILSON: 'I don't know what else we could have done for him. . . . He hated school. He used to get asthma, and we always noticed it got worse on Sunday nights or Monday morning. He's often been to school and got so bad on the bus they've had to send him home. We used to live in a block of flats, and once he crawled up to the third floor and we found him there in a state of collapse. We took him to the chest hospital, everywhere; but it turned out it was psychological, because of all the bullying and so on. All this only came out later; he only told us about all that recently. You don't know what goes on in their lives, even though you see them every day.

'I suppose he's always been inclined to find any trouble if it's going. Before he started at the College of Further Education, he'd been mugged by this gang in the flats where we lived in Stoke Newington, and he'd told the police. Then the day he started, he'd got both his hands in plaster: he'd cut his hand a few days earlier and had to have a skin graft. These kids could see he was defenceless, so they set on him and kicked him unconscious. He was blind in one eye for twenty-four hours. That was their way of trying to get him to drop charges against them for mugging him.'

Mr Wilson: 'Poor old Steve, things always seem to go wrong for him. I suppose he might feel he hasn't had as much attention as he might like. Perhaps he's been a bit left out of it at times. But if he'd seen us when we thought he'd been executed, he'd've known what we feel.'

Mrs Wilson: 'When he went off to get that flight, he said goodbye to us, and then he said, "There's a letter for you upstairs." One for each of us. And he said in his letter he felt he hadn't got everything his brother had – he's settled down, got a lovely wife and child, she's nearly four; and Steve's brother'll be twenty-one next birthday. He feels it, he wants the same things for himself.'

Mr Wilson: 'He wanted to prove himself in a way. You know, "I'll show 'em" sort of thing. He might come out with all this bravado, but underneath, he's still a little boy. He's immature.'

Mrs Wilson: 'That's what they took advantage of, those who were organizing it. When Banks went out with them to Zaire, and handed them over to Callan, Steve's mate heard Banks and Callan arguing, and Banks said to him, "You won't get any more bodies." Bodies. That's how they thought of it. It was a trade in flesh. That's how they regarded life, human life. I'd like to get my hands on him, I would. . . . I'd find him, even if I had to take three months off work to do it. They told all these lies to the newspapers, it was in the headlines, "Boy Soldier Refuses to Come Home." They told the papers that Steve was driving a jeep, 700 miles from the combat zone, delivering food and supplies. Well, Steve can't even drive. Then when he did come home, Aspin rang up and said, "I got your boy home, Mrs Wilson." He hadn't. He hadn't been anywhere near the place. Banks said there would be money in compensation for all those who'd been bereaved, £10,000. Not a penny of it has been paid out yet.'

Mr Wilson: 'Steve saw one of his mates last week, one of the blokes who had to pull the trigger on those boys. I bet those men don't sleep at nights. It'll haunt them to their dying day, what they had to do. I shouldn't be surprised if you hear in the end that they've committed suicide.'

Mrs Wilson: 'Well, I hear Steve moving about sometimes, late at night. Last night till two o'clock I could hear him. I think it's the best thing for him to start work – he's starting tomorrow in a wine shop, get back to normal. It's an indoor job, I hope he

lasts, things sort themselves out. He's getting engaged – a girl he
met just before he went to Angola. But he's applied to join the
army as well.'

MR WILSON: 'The trouble is with kids like Steve, there's too
much individualism. They're too individualistic. What they
need is a time in the army; then you have to co-operate, you
can't just go your own sweet way. . . . They expect too much to
be laid on for them. When we were young, we had to find things
to do, we had to make our own fun. I mean, I know we had
bombed houses and that to play in, but there's life to be had,
even here in Edmonton, if you can find it. It must be. . . . We've
only been here a few months, so I don't know. I don't want to go
out. I'm all right here. Me and the missis, we might go and have
a drink or go out in the car, but when I've done my job, I just
want to come home and be on our own. We've got a decent
home together now. That's all I want. We have a few friends,
family over to see us. I don't want to be bothered with anyone
else. People come and tell you all their troubles if you let them, I
don't want to know about it. We've had our ups and downs over
the years. I left her for three years, but we've got over our
troubles with nobody else's help.

'We had a harder time. I was in London all through the war.
My father was killed in the war. We were more or less brought up
by my grandmother, she ruled us with a rod of iron, but we
loved and respected her. We had a sense of responsibility, we
didn't expect everything to be laid on for us all the time. I bet my
dad'd be turning in his grave if he could see what's happened to
the country he fought for, so that we should be free. All those
who don't want to work, the Social Security just dishing out
without question. Look at the Government, they sell out to the
Common Market or the unions, it's a sell-out all along the line.
Enoch Powell's the one. I've listened to him for fifteen years,
and everything he's said has come true. I'm not saying some of
them aren't doing a good job of work: doctors, nurses. When I
lost this finger' (he indicates the third finger of his left hand,
which is missing) 'it was an Indian doctor who saw to it; but
there's too many not doing any work. Not only blacks, but the
Irish and Scots and all the other foreigners. They get privileged
treatment. If two people are in court for the same offence, and
one's black and one's white, the white bloke'll always get the
stiffer sentence.

'Trouble is there's no co-operation or trust between people. Everybody's always quarrelling. You see politicians on the television arguing. Why can't they get together for the good of the country. People can work together, they've done it before. In the war we used to be all together.

'When we had all this publicity, we had some crank letters. One read, "Listen sonny, if you want to play at soldiers, ask your mummy to buy you a nice coloured box full; don't play at things you don't understand." There's one here addressed to me, says he was an ex-commando. "Dear Hypercrit" – look how it's spelt – "instead of bellyaching to the papers, you and your thickheaded son must both be thick as two planks not to know the score if you go on an outfit like that one." Why are they too scared to put their names at the bottom?'

Steve is beginning to feel a sense of anti-climax after the excitement of the past months. He says he would like to drive long distance, trans-Europe. He longs for excitement and adventure. He has itchy legs, wants to be on the move, to get away. He feels restless and unfulfilled. His feelings about the experience of Angola are ambiguous.

STEVE: 'I wanted money. If I hadn't been conned, it would have been all right. I wouldn't have gone if I'd known the way it was going to turn out. No way. I've had a good life up till now. I've done more in my seventeen years than a lot of people do in a lifetime. I can afford to let the future take care of itself. I've done a lot of things. I've travelled more than my dad has in his whole life. I don't care if I die tomorrow. Well, I do care, only I'm not worried about what happens to me. Some people might think I'm a right nutter. I haven't got a very high opinion of myself. I don't think it'd matter much if I got killed. . . . I've always been one to do things on impulse. If I feel like doing something, I'll do it. I'm ambitious. I've always been ambitious. I want to be the richest man in the world. Don't think I'll make it, somehow.

'You see this flat. My mum and dad have always had to work hard for everything they want. If they want something new, furniture, telly, a holiday, they've got to work for it. Well, I want to be able to just go and buy anything I want. Work, I don't mind work. I'm happiest when I'm doing something. It's sitting around here that gets me. . . . I don't mind work; but then I want to retire somewhere in the sun. . . . What I can't stand is being in one place all the time. I want to be a speedway driver, but it costs £40 a lesson. Well, where can I get that kind of money?'

The telephone rings.

'Hello, wanker. . . . No, I had a blow-out on the bike, so I never got there. . . . I might go away for the weekend, I don't know. If I don't, I might come round Sunday afternoon. Listen, I might be getting engaged at the weekend. Yeh . . . Naoo, I haven't told her about it yet. No, she'll do what I tell her. See you. Ta-ta.

'I'd like to settle down. Well, I would and I wouldn't. But this one, she's a real little charmer. Sweetest girl I've ever met. I don't want to be tied down though.

'I never went to school for about two years. In the end, they gave up, didn't even bother. What a place. I used to hop it, go hitching. I went all over the country. I had a social worker. She was nice. A right nympho.

'If I hadn't seen this article in the Sunday paper I would never have gone to Angola. When we went, Banks promised we could have all the beer and women we wanted. The only women I saw were all pregnant and black. They were horrible, and they cost £35 a time. There was only one bloke went with one of them, and we took the piss out of him rotten.'

Steve takes out his press cuttings. A scrapbook with a drawing on the cover of a 1940s-style movie star, multi-coloured and smiling, with *My Scrap Album* in italic handwriting. There is a notebook called Summit Students' Pad, which has been erased, and the words *My Personal Diary of Angola* substituted. Steve has kept all the press articles about himself and his photographs, including some grainy photographs of his mother and father, their faces contorted with pain and tears.

'All the stuff in the papers was a load of lies. They said I refused to come home, then they said I'd been shot, then they said I wanted to stay in Kinshasa. It was ridiculous. This mate of mine who just phoned, he wants me to go into business. I wouldn't mind that. Only thing is, he wants to con people, and as I've been conned by Banks and Aspin, I wouldn't want to do that to other people because I know what it's like. I want to make money, but I won't do it crooked. . . . I have got something in mind, another mission. I'm not saying what it is. It's not war. It's not peace. It's half-way between war and peace. I'd like to have enough money to get a place of my own for when I get married.'

He puts on a record of Hits from the Fifties. *Bird Dog*; *Dream, Dream, Dream.*

'I believe there is a life after death. I know it. Anybody who says there isn't, I'll smash his face. I've had experience of it. When my grand-dad died, right, he lived in this flat, and I used to go and stay with him sometimes. He always did the same thing, he had a routine for getting up in the morning at six o'clock: you could hear him moving about, washing in the old enamel bowl in the sink, you know, the clatter it makes, and going downstairs, you could hear everything he did. Well, when he'd been dead a week, I spent the night there. And next morning, I heard every single thing he did, he done exactly the same as he'd done every day of his life. I heard the bowl in the sink, I heard the floorboards creaking. I heard him come downstairs. He'd been dead and buried a week. So don't tell me there's no life after death. . . . Might have been his spirit. . . . I could give you hundreds of examples. I believe that everybody comes back to earth. Five times, yeh. And each time, you get to a position of more power, a higher position every time. That's why people aren't the same, they can't be equal, because they're all at different phases of their existence. The people who are at the top now, they must be on their fourth or fifth existence, like doctors and scientists, things like that. . . . I think I'm on about my third. So I've got two more to go. . . . I know somebody who's a reader of what you used to be in other lives. My girl, she's on her second now. On her first, she used to be a serving wench. You can come back as anything, black, white, it doesn't make any difference. I might have been anything, murderer, beggar, anything. The only thing is, you go on getting higher and higher, until everybody has had a turn. I don't believe in God, like that, not angels and devils and all that. We sometimes have a go with the ouija board, only it can be dangerous. You know, somebody is the scribe, and the spirit writes things through the person, but it can be dangerous, because sometimes people can go mad doing it. Not the glass, that's nothing, because anybody can cheat doing that, but you can't cheat the ouija board. I'd like to be a medium. I know I've got an aura. I'm psychic.

'I suppose life's been good to me. I don't know what I'll do. There's always the Rhodesian army. I'd join if I thought there was a chance. You need a bit of excitement. I liked Africa. We ate sardines and rice every day. We used to wipe our arse on leaves from the trees. I don't know what trees they were. I used my FN rifle three times; twice it was an accidental discharge, and then I got a bullet lodged in the breech. The third time was when we heard these people in the bushes and we knew it couldn't be any of our guys, so I just emptied a magazine into the bushes. . . . I didn't go and look at their faces afterwards, but I think there must have been about nine of them.'

He sets out the uniform on the sofa: camouflage jacket, olive drab background, with cloudy patches of dark green and brown, lightweight; American issue webbing, plain olive pants, four ammunition pouches in the belt. The uniform was issued in Kinshasa. Boots were DSM Dutch military, of tough grainy leather, thinner calf-length leg. They all wore the underwear they went in. Steve's own knife was taken away at the airport. 'That was only a lucky charm, really, frighten the kids at football matches'; ordinary military socks; a dagger, called 'Auntie's teeth', with a black leather handle, metal painted black so it would not glint in the dark. The dagger was worn in a pouch on the left-hand side, tied with a piece of bootlace so it was firm.

Although Steve's experience was extreme, his feeling is that of a whole generation of young working-class people. Many of them have been severed from the working-class tradition; they will never experience the kind of work situations which forged the collective spirit of the labour movement in the past. Their energies are under-used. They need to give something of themselves; but being suggestible and volatile, what they do give themselves to may well be random and arbitrary.

Steve's expedition to Angola was treated by the media as though he had tried to live out a dangerous fantasy; by a piece of good fortune, he had survived, and come back to reality. But there is a very grim sense in which the reverse is true, as he himself said. He went out to Angola and confronted the reality of civil war, and then came back to a life of fantasy again.

5

PARTS OF BRADFORD look as though they had been abandoned; as though the people had deserted the worn-out housing and exhausted landscape and gone elsewhere. Ruinous streets and collapsed workshops evoke a population that has been forced to retreat by some natural disaster. The neat chocolate-brown parlours, scenes of ritual celebration and layings-out, have been profaned by casual occupancy – dossers and young people using them simply for a night's shelter, have left a debris of empty cans, cider bottles, ordure and ashes.

In a house in one of these ravaged terraces, Mrs Collins lives among the ruins of what was once an extended family. The obligations and duties that once held them together still work, faintly; but the individual members long to go their own ways, and are held together now only by the fragile bonds of Mrs Collins's need. Their being together is full of strife and dissent, as each member clashes with the others in a competitive search for the answers to their own wants and preferences. There is something sullen and fidgety now about the sense of sharing; so much so, that escape from the family is the principal object of the younger members. They do occasionally try to move away: go down South, go and live in Leeds or Manchester, only to find that something still brings them back, so that for most of the time the idea of escape remains a fantasy.

But this crumbling example of extended family gives only a weak idea of its former strength. It meant that the family absorbed pain and suffering; protected its shame, cradled the individual against some of the consequences of his own wrongdoing, muted the keenness of loss, assuaged the pain of bereavement. Although it evolved as a response to an environment of poverty and insecurity, it contained as well an existential component that expressed a humanitarian philosophy of courage and reciprocal support against suffering. It is this humanitarian component that has been destroyed by the terms on which our improvement has been achieved, and it is this that escapes us now, for all the advances that have been made. And its absence brings home to us every day some of the unfreedoms of our liberation. Human skills (no less than work skills) absorbed unselfconsciously by the family have been taken away from those who exercised them without effort and laboriously invested in professional social workers, who have to be taught them: an act of human plunder.

The sharp individuation of people within the diminished circle of the smaller family unit highlights our own isolation as much as it enables us to pursue needs and personal ambitions that were obscured in a more crowded family place. Mrs Collins hovers between lament on the ingratitude of her children, the defection of her brothers and sisters, and an intense and crushing relationship with Stephen, her youngest child. He is vulnerable through being backward, dependent and over-weight. She is locked with him in an embrace of terror, like people clinging together for support in a shipwreck. The child's weaknesses tether him to her in the place of a decayed sense of duty and obligation: an emotional dependency has replaced the mother rôle. She clings to him as the guarantor of her future, and the relationship imprisons them both. All the anguish that would have been dispersed and mitigated by the extended family is concentrated on one weak and uncomprehending child – on him who is least able to cope with it.

Mrs Collins is in her late forties, harassed and anxious. Her family extends through three marriages as well as by generational continuity. She is the centre of a still substantial network of people, who turn to her for support, advice, money and shelter. She is the traditional matriarch, self-sacrificing, long-suffering. She needs someone to worry about and someone to blame; and the focus of her distress and frustration changes from week to week, almost from day to day. She will pour out all her disappointment in the unreliability of Lennie or Joan, two of the grown-up children, and the next time you see her, this will have been forgotten, displaced by the troubles brought upon her by some other member of the family. It might be that Lennie's wife thinks she's too good for the family she has married into, or that Lennie has learned to despise them, accusing his mother of living like pigs in dirt; or that Joanie's Roge has nicked something, or had the gas cut off for not paying the bill; or Tracy, who is fourteen, refuses to go to school and has moved into a flat with a fellow who works on the buildings and is over thirty; or Mark, who is getting money from somewhere and is running wild, and whose father never comes anywhere near; or above all, Stephen, with whom Mrs Collins has an all-consuming involvement. She cannot leave him alone, but goads him all the while into affirmations of his love for her.

Mrs Collins is always on the verge of final disaster. She communicates her anxiety in such a way that many social workers have been deeply affected by her worries, and have been mobilized with great urgency on her behalf; only to find that the emergencies evaporate immediately. Mrs Collins has always been through the final breakdown of a family relationship, she has always just suffered the ultimate disillusionment about one of her children. 'He used to be the sight of my eyes before he married her.' Wherever she has lived, she needs to be re-housed, although she always tries to get back to the familiar streets that seem to have such an affinity with her decaying sense of family. The place where she lives always absorbs a great deal of her dissatisfaction – as though the plaster itself were porous.

She lives in a comfortable neglect. The house is always warm; the gas fire burns through the summer, tea is always ready in the hot back room; a closed impermeable world. There is a buff leatherette suite losing its stuffing, a mauve carpet. The wallpaper has been removed to child level. Above, the only ornament is a text carved into a piece of varnished wood, 'She offered her honour, He honoured her offer, And all the night long, He was honour and offer.'

The permanent crisis shifts all the time; and she is threatened by unpredictable but certain tragedy, which indeed did occur.

Her daughter Joan had been separated from her husband and was living with Mrs Collins. She had two children, Scott, four, and Natalie, three. While playing with his sister in the living room, Scott received a serious head injury, and died in hospital a few days later. He was said to have fallen against an onyx-topped table; but because of the mysterious circumstances of the accident, the hospital refused to issue a death certificate. Mrs Collins was visited by the police several times, and one night spent four hours at the police station being questioned. The hospital doctors said that the child seemed to have suffered a blow that could not easily have occurred in the course of a mere fall. Mrs Collins had been in the kitchen, had heard a scream and called to the two children to behave themselves. When she had gone back in the room, she had seen Scott lying on the floor.

Although she knew she was not responsible for the accident, she was tormented by a sense of guilt, displaced in part from the fear that she would be unable, in the long run, to hold the warring members of her family together. She had always been surrounded by children, and Scott was one of her favourites. Was it a punishment to her, because she didn't deserve to have such lovely children to look after? Had she done something that she was unaware of that had offended God? But even worse than this, she kept returning to the idea of the child not being given a funeral. The body had been laid on ice, and was not being allowed to rest properly. On him she projected some of her own turbulent anxiety. She said that the police had insisted that she had showed no grief when she was told of the child's death. 'But they don't see you when you're lying awake crying at night, do they?' The denial of the funeral preyed on Mrs Collins all spring; she became worn and haggard. 'I think it's the worst thing you can do to a child, to deny it a proper burial.' In a family still governed by the importance of ritual, this infringement of custom added incalculably to her distress.

The doubt remained for nearly six months, and then, at last, an open verdict was returned.

When the funeral did take place, it was overshadowed by the fact that Social Security had told her that all they would pay for would be a Minicab, with room for the mother and father of the child alone, who would have to carry the child's coffin on their lap.

This event had a decisive effect on the family; and the bonds between them, already weakened, slackened still further. Joan remarried and went to live in Batley. Mrs Collins's relationship with Stephen became even more obsessive. The electricity was turned off because she could not pay the bill; but Stephen, who was afraid of the dark, became seriously disturbed. He was directed to a school for maladjusted children. Mrs Collins asked everybody for interpretations of her relationship with Stephen. Why was he always naughty to her, why did he have to test her out all the time? He knew she loved him. A blind symbiosis of dependency existed between them, which they both partly resented, but which neither could bear to do without. Stephen began soiling again; the bedding was ruined. He had to go on a diet.

Lennie's wife, Carol, wanted to move. Lennie quarrelled with his mother for her lack of ambition, her apparent contentment in the overcrowded and ramshackle house. 'Look at them, they're all the same, all the women in this family. They need a rocket up their backsides. They'd live in a midden and not notice it.' Lennie and Carol set their hearts on getting out of Bradford and buying a house. They had learned to define themselves against the social values of Mrs Collins, which derived from a tradition of poverty. For them, everything that denies that tradition is good — being modern, trendy, fashionable, ambitious, competitive. Lennie said, 'I could go anywhere, be anybody. I might emigrate, get a Lotus Elan, go abroad. I might go on an oil-rig. This country's finished. Nobody's got any ambition. My mother and sisters, what have they got, what have they done? Nothing.' His mother says, 'You haven't got so bloody much, you haven't even got a job.' 'No, but I will have. I've got a bit of ambition, and I've got dreams. You have ideals, and if you want things badly enough they come to you in the end.'

Lennie clings to a traditional male rôle, exacting deference for a position which in fact he does not hold. His insistence upon what is his due, his expectation that the women will dance attendance on him, belong to a time when the rôle of breadwinner meant the difference between eating and going hungry, survival or the workhouse, literally life and death. In a context of unemployment benefit and a wife's superior skills (Carol had been a secretary), a house shared with his mother, his male pride seems inappropriate; and can be fulfilled only in fantasy. Fantasy comes to have a crucial social function in a changed reality – one of diminished rôle and redundant skills: it becomes a means of self-expression, absorbs energies that are not required, drains off aggression and frustrations that might contest the way things are.

Most evenings Tracy goes out. She has had her ears pierced, and she is wearing small gold rings. She has a flimsy batwing blouse and platform shoes; she totters out, impervious to the freezing night, with a pile of records, and she never tells anyone where she is going.

Mrs Collins feels her waning power over her other children; and needs to reassert her emotional hold over Stephen the more strongly. She could control him by saying that she was ill, and seemed surprised and gratified to discover that this raised him to such a pitch of anxiety and concern that he would always do whatever she told him. 'I've only got to say "Mummy will die" and he's gentle as a kitten. I've only got to pretend to cry, and he'll come and comfort me.'

Tracy scarcely ever went to school. She was always involved with teachers in arguments about manners or language or insolence. Occasionally, she would be sent home from school, and this legitimatized an indefinite absence. At the end of term, Tracy and her mother sat brooding over her report. It said that it was impossible to judge whether Tracy had any ability in any subject because she so rarely attended any of the lessons. She had been away for three-quarters of the term. For weeks she claimed to have no shoes and refused to go to school in her best ones. Then she had a throat infection; then stomach ache and then 'troubles' connected with her age. She said she didn't care. It didn't matter. School was boring. Everything was boring, except boys and clothes and records. She was as far as she could be from her mother's values. She was an intelligent girl; but her appetites had been excited, and her abilities lay untouched. She was getting engaged anyway. 'I've been to see the ring I want, it's a diamond in a claw setting. Twenty quid. He can afford it, he's well off, he's got a car. I'm not going to get into trouble, I know what I'm doing. I don't want to finish up with a baby and having to get married. I want something better than that. I've seen what's happened to my sisters. I don't want to finish up like them. They're both trapped, because they couldn't wait. The girls at school, they all come in making out they've done it, and they dare each other how far they'll go. Jackie comes in and says 'Last night he did this', and Joanne says 'Oh, that's nothing, mine did that', and I don't say a thing, but I'm thinking 'Yeh, which one of you two is gonna come in crying and scared stiff because they've had to rush off to see the doctor. I want a decent life for me and my kids, when I have them. . . . We had a visit the other day from my old man. A stranger. I was here in the house on my own. He knocks at the door and says "Can I come in?" He says "How old are you now?" I says "Nearly fifteen." He says "Are you really? I thought you were about twelve." Lying so-and-so. He knew. That's why he came round. His own daughter. He says "Let me see now, what's your name?" He couldn't even remember it. He says "Oh, I'll have to see more of you." I says "Not if I see you first." That's the kind of man my father is. . . . I haven't got much, but what I have got is precious, and I'm not throwing it away.'

Mrs Collins says: 'I'd rather have boys than girls any day.' Tracy: 'Well, thanks very much.' Mrs Collins: 'No, I wouldn't change the ones I've got, only boys don't land a baby on you. . . . Both of mine, Joanie and Chrissie, it was the same. They were full of it, when my husband left, "We're not going to finish up like our Mam", but here they are, both the same as I was, for all their big ideas. Mind you, Tracy's different. . . . Only I wish she wasn't getting engaged.'

The engagement lasted three months. It was followed by heartbreak and an overdose; and then, not long afterwards, a new engagement.

Through all the loss and departures – Tracy moved into a flat with a woman whose husband had left her, Lennie and Carol got their house in Leeds – only the relationship with Stephen remained constant. 'Even if he's in the other room, he keeps running in to see if I'm all right. He says "Are you all right?" and if I look sad, he says "What's the matter, Mam?" He says "I don't want you to get old, because old people die." ' Mrs Collins says the family accuse her of treating Stephen like a Mummy's boy. She says they complain she's turning him into a 'cream puff'. 'Only he's different, you can't treat him the same as the others. I daren't let him go out on his own, not far. . . . I worry if he crosses the road on his own. . . . If anything happened to him, I'd never forgive myself. . . . He doesn't want to go away from me, he doesn't even like playing out, he's all the while running back to see if I'm all right. . . . I mean, I know nobody'll want him when I've gone. Nobody'd put up with him like I do. I can't see anybody else in the family looking after him. That's why I shall have to help him be independent. I've told him about dying and that. . . . I say to him "Stephen, when a person gets very old, they die. They go away, Stevie. They have to." And he says "Don't die, I don't want you to get old." He does need me. I know I'm too soft with him, I'm the softest cow on earth.'

She feels half shame, half pleasure in her relationship with Stephen. His dependence on her promises her a secure future; but she also realizes that he ought to be able to detach himself from her emotionally, or he will suffer. She defers a decision. He's still young, there's a whole lifetime; and it is the one relationship which is constant in the turmoil and loss; the one commitment that will not weaken. It is her only certainty in the ruins of the broken and dispersed family. Because of her own isolation, she cannot bear to let him go. Stephen is her comfort and support. It is not easy to see where his will lie.

Changes over which we have no control reach deep into our lives, affecting our deepest relationships, re-arranging, modifying them, despite ourselves. The anguish of Mrs Collins isn't her unique experience: she is a victim of an excruciating epic of violence imposed on us under the cloak of material progress and improvement.

Mum, the formidable and eternal Mum, virago, domestic lawgiver, comforter and martyr, is dying. Ma Joad, Ena Sharples, the East End Mum, the watcher on the doorstep, the layer out of the dead, is herself fading away. You can watch her die. Like everything else, it is a public spectacle: on the television adverts the children instruct her as to how she should best provide for them; what she should buy, which supermarkets she should use, with what tasty items of manufactured food she may win their hearts; and vacillating, confused, she complies. Her functions have been usurped. She is becoming extinct.

The rôle she had, the domestic supremacy, was in part a consolation for her inability to express herself outside her marriage and family; and in this respect may always have been a makeshift, a substitute for forbidden personal satisfactions. But her human and domestic skills were real – the counterpart of those her husband applied to his work – and the surrender of them cannot be made without pain. She always made the most of her position, lamenting the ingratitude of her men, pro-claiming her own selflessness and sacrifice. All that repressed energy which went into consoling the bereaved, forgiving – but never forgetting – the wrong done to her, advising, interfering, setting other people's lives to rights, gave her an undisputed place and purpose. She never flinched from any of her duties, however distasteful. It was she who always identified the bodies and washed the dead, and visited the sick-room, scorning consumption and diphtheria. It was she who kept together those sprawling and haphazard assemblages of people called the family, and who kept alive a sense of commitment to others in accordance with the precedences of kinship. She may have been a battle-axe: outspoken, dogmatic, incorruptible, a model of

pig-headed and self-conscious rectitude. She always knew what
to do in a crisis. She was always being sent for; and she never let
anyone down. Her enduring power was acknowledged by her
sons, who tattooed her name in their flesh, making of their body
a shrine to her who had taught them right from wrong; and they
affirm it now at her funeral, MUM in daffodils or carnations
emblazoned on the black limousine that slows the traffic and
commands the attention of even the most indifferent passers-by.

Mum's own needs and preferences had no place in the way of
life of which she was a kind of mistress of ceremonies. For some
women this rôle may have been an odious constraint; and it is
no doubt they who cry liberation with the greatest passion. But
some women expanded and flourished in the rôle. Mum exulted
in it.

You can see her now, in her agony, in any doctor's surgery,
where she sits, haunted and diminished, seeking diagnosis of a
malady which no one seems able to place satisfactorily. Is it old
age, is it a prolonged menopause, is there a growth? Where does
it come from, this nameless grief? She is on tranquillizers, which
numb the obscure ache but don't drive it away. Her children live
too far away to visit regularly, but they have paid for a telephone
to be installed, so that they can keep in touch. She carries their
photograph in her handbag, and shows it to anyone who will
look, when she sits on the benches in the grassy places where the
old houses have been cleared. She is wasted and ghost-like now;
once monumental, she has lost weight. Her hair is white, she
begins to look frail. She is surprised when younger women,
strangers, take her by the arm as she crosses the road. She goes
to the pensioners' clubs, where she will quarrel over the last
sticky bun or a seat at the pantomime; inconsolable, unable to
find relief from that elusive but persistent pain that is always
with her.

When she was struggling for the family and the children were
still at home, she looked forward to this time, when they would
all be grown up. She imagined herself, in the middle of her
grandchildren, telling them of her youth, of her resourcefulness
in adversity, her triumph over poverty and want. But the
grandchildren are few, and seldom seem to visit. And even when
they do come, they ask her what she's got for them, what they
can have. They want prizes and rewards. They don't want to
know about her life. She, their own past, has been expunged;

and she feels as though she is already dead, but somehow a spectator of her own absence. Her experience is not validated by any of her young. They see her sense of duty as repression, what she saw as caring, a substitute for living. And she tries to console herself, looks round at their ranch-style house on the new estate, and says that it was her efforts that made this way of life possible; and then reflects that it is this way of life that hurts her so.

She comes from a generation of women which is not being replaced: her daughters will never grow into the rôle which their mother has so unwillingly set down. Her daughter will acquire no wisdom, no experience to transmit that is not everybody else's experience and public wisdom. So many other people have taken over the mothering function, people far more knowledgeable and better instructed than Mum ever was. There are social workers, health visitors, pediatricians; but above all, there are food manufacturers who know what vitamins her children need, who know how to provide the goodness which Mum provided only haphazardly with her ham-bone and shillings-worth of root vegetables simmering all morning on the gas stove. Mum's daughter has remained a girl herself, despite the apparent maturity of her growing children. She spends her time in terror of losing her husband and children, feels unworthy, purposeless, abandoned; above all, alone. She feels guilty and inadequate towards her own children, and buys them the things which the ubiquitous voices in the air tell her she must buy in order to be worthy of them. She is the distraught mother who consults the Child Guidance because her child has lost interest in the £200 worth of toys she bought him for Christmas. She is the anxious woman who tried to explain to her five-year-old that Mummy must go out to work or Natalie won't be able to have pretty clothes. She coaxes her child into expressing ever more urgent needs, and then drives herself to satisfy them. She lives in constant fear of the nightmare in which she loses her looks, her figure, her youth; the only things she feels she has, and things she is certain to lose. Mum never worried about that. She didn't care if she was fat; she wasn't preoccupied with the loss of her husband's affection; and in any case he always said, 'You don't look on the mantelpiece when you poke the fire.' She grew into being Mum, comfortably and without effort.

Her daughter cannot grow into the rôle now, even if she wants to. There is simply no place for it. Even if a woman chooses to adopt a traditional Mum rôle, if she stays at home, determined to look after the children, she cannot do so without constant reference to all the instruction and advice that assail her from outside, the benevolent carers on television and in the newspapers, who somehow prise her whole life open, correcting attitudes, eliminating instincts, refining understanding. Only the world of manufacture and expert knowledge possesses the indispensable adjuncts to proper parenthood, without which no child can be expected to grow safely to maturity; and she is compelled to obey.

And Mum herself, no one goes to see her now in her little terraced house or in the council flat, unless it's to ask favours – a bit of baby-sitting, have the kids for a few days while Jeff and Sheila have a winter break; lend them her life savings of a few hundred pounds to buy a new car or help out with the deposit on the house. And she sometimes sits with the grandchildren she adores, and wonders why they are not a bit more like children; sitting beautiful and immaculate as Barbie dolls; but somehow unapproachable, their eyes already fixed on a not distant future of excitement and plenitude. And she feeds them even more illicit treats and sweets and rewards, in a vain hope of attaching them to her; catching something of the altered feelings about children, she too begins to appease them, placate them; sensing their power, their despotic reign that has ousted hers.

What has become of them, the next generation of women whose energies had to be used up in the circle immediately surrounding them? Because that energy did find an outlet, even if, at worst, it was only monitoring everybody else's behaviour or exulting in their own martydom. They are now left with the opportunity to express an identity of which they felt they had been robbed. Have some of them managed to find the long-repressed self by changing into breathless media women, those jazzy reporters with their big glasses and show-me-where-it's-all-at voices, telling us about a scandal in Doncaster, or shocking practices in Birmingham? Are some of them now in the army of social workers who sip prudently at cups of tea from the wrong side of the cup in council flats, while the less fortunate daughters of Mum confide their unhappiness, their frustration, the details of their hysterectomy, their broken marriages? Are some of them perhaps in factories, making clothes or toys – electric-blue teddy bears six feet high – which others will buy to make up to their children for their absence from the home and their own feelings of guilt? Perhaps some of them are in schools, instructing children how to find themselves and give expression to their needs and wants. Some are almost certainly in the food factories, preparing the instant meals they will be grateful for because they get home exhausted from preparing instant meals in the factory all day. . . .

The process has come full circle; and the meaning of Mum's death becomes a little clearer. The release from individual mothering has exploded into career structures that serve exactly the same purpose, but in a way that is depersonalized and professional, and consequently more efficient and homogeneous. The release of energy from bondage to hearth and home is immediately absorbed in pursuing the same end, but in a more roundabout way: one that can be calculated in money terms. What an elaborate circle of vanity it has been. Women give expression to their long crushed selves at last; but the sterility of the institutionalized relationships that have replaced the universal and instinctive knowledge of Mum satisfy neither the givers nor the recipients of them; their lives are corroded by guilt at the defection from their own depleted families; and they try harder to buy more things for their young, who have been partially relinquished to the superior caring power of the agencies whose function it has become. But young men do not tattoo themselves with the name of a schoolteacher, nor with the names of the manufacturers of their favourite food, spaghetti rings or instant whip.

So Mum lives on, in a dispersed and attenuated way. Her labour has been infinitely divided, and multiple skills once vested in individuals have been torn from them; ironically, in order to preserve the *status quo*. What Mum could once do as a matter of course has been parcelled out into a hundred jealously guarded specializations. But she herself has gone; and her tombstones are perhaps the great slabs of dwelling places which rise over the cities like the funerary monuments to a race of extinct giantesses.

Part Three

CITIES, OLD AND NEW

NOTTINGHAM

IN NOTTINGHAM I met a lot of people who had worked for much of their lives in some part of the labour movement. Many of the old activists are proud of the increased importance of the trades unions, and see the present as a time of relative ease, compared with their past of scarcity and absence of comfort. But many more say that the hopes of the labour movement have been disappointed, its aims not realized. They feel bitter at what they regard as the slow extinction over the years of an ideal that they know cannot be easily re-kindled; and it was to them that I turned for some illumination of what they mean by disillusionment and betrayal. There is something moving about those austere interiors, the old encumbered parlours, the ticking of an old clock, the fire smouldering in the grate even in summer because as they get older they feel the cold more. Often they feel isolated within their community, because they have held fast to their beliefs, while the majority of the working class seem to have accepted a growing dependency upon the values of capitalism, and increasingly acquiesce in them.

In a sooty terraced house in the shadow of the Players factory, the widow of a former tobacco worker sits in a wooden rocking chair, hands swollen with arthritis, head moving with old age, as though in affirmation now of a world she has always denied.

Her grandchild, a little girl of eight, comes in after school, to wait with her grandmother until her parents leave off work. The child has a key to the front door on a ribbon round her neck, and she lets herself in. The old lady's face is illuminated with pleasure at the sight of the beautiful little girl.

But the child goes straight into the kitchen to see what is for tea. She is cross because the biscuits are not chocolate. 'I don't like fig rolls. I hate them. What did you get those for?' She sits on the floor with her doll: a tiny malevolent figure with idealized features – red lips, large eyes with long lashes, elaborately dressed auburn hair and red fingernails. She looks up and says, 'This is my twin.' The old lady is full of apologies because she hasn't got the right biscuits. She explains to me that the little girl can't understand that the supermarket is too far away, and to go there she has to rely on a neighbour's car. 'They don't understand as you get old. Sometimes I think she feels I do it on purpose.' She tells me that she would do anything to protect her grand-daughter from the life she led. She had been in service at thirteen, and cruelly treated in a big house in Derbyshire.

But the child will not be required to experience anything her grandmother knew; and between them, despite all the feeling and good will, there is no common ground. The grandmother says she has been sheltered; which means that she has grown up at a remove from any of the processes that provide things. The only thing that matters to the child is the availability of the things she wants: it doesn't matter where they come from, how they are produced, how they originate, or who might suffer so that she might enjoy them. There is something deeply shocking in the abjection of the old woman in the presence of her grandchild; the old lady who started work at thirteen, who adores the girl she sees as her own creation, but who, somehow, troublingly, elusively, is not of her, feels no strong sense of continuity or even kinship with her.

The little girl tells me it is her birthday soon, and what she might have; what she has been promised. She asks me if I like her dress, her shoes. She had wanted a different kind of shoes, but her daddy couldn't afford them.

I was reminded of an old lady, in Bradford, talking of a pair of boots she had had, perhaps seventy years ago. 'I always went down to the foundry on Friday night, and I went shopping with my dad. That was always a great treat. I'd look in the foundry, and he'd smile when he saw me, and put me on the bench while he got his things on; because the floor was all wet, and he only had a board to stand on. One Friday, he'd been working overtime all the week, and he took me along to a shoe shop. I said, "What are we going to do here?" And he said to the girl, "Will you get the pair of boots I looked at at dinner time?" And she brought out a lovely pair of boots, real leather soles. And I'd only worn clogs up till then. He said "Do you like them?" I said, "No, you mustn't, I can't wear those." He said, "Yes you can. Would you like to keep them on?" To think, he'd been working overtime all week, he'd taken the trouble to go down there and have them put on one side for me. . . . And he stood in all that water. He was crippled with rheumatism. When he had to leave work, I went down to the mill and I asked for a job, and I was only a little tot, and they said, "Who have you come for, have you come to look for your mother?" I said, "No, I've come for a job." They said, "You're too little," I said, "I'm twelve." They said, "You'll never reach the loom." I said, "I'll stand on a box then." And that's what I did.'

The testimony of the old militants is always similar: their anger at the conditions in which they grew up is muted now by the years, but not the determination to keep faith with the suffering of their parents. They have brought up their own children with a lively awareness of it; and generally their children do retain a diluted but affectionate commitment to their parents' beliefs, even when they are no longer really interested in the stories of poverty and struggle, which sound to them like the exaggerated ramblings of ageing exiles. Sometimes they will chide them gently and tell them not to go on about it; or, having heard it many times, they get up and leave the room, or hide behind a newspaper. The generation that has replaced them has not been subject at first hand to that experience, not its intensity, not its passion. The end of poverty weakened the transmission of values that grew out of it; and a stronger influence than parental experience for them has been the mesmeric power and promise of the spectacle of capitalism. The old have seen their young recede from them; and while they have remained in the same place, they nonetheless inhabit a different world.

'When we had nowt, we threatened the rich. Now we act like they did. We know what we have to lose when we see today's poor, and we do see 'em, every day. They might be on the other side of the world, but they come into your house every night of the week, on that thing' – he points to the television. 'Just so we know. Today's poor are black and hungry. You'd think we'd know what it was like, we've been there as well.' – Miner, fifties.

'What can you tell them about means test, parish relief, pauper's graves, workhouses, pawnshops? They were our teachers, those things.'

'My father was a miner. He went to work in the dark, he came home in the dark, he worked in the dark; and now he's dead in the dark. I've seen him come home and throw his money on the table, and put his head in his arms and shed tears at the amount of it, because it wasn't enough to keep his family on.'

'When I started work, well there were three factories in the village, and if you couldn't get on in any of them, you had no choice but to go to Nottingham to look for work. My mother wanted me to get a trade in my fingers, so I got a job in a hosiery factory. Ten shillings a week. The trouble was, I had to travel all the way from Heanor. That cost 7/6 a week; which meant that I had half a crown left.'

'People aren't satisfied, only they don't seem to know why they're not. The only chance of satisfaction we can imagine is getting more of what we've got now. But it's what we've got now that makes everybody dissatisfied. So what will more of it do, make us more satisfied, or more dissatisfied?'

'I started work in a hosiery factory when I was thirteen. I had to turn half-hose from one side to the other with a sort of peg-brush, and tie them up in bundles of five dozen. I got 6d for 2,400. You had no facilities for making tea: you could do it with the water exhaust from the dye vats. In your dinner-break you might boil your egg in the vats, boiling dyes. Your egg might come out red or blue. You had half an hour break for breakfast, an hour for dinner. People used to go home for their breakfast and again for their dinner.'

'After the First War, this country was in ferment. You could go into many a pub in Nottingham, and at closing time it was nothing to hear everybody get up and sing the "Red Flag". My father was in regular work, in a hosiery factory. My grand-father had been a miner at Pinxton; he'd taught himself to read and write, and had been a local preacher. My mother was a devout Christian. I was always a Baptist chapel-goer, and when I went into the army at eighteen I'd never thought about it. I just accepted. Before we came back to England in 1919, our colonel warned us against Red agitators. If he hadn't mentioned them, it wouldn't have occurred to me to think about it. But when I got home, I began to look around. I worked against a lad who'd been brought up in an orphanage, but he had the finest turn of mind of anybody I'd ever met. I think I owe a lot to him, his comradely tutelage. He introduced me to Mazzini's book, the *Duties of Man and Other Essays*; that book influenced me almost more than any other. I got my political education through the

National Council of Labour Colleges. Education for Emancipation was its slogan. When the Labour colleges were closed, the labour movement lost its last chance to provide any mass education for its members. I joined the ILP. I remember during the Depression, we had such a sense of elation, not at the living conditions of the people, but because we felt we knew and understood what was happening, when to so many it was a mystery. We really thought we would see socialism before we died. I don't now. It was an exciting time: I enjoyed doing battle with the parish, to get relief or food tokens or whatever it was. I never enjoyed spending it: it was simply the fight that I liked. At the moment, we're living through times very similar to the '30s, but unlike them at the same time. It's a kind of mirror image of what was happening then. In today's climate, the only arguments that make any popular headway are Right-wing ones. You've had a liberalizing of the surface of society, and that becomes the scapegoat for all that's wrong, without reaching the root problems. In the '30s it was so different; even more so in the General Strike.

'You can't ruin the capitalist system simply by taking money off it, and that's all the working class is doing. You can't beat them economically. There's got to be an awakening of the working class; a spiritual awakening. I don't know whether it will come. I've always thought of myself as a revolutionary rather than a rebel. A rebel, to me, implies someone who doesn't know what he's fighting for, only what he's fighting against. A revolutionary should be more intelligent than a rebel, and more constructive. When I was young, we came close to a moment of real change; but now we've receded from it again. I can remember during the General Strike, we went into the Palais-de-Danse with our banners. Everybody stopped dancing and cheered. That showed the depth of people's commitment. Imagine doing that now. You wouldn't get past the door.'

The Meadows. Close to the centre of the city, one of the ugliest slums in the Midlands was still standing at the beginning of the '70s. A series of streets and courtyards and dark terraces, a strangely evocative place it was, a survival of a large area of Victorian building, almost intact: yards without sunlight, covered with a permanent sticky velvet of moss, willowherb and grass growing out of cracks in the brickwork, outside privies overflowing, ruined wash-houses, leaking roofs, broken glass, houses infested with rats and cockroaches: a demoralized and despairing place which had once been a stable, if poor, working-class community. The Meadows Association of Tenants and Residents was started in 1972, a vigorous and committed community group, and supported by some university students who had moved into the area. But by the time the group began, the community had for the most part already deserted the places where the community work was concentrated. All those people who could afford to leave the Meadows had already done so; and this included a large proportion of the people in regular and reasonably paid work. Those left were, as in so many of the areas where community action was focused in the late '60s and early '70s, the dispossessed: single-parent families, the unemployed, the old, the migrant, the disabled, mentally ill. Often, these groups were mistaken by the university students anxious to help them, to be representative of the working class, rather than the residue that is left when those who can do so have already departed. The poor sometimes became objects of fantasy for radical students; and I can recall a few occasions when old-age pensioners or depressed unsupported mothers have been the puzzled recipients of exhortation and rhetoric; slightly shocked but quite impervious.

The Association was formed, first of all, to get essential repairs carried out while people were waiting to be rehoused; and then, to enable those displaced to have a say in the planned reconstruction of the area; to be allowed to return to the places where many of them had lived all their lives. There was much talk of reconstituting broken communities, salvaging something of worth from the wholesale removal of thousands of people from a long-established working-class part of the city. The activists in the Association tended to see the work as a struggle between malevolent functionaries protecting a cruel bureaucracy and an idealized working-class community. Its real achievement was to take the council to court for failing to carry out repairs on property it owned, and winning the case; which set a precedent that was widely imitated elsewhere. In 1972 the demolition was just beginning. The council had conceded that efforts would be made to re-house those who said they would like to return to the Meadows when it was rebuilt.

By 1977, most of the area had disappeared, and the first phases of rebuilding were already complete.

On one side of Kirkwhite Street, half-demolished houses, three storeys high. There is a long ginnel, opening out on to communal backyards of brick and slate, overgrown with weeds and wild flowers; everywhere the dereliction is in flower, an eruption of fireweed that is like an organic part of the flaking red brickwork. Outhouses and wash-houses have collapsed, the yards are littered with pieces of furniture and ornament which have been left behind, as no longer appropriate to the change of environment which the people who lived here were anticipating.

On the other side of the street, opposite the three-storey ruins, there is a newly built old-people's home. Some of the former inhabitants have indeed come back to the place where they were born; though perhaps not as they had imagined it. Behind the windows of the home, you can see the pale smudge of the wasted faces of old women; and as the summer afternoon sun shines on the decaying houses opposite, these are reflected vividly in the windows of the new building; so that for a moment it looks as if the old women are in both places at once, visiting their own past like ghosts; and briefly, the plain new building, with its flowerbeds, picture windows and rubberized floors, is invaded by the tenements it replaced.

Although some people have returned to the new flats and houses, many more have not. The community, which before demolition still seemed natural and coherent, no longer matters when the physical structures have been removed. In retrospect, it now seems to the people that it was merely chance that threw them together, rather than social and economic forces, against which they knew they had to unite or perish. The setting itself reveals a new purpose that was hidden by the old squalor. The responses are the same now as they are on any new estate: the cost, the expense of the things needed, new furniture, new curtains and carpets, new equipment and utensils. It seems that new people are required too, and many try to live up to the images which these new living spaces impose. The working-class past is extinguished. It is something ugly and shaming, and the overwhelming need is to expunge it. The emphasis on the domestic interior draws people away from old associations;

these wither and are not replaced. The initial excitement of the new house lasts for a time; but then it abates, and debt and discontent are left.

The Meadows is perhaps one of the most dramatic examples of the transformation of what was an appalling slum into a modern and carefully designed estate. It has all taken place in less than a decade, and as such is a symbol of the altered relationship between capitalism and the people: out of the squalor, poverty and denial of basic needs, suddenly appears a promise of a better life. But the thing that has given us new hope brings with it a corrosive kind of poison that alters our patterns of human association, makes relationships appear unfulfilling, friendships unrewarding, the demands of kinship onerous and unwelcome.

Mr and Mrs Dunn live in a one-storey council house in a vast grey estate in the city. The roads are long, with arid vistas of concrete. Everything is hard on these estates: glass, concrete, metal, brick. A children's playground is made of more metal, growing out of unyielding stone. The lamp standards are concrete; the houses are interrupted only by a petrol station, squat metal pumps on plinths of brick, a pub with a yard of flinty asphalt.

Mr and Mrs Dunn, now in their late sixties, have worked all their lives for the labour movement. He has kept his optimism – 'I look abroad, to where socialism has triumphed' – but his wife sometimes loses heart as she listens to the women in the street:

MRS DUNN: 'Oh it was there, believe me. The working class did have the capacity to be creative. When the Armistice was signed, the same day, there was such a party in our street, and we did it all ourselves. Somebody could play the accordion and the piano, we sang and we danced, and the women all baked and cooked, things they'd been saving till after the war; they cleaned the street, somebody swept it, and they made decorations out of next to nothing. I was only a child at the time, but I remember the spontaneity and resourcefulness of those people.

'They had the ability to enjoy some of the good things of life; I don't mean having culture rammed down their throats, but we loved nothing so much when I was a kid as going to my auntie's and listening to her records. She had an old gramophone: there'd be the *Messiah*, the Nuns' Chorus, the Triumphal March from *Aida*, *Trovatore*. And a lot of people had read Shaw, the pamphlets and the plays, Robert Blatchford, H. G. Wells, Dickens, Thackeray. Ordinary working people, some of them who'd left school at thirteen or fourteen. Above all, they weren't afraid of ideas. We went to see travelling performances of operas; we saw *Carmen* I remember. We had to queue for hours to get a seat in the gallery. There was this hunger for something that was better, you could feel it, it flowed like blood through the people. Now, well, I know all those things still exist, only it's somehow harder for the working class to find them, they're offered so much that's superficial and empty. There's no leadership any more; people are adrift.

'My father was in the shipyards in Hull during the First War, directed labour. We often never saw him from Thursday to Sunday. My mother was a semi-invalid. I was the oldest, so I had to take her place in a way. I got a scholarship to the grammar school, but by then my father was out of work. We moved to Nottingham and a I had a job at Lewis Meridian, 8/– a week, making up hosiery. I thought because I'd had a bit of a grammar-school education, I was going to cakewalk into a clerical job. The first job I went for, I got there at seven in the morning; there were already a hundred girls queuing. I went back eleven times to Meridian before I got a job. The woman who was in charge, when I went for the eleventh time, she said "Haven't I seen you before?" I said, "Yes, ten times." She said, "That's two more times than Robert Bruce, you deserve a job." But that's how it was. You were at the mercy of someone taking a fancy to you, or pity. Caprice. Anyway I stayed there. Oh, they were strict. There was a supervisor, oh, she did tyrannize our lives. We used to call her the shithouse cop, because it was her job to time you if you went to the lavatory. I got a learner's wage to do finished mending; that is, cutting in two pure silk stockings that had been finished, and taking out damaged bits and replacing them. They made lovely stuff; only we could never afford it.'

MR DUNN: 'My grandfather was a miner. All the boys in our village went into the pit, the girls to service. That's all there was. My mother used to go out to do washing at the washtub. She brought it all home; we never saw our fire for other people's washing round it. My father was a Methodist, and I always went to Sunday School. You never doubted what you were told. You thought that's the way it was, everybody believed it. The first job

I had was selling essences for herb- and ginger-beer. I eventually got an apprenticeship in the hosiery trade. It was there that I met blokes coming back from the war, some of them atheists. I'd never met anyone like that before. It was a revelation to me. The bloke I was apprenticed to, he used to talk to me, and within a few months, I was attending ILP meetings. One thing I shall always remember. On the wall of the room where we met, there was a banner. It read "The World is my Country, to do Good is my Religion, and Mankind is my Friend" – Thomas Paine. That has always stayed with me.'

A house in Sherwood, apparently typical of houses on post-war estates. But it isn't quite what it seems to be. Fred Croome, secretary of the NUM branch at Claverton Colliery, has made almost everything inside the house himself: the new coal boiler for the central heating, the colour television, the hi-fi equipment, the plumbing and carpentry and decoration. The range of skills he has mastered is a powerful denial of the vast division of labour which makes people feel helpless at the prospect of creating and making things. He is in his late fifties; one of those people in the labour movement of whom it is said 'There won't be any more like him', but who, in spite of everything, still seem to be there.

'There is a lot of energy untapped in the labour movement. It's surprising what people can give if they're asked. In the colliery the union organizes a wide range of things beyond its negotiating rôle; which is as it should be, of course. We've three jazz bands, a silver band. The sharing of life at work is a very precious thing; it's right that you should build on that. You could say it's the same people who take part in everything, the same few. But there you are. Things have to be done, don't they?

'My grandfather came into this area when they were sinking Basford Colliery. He travelled here in a cattle truck. He was a Methodist lay-preacher, came from a large family. The men went in the pits, the girls worked at the laundry nearby. My father left the pit in 1926 after the General Strike, but he did go back when they were appealing for colliers after the war. This area where we are now used to be a coal wharf and brickyard. It's said they once hung a bloke on a tree at the back here, a scab. I've always been involved in the labour movement. I grew up with it in my blood. We lived in a street with a Labour Hall in it; my mother served soup to the Jarrow marchers.

'There's a lot of unused power in working-class people; initiative and the ability to do things for ourselves. We've tried to tap some of that in the union. In the miners' strike in 1972, at Claverton we started a shop to help out with cheap food and so on, and it's still going strong five years later. We sell a good range of things: eggs, hi-fis, shoes, skirts, anoraks, kids' clothes, tea and coffee. A lot of the lads pay more than we ask, and what we do with the money that's over, we help to finance others who are on strike, in other industries. Working-class institutions should reach out, give a lead, inspire, not just be reflections of capitalism.

'There is something special in the mining industry which you don't find in some others. There is the sense of adversity, the lads together, there's no women in it. I don't mean that in any way detrimental to women, only that everybody is the same, you all understand each other. There's always the danger of injury and accident, that welds everybody together. You drink at the Miners' Welfare Club together, your social life is in some ways an extension of your work life, not cut off from it. Even people who've come out of the pits go back to drink with their mates; once you've been a miner you can't think of yourself as anything else. It's very much a community still, even though you don't all live in the same place round the pithead; not in Nottingham anyway. You perhaps wouldn't think the spirit was still there, not until you come to something like the 1972 strike. But then there is a tremendous surge of feeling, the collective memory of what the miners have been through. On the first morning, the lads got the banner out and formed up behind it. The police came, mounted as well, and charged us. At Gedling they got into trouble keeping the NACODs out, so they asked us for help. Five or six hundred of our pickets went over there, to give them a hand. The police were there, they'd got a crack mounted squad from Leicestershire. The lads stood solid. We had one lad taking photos, and a video of the police charges. I reckon the police learned a thing or two from us, they've started doing the same thing themselves now. Then there was a call to go and picket at one of the ports, where there was a coaster full of coal supposed to be docking. I went out with the loudspeaker van, and we got a

busload of pickets in five minutes. We organize things properly.
We get all the women involved as well. We talked to them and
explained our objectives. We had meetings where over a
thousand women came. It's no good if you neglect the women.
A lot of men just say to their wives "We're going on strike", and
that's that, no attempt to explain. Some of the women were
trying to persuade the men to accept what they were offered.
They didn't realize at the time that rents were due to go up, food
prices were due to rise. You put it in context, win them over. And
they were solid, 100 per cent in support of us in the end.

'What we did in the strike, we went to Grimsby and got three
ton of fish every week; wholesale groceries from the Co-op,
sugar, butter, cheese. Some of the lads even said they got better
fed on strike than they did when they were working. We cut up
the fish ourselves and sold it. We were dealing with over £1,000'
worth of groceries every week. We're used to doing things, our
branch. We've got a lot of experience over the years of
organizing things. We've got an electric duplicator, so that we
can keep the lads informed, get a leaflet out in no time. We've
even got our own computer; we've public-address systems,
roundabouts and swings to raise money at galas and fêtes,
booths and stalls. We lend our equipment to charities, to local
Labour parties; our jazz bands go on marches and
demonstrations. We've raised money for handicapped children
– this year we raised £700 for a minibus for them. Recently we've
given money to NUPE to help them fight against the cuts in
public expenditure, we've given £60 to the Langley Mills strike
fund, that's a furniture factory. We gave £25 in picket supplies to
them – calor-gas fire equipment, a brazier, hot-water boilers,
urns for soup and tea. We helped the strike at the Savoy Hotel
down the road. In fact, my son was on the picket line, he got run
at by a car, picked up on the bonnet. We helped the jockeys
strike. One of the lads at the pit had a couple of sons who were
apprentices. We helped the building workers and the NUPE
march in Nottingham; all of this in the last few months. We've a
very good relationship with the nurses at the hospital, and with
the National Union of Public Employees. A lot of them use our
shop – it's open to all trades unionists.

'The trouble with the labour movement isn't the movement
itself, but the way it gets reported and represented. Newspapers,
television. There's no working-class press. When you see what

you know to be your own life and experience misrepresented all the time, and you know that's what people take for truth, well, you realize what a struggle we have. We had this vote against the productivity scheme – well, they're trying to get it reversed now. We had to fight it, but I've yet to hear anybody in the media give a sympathetic hearing to why we're fighting it. They just assume that Arthur Scargill is some kind of extremist – it's rubbish, it's a humanitarian argument. It's not a question of cash in the hand, it's blood in the hand. It's a return to the system we had twenty years ago, the old contract system. Twenty years ago I was earning over £100 a week on that system, but it's wrong. It divides people, it sets man against man. You've got to have a collective working system in the pits, you can't have competition like that. The other day I buried a bloke from the pit, a bloke I first worked with when I began. The contract system meant getting paid by what you could produce – like this productivity scheme – and I was remembering, this lad we buried. . . . In the headings sometimes, you know, you get short of air; once this lad was working alongside me, and the air was running short and he passed out, fainted. And all I did was sit him on the side, and went back to the coal, because that meant money. . . . That's the way the system affects you, your humanity. It takes hold of you without you being aware of what it does. This lad, he died of cancer; and when I thought of that incident, I wasn't proud.

'I was going through our death-fund book recently. When we were fighting for the abolition of the contract system in the '50s, there were 500 or 600 accidents in 1959. I sent the book to Scargill when he was campaigning against the productivity deal. It means less safety, less concern for each other. It'll divide the industry. They think that if they offer money, everybody'll take it. That's the trouble – money is seen as the be-all and end-all. But all the people who have fought and struggled, your traditions and loyalties, you can't bury them, it's like burying your father and grandfather. You've got to keep faith with what they suffered and struggled for. The argument that says, "If it's money, take it, and damn everything else" is the biggest danger to the labour movement; that's when you start to forfeit your humanity, and accept the values of capitalism.

'I see my job as a link in a chain. I do a bit of everything. For one thing, I go to all the funerals of our members who die. I act as a link between all those who've retired, and I'm a link with the community. At our pit, we treat the old just the same as if they were still working. We always send a wreath and go to visit the widow of any retired miner who dies. We give the miner £25 out of union funds when he retires; and the next of kin gets £170 when he dies. We take the old people to the seaside every year, give them all £1.50 to spend, fetch them and take them home in buses. We've 700 old people from the colliery I'm still in touch with. Then there are the common-law claims for accidents, the National Health claims – a lot of the work is form-filling; negotiations with management of course. I've been branch secretary for seven or eight years now, I know the job well. I think in our industry we've preserved something of great value that has been lost in many other places – that is a sense of our working-class heritage, our sense of community. And we can see how much there is within working men and women, all the energy and creativity that is never called upon in any meaningful way; and we try, as best we can, to harness some of that in humanitarian projects.'

A house opposite an old lace factory which throws a long red shadow over the street. The street is built on the site of a former mining area, rising and falling, so that at night you can see the lights of the city, chains of blue and yellow between the old terraces. Dead leaves from the plane trees wheel in the cold night wind, and as they turn against a sky lighted in dull orange from the glow of the city, they look like extinguished stars.

Inside, the house is warm and comfortable. The coal fire in the grate punctuates Arthur Palmer's conversation; the soft lapping of the flames against the coals, the metallic burst of sparks, the collapse of the consumed pyramid in a cloud of ash and cinders remind me of the gentle domestic music of childhood.

'I left school in 1934, and I was out of work from July 1934 until February 1935. So when I look round now, my feeling is that I've been here before. It's like living through the same thing all over again. Of course there's a difference now. I used to go round all the factories, begging for work; and at that time, there were twenty or thirty men at the pit gates every morning. I never wanted to go into the pit; but that was the only place I could get taken on, so in the end I had to go. I remember the date: 11

February 1935, it stays with you. I cried my eyes out when I knew that this was going to be my life. My father was a miner; he'd come down from Sunderland after the '26 strike. But in another way, I was chuffed to be working.

'I've done every job except shaft-sinking. We lived in Yorkshire when I first started. Since then, our work has changed, and with it our social life. I started pony-driving into the tub stalls. The tubs fetched the coal out, and where there were tub stalls there was a working area where three or four blokes could work together; there was what we called the flash-sheet, where the tubs spun round and were taken back to the coal face. I was amazed to see the blokes fighting over who should get the most tubs; but outside work, they all bought each other drinks. There was an overall comradeship, but inside there was this competitive element as to who should make a copper or two more. But it never lasted after work was finished.

'When I came down to Nottingham, I noticed there wasn't the same mateyness, the same mining spirit I'd known in Yorkshire. Longwall facework was more predominant in Nottinghamshire, it was established earlier here. I'd not been working here long when I was talking to an old miner, and he told me of an occasion when three or four men had been working together, and one of them was injured, quite badly. All they did was lay him on one side, and get on with work. They didn't dare take him out, because of what they would have lost in pay. That's how the system dehumanized people, you see. Anything that sets money higher than humanity will degrade human beings. I hadn't been here long when I saw an incident that shocked me. I was working on what we call the Panzer unit. Three men worked together, it was a steel chain that hauled a machine up and down the coal face. It cut the coal off and ploughed it back and deposited all the stuff on the cutting track. The rope suddenly flew, and me and my mate just stepped off in time, but this other bloke, it caught him and broke his leg. I knew his leg was broken, because you could see it was at an angle, like. I stopped the chain and shouted for help. The gaffer yelled, "Let the chain go." The chain had to go on; it couldn't stop work for an accident. I found that shocking.

'I think a lot of the breakdown in social life is a result of changes at work. Mining has become more like an assembly line in a factory, you're part of a machine. Attitudes have changed.

They're all hard-working blokes, no trouble over that, but there is a certain lack of comradeship. At home, I was brought up in the atmosphere of the working-men's clubs as soon as I was old enough to join. The clubs were everywhere, moved by a spirit of friendly rivalry. I think the sense of avarice that you find everywhere hasn't left us untouched; the tendency to skive a bit, get a bit extra, fiddle overtime. It makes the work of the unions more difficult. Union discipline is harder.

'I think our Gedling Colliery is more trade-union-minded than it was. People are more conscious of the union. Originally, I got elected as a workman inspector, because I didn't like some of the inspectors' reports. They only came round every three months. I worked with an old man who'd been a workmen's inspector; he could see lots of things wrong, but lacked the courage to say so. The workmen's inspector had always been treated with some contempt before I was elected. I decided that was going to change. For instance, the guards on machinery, wire mesh round moving machinery, should always be bolted securely into position, but they were just being leaned against it or wired up. We had to raise the standard of safety, and management started to take notice of us. We have built up a respect for the union, I think, awareness of what it stands for. Gedling had the highest vote against the productivity deal of any of the pits in Nottinghamshire.

'When I first came here, riding time used to be 6.00 to 6.30, but if you weren't down the pit by 6.00, you couldn't get a job. Even if you'd got a regular job, the chargeman would use it to keep a hold over the men. It was like a hangover from the old butty system which officially ceased at the end of the '30s, but it lingered on with the chargemen. Because management appointed them, they had tremendous authority. On Fridays we used to do a double shift under the day-wage system. The chargeman said to me and my mate, "Everybody on this face has bought me a drink, bar two." I said, "If my work isn't good enough, I'm buggered if I'm going to start buying jobs." There was always some backhander there, some bribery. I never saw much of that in Yorkshire.

'I've always breathed the atmosphere of the pits. In Durham, I remember, I used to go to my granny's, and there'd be all these lads coming through the house – my grand-dad was Lodge Treasurer, he'd be paying people their strike pay or whatever. I can remember my dad coming home from the pit, no pithead baths then, he used to come home in his pit-muck, rub his hair, and there'd be a paper full of coal come out of it. He'd rub his lips with a wet sponge, have his dinner and then fall asleep. I've even seen him fall asleep over his dinner before he'd finished it, he was so buggered. I've seen him come home with ribs broken when there'd been a fall; he always had knocks and cuts, bruises and scars all over his body.

'I shall never forget my first day at work. You feel so insignificant. When the cage gets half-way down, it seems to go into reverse. You have the sensation you're going back up when they halt the momentum before getting to the pit bottom. Then it opens out into a huge gallery. My first job was coupling tubs on, that's the lowest job you can do. I always had a big appetite; my mam used to pack me apples and bread and a flask of cocoa for snap time; we ate in a cabin, we called it, really it was a hole in the wall.

'We were talking in the pit one day, and somebody said there was no Miners' Welfare at Gedling. And some of us got together and organized the Welfare on Mapperley Plains. We put on dances and entertainment. I was MC for five years. That was how I first came to be active in the union, and it developed from there. But what really had a vital effect on me was a day-release course I did on industrial democracy. There were a lot of things which I'd always known, but never spoken of, never put into words. I think this happens to a lot of blokes. It's a lack of confidence in your own ability that holds you back, and that makes you accept that other people should make decisions for you, when you're perfectly capable of making them for yourself. Because you're never sure of your argument, you feel inadequate. You think words belong to those who own everything else; you only borrow them. When you're faced by management, even though you know your own case thoroughly, it becomes half-baked in expressing it, because you haven't got all the information they have, and you're not so familiar with the conventions and procedures. But your confidence grows with doing things. You have to be so strongly motivated that you think, Dammit, I'm going to say what I feel, and you say it so vigorously that you make your point anyway.

'When I see what has happened as a result of decisions made by management which I knew were wrong, it makes me feel that the work force themselves should be running the industry. And I'm sure it's not so different in other industries. I've carried out wrong decisions, knowing they were wrong. I've done development work, I've been on heading new faces, driving new roadways on five jobs, not one of which has turned a cobble of coal. I was working on one four-and-a-half years, driving through a fault in the original seam. We got half-way down and we were told we were to go into what was called the Main Bright seam. It had been worked twice in the past, and closed because of bad geological conditions. I said, "This won't work." It was four years of real struggle, in the worst conditions I've ever known, and I'm neither a hero nor a coward. We got into the coal, tried to head a few faces: water, subsidence, it was hopeless. Management decided to get in some outside contractors, specialists at driving roadways and drifts. After we'd worked all that time. Management said, "Well, they're coming in." I said, "They're not." The union passed a resolution of No Confidence in management, and demanded the withdrawal of the contractors. We had a meeting in the canteen, all the blokes, 250 of them, supported me.

'That was on the Monday. On the Tuesday I was sent for. I put my case. They'd already spent a quarter of a million pounds on wages alone. Between 1955 and 1969 the pit had dropped from a £1 million profit a year to a loss of £200,000. I had good grounds for my argument; and although the full-time union officials made us rescind the No Confidence resolution, my argument was substantiated. There was an enquiry into the running of the pit; into the bad planning and wrong decisions, machinery that didn't work, schemes that couldn't be realized. They ignored the fact that we at Gedling had special knowledge that no outside specialist teams could have. We had driven tunnels through those faults already. The outside contractors said they would need just seven weeks to drive out of the Main Bright seam into the Hazel seam; and we'd been four and a half years driving out of the Hazel into the Main Bright. Our resolution was withdrawn. As usual, when workers are faced with a challenge from management, supported by full-time union officials, they usually back down. But they never contacted us to see what kind of a case we had. Needless to say, the whole project was abandoned. The conclusion of the investigation into the alleged bad planning, of course, justified all the actions of management.

'We have to create in the work force the ability to recognize our strength and to be able to take control of our industry. Blokes are treated as a number, as a piece of equipment. You have to persuade them that they can do things they've never dreamed of. The workers ought to be able to allocate themselves rôles in society, not wait for it to be decided by forces outside them. They should determine themselves who gets the highest pay, according to an agreed rate of social priorities. We haven't yet begun to take the decisions we're capable of. However many experts and managers and advisers you can create, however much you can blind the workers with knowledge, it'll never equal that of the people who work in the pits. It is the same with every work place: you reduce the function of the individual worker, you make him into an isolated unit, dazzle him with the mystery of the machine he operates; it gives him a feeling of inferiority. When he realizes what he is capable of, there'll be no limit to what is possible. It's only the fear that everything in society is organized down to the last detail in such an expert and complex way; but your own evidence tells you all the time it isn't. You don't even trust your own perceptions any more. Everything tells the worker of his own inferiority: the cleverness of all the experts, even his own heroes of the pop world or football get inflated into something huge and intimidating, which helps to keep him in his place.'

The Victoria Centre in Nottingham. What is most striking is the silence of the crowds. You can hear a mildly euphoric music above the shuffling feet on the marble causeways, and the splashing of a great coloured cascade in the middle of the ground floor. The space is like the nave of a cathedral; the shop fronts are stained-glass windows, full of stylized models in expressionist poses.

This place is a permanent exhibition, part kermis, part communion. Here, all human pleasures and aspirations have been captured and priced. The display combines the search for happiness with a sense of the great public rituals that have decayed. The names of products – Jupiter, Saturn, Aztec, Odyssey, Vivaldi, Windsor, Savannah, Olympic, Capri,

Imperial – represent a cosmic ransacking of time and place, to describe beds, duvets, fashion valances, chairs, dining tables, digital clocks; a piracy that creates an impression of effortless mobility and power. Revolutions and miracles are advertised in the preparation of dessert foods and the washing of underwear; and in this way, politics and religion are put in their place.

Things are full of promise; not only of well-being and comfort, even immortality. Siliconized polypropylene, 'no deterioration', 'there for ever'. You are invited to sleep on a white cloud filled with soft Dacron, serenity Latex foam, four-poster beds, a home solarium, interior log saunas, marble caskets for bathing, water massage in sealed cabinets like up-ended coffins. Leisure and escape are everywhere; relaxation and sleep. Everything is caressing and somniferous. A girl sits in a hanging chair suspended from an ornamental gibbet; and another girl is being paid to sit with no clothes on, but wrapped in a duvet, in a deep-freeze, the thermostat of which is set at −10°C.

Everywhere there are objects to save labour; many of which imply time spent in activities hitherto unimagined. They give the reverse of the freedoms they promise, because they create a self-determining universe, limited by the things that are there to release you from a bondage which they themselves impose. This place proposes a world which manages to combine the beatific vision with the occupational therapy workshop. The whole process is the counterpart of what is happening in our work-situations – to rob us of our functions, to crush us into passivity; to make us forget old skills and abilities, to usurp a sense of achievement, to erase old habits and customs, to assault our creativity, to colonize our imagination. Only fantasized extensions of what already exist can be admitted into our lives. This may be one of the reasons for our obsession with outer space in the 1970s: it is the last refuge from that overburdened, cluttered inner space in which there is no longer any room to breathe.

Saturday morning in the Victoria Centre. A crowd gathers where a woman's voice is heard above the subdued murmur of the people shopping. She is crying. This already sounds incongruous; as though someone were laughing in church. A man is with her, coaxing and anxious. They are perhaps in their early forties. He wears a raincoat and grey flannels; her face is distraught and pained; beneath her eyes there are dark bruised-looking patches. The sound of their conflict is magnified by the hush of the shopping area. 'Come on duck,' he says to her, 'you've got your new shoes.' Her cries become louder; a sustained howl. Some security men appear, and look at her. The crowd keeps its distance. The man is embarrassed. He explains to those people nearest to him, as though he owed them an account of the disturbance, 'She's not well.' He turns back to her, and tries to urge her away. 'Come on, we're going home now, we'll have us dinners. We got your nice new shoes.' His voice is protective and reassuring. She is wearing a pair of high-heeled cork and plastic sandals, bright yellow and at odds with the shabbiness of the rest of her dress: they gleam in the subdued shadowless light. The howl rises higher; a desolate cry of pain. 'She's been in hospital,' he explains to the crowd, as though to dissociate himself from any accusation of ill treatment. Her cries echo round the precinct, but she refuses to move. The girls serving in the open-fronted boutiques come to the edge of their stage; the older women with blue rinses and mortuary chapel smiles. A moment of deep unease. Perhaps we recognize that her cry is not gratuitous. It is the cry of a human being in the process of mutilation to fit a pair of plastic sandals.

The spread of material goods to people who for so long wanted even basic subsistence should have given rise to a song of celebration from the voices of millions of people who in the past worked without reward or hope; but instead, the release from poverty has been accompanied by a jangling dissonance and harshness.

In the way that poverty in a monastery differs from poverty in the slums of Victorian England, so there is – or could be – a world of difference between the distribution of an abundance according to arbitrary ideas of competition and merit, and its distribution according to what is fair and equitable. The things which should have liberated us have failed to do so; not because things are not liberating, but because they are annexed and controlled by others for profit. They serve ends other than their apparent function; and it is from these that the sickness in our plenty arises. We are tyrannized, cowed and beaten by our abundance; anxious and addicted; passive functionless dependents. And instead of an end to the ancient struggle for survival, we have accepted to go on with a symbolic and attenuated version of the same drama, as though it were not a tired and redundant game; and the whole economic and social structure exists to support this sterile fantasy. What we call our standard of living is often no such thing. Far from being a precise description of our situation, it is really a metaphor for our dependency on capitalism and its products, its system of rewards and profits, and the falsehoods that flow from it, the morality and values which are none at all.

We have to balance the kind of consumer freedoms we have against the spoilt humanity, the ruin of so many human associations, the hope of a better life which has been deformed into fantasy and delusion. We have to separate the values by which we actually live from those by which we believe we live. Societies seldom act out what they claim to believe. Belief-system is always more or less a patina, an official justification for the real dynamic that keeps the society together. If, in the structures and institutions evolved precisely for humanitarian purposes, to alleviate poverty and care for people, we consider ourselves to be caring and civilized, it is because this has become an ossified official ideology; beneath which violence, racism, the corruption of human associations go unchecked. If caring is undertaken by paid functionaries, everything else is left to the market-place – friendship, sex, loyalty, conscience, virtue, charity, tolerance are all on sale.

Because of the undisputed desirability of things, all negative feeling flows into our human relationships; and this is accepted as the price we have to pay for our improved living standards – or rather, they are not seen to be part of the same process at all. They are felt to belong to a different, and unconnected, domain. On the one hand, we know what we need for our personal happiness; but on the other we know that other people are venal, indifferent and rapacious. This is the hidden contradiction, the conundrum of our loneliness and discontents.

It isn't what these processes do to other people that we should look at, but the way it affects ourselves, our relationships with others. Those to whom we have made a commitment become as perishable and interchangeable as the goods that wear out before they are paid for. We make expiatory gestures to our children, lavish things upon them, because we can never spare them quite enough of ourselves, because we are no longer sure which part of ourselves to relate with anyway. We are reluctant in our duties to parents or kin, impatient and guilty at the telephone call and the long car journey that call us to the bedside of a dying old man. Our friendships are arbitrary and functional, can be taken up and forgotten with every move of house. We should consider the conflict and division within the compass of our own lives, the fear of violence and treachery from strangers who live where neighbours once were; the fear above all of our inadequate selves, and the anxiety that we might not be good enough for the duties and obligations imposed upon us by the images of perfection all round us. Human sacrifice is felt to belong to primitive societies; but we sacrifice human beings no less than if we ceremonially offered up our children to images of metal and stone by tearing out their hearts.

And yet, confronted by all this, when you ask people on the Left what vision they have for the future, for socialism; how you can best describe, represent, urge the advantages of socialism on the mass of the people; significant silences occur. Our eyes and minds are so full of the things that surround us, and the desirability of what they tell us, that there is no room for another vision. Our senses are flooded, our perceptions brimfull with what is; with the result that what might be eludes us, defies description. The vision of an alternative is thin and diluted. Many people on the Left say they know what needs to be done; but there is rarely a positive feeling for the alternative which will flow from the changes which they prescribe, and it sounds like a litany, an incantation. What they say is often banal and threadbare. Its old passion has deserted it. Passion is far more vigorous in the rhetoric of the Right. The vision of the Left, if it isn't simply more of what we have now, turns out to be the abolition of the House of Lords; an end to privileged education; greater sporting facilities and provision for the arts; an absence of litter in the streets, improved public services and less advertising: scarcely the kind of objectives for which most people are prepared to jeopardize all they feel they have gained. Because we are still obsessed with our recent poverty, the promise of an end to it still has something of the quality of a mirage.

Neither description nor analysis captures the feeling of what has happened in these working-class cities. The sense of anxious dependency, of which these shopping precincts are merely material symbols, is perhaps akin to the cargo cults recorded in certain islands of the South Pacific. In Nottingham I met an actor with a community theatre group, and he told this story:

'There was once a girl who worked in a mill. Her parents were both mill workers, and her brothers and sisters, too. They lived in a tenement in a great grey city overlooking a coalyard and the railways. In the mill where she worked, they made beautiful fabrics, silks and velvet, which went to London and Paris for the benefit of those who could afford to keep up with high fashion.

'One day she was working at the loom, when the machine broke; a beam flew out and struck her head. She fell, unconscious, on the stone floor. She was taken to hospital, where she was found to be still alive, but in a deep coma. And so she remained for more than a year. She lay with her eyes closed, scarcely breathing. Her mother sat for long hours by the bedside, knitting and talking to her, although there was no response from the sleeping girl. Her father called to see her every night after his day's work, although she could not know it. Her brothers and sisters saved their money, not only to pay the hospital bills, but to buy things for her that would nourish her weakened body. Her workmates took it in turns to go and sit by her, hold her hand for a little while. After a year, when people had begun to despair of her recovery, she stirred, and consciousness seemed to be returning. One spring morning, she opened her eyes and looked at the anxious people all around her. She smiled at them; but she recognized no one. She had no remembrance of the mill where the accident had occurred. She didn't know her parents. Her brothers and sisters were strangers to her. They talked to her of a shared childhood which meant nothing to her. She didn't even know her own name. She had forgotten her home; she had lost her skills at the loom. She had no memory of anything that had gone before. Despairingly, her father and mother tried to talk to her of her own past, but it troubled her and made her unhappy. Her friends tried to rekindle some memory of what they had experienced together, but were met with blank disbelief.

'People felt sorry for her, and began to bring her things to console her. They deprived themselves of necessities to be able to offer her little luxuries. She was given beautiful clothes, make-up, jewellery. While she had slept, the town had become more prosperous. New machinery had been installed in the mill, which made work easier. The shops had become well stocked with new merchandise. The people were less poor.

'She became something of a local celebrity. People were fascinated by the woman who seemed to have shed all memory of who and what she had been. They brought her presents; lotions and scents, food, clothes and shoes. She was given television and music, picture books: great coloured catalogues and brochures from which to choose things as a comfort for her loss. Little by little, she began to compose for herself a new personality. "I am the girl who had a new dress last week," she would say, while friends and doctors alike nodded approval at what seemed to be a return of sorts of memory. "I am the girl who wears such a scent, who prefers such a colour, whose hair is given lustre by such a product, who relies on such a substance to keep her skin soft; who feels like a princess in such a gown, like a whore in another."

'The story has a happy ending. Not that her original sense of herself ever did return. She never discovered who she was; she never knew where she had come from, in what place she had grown up and with whom; only, in the end, it ceased to matter.'

2

BLACKBURN

BLACKBURN, LIKE MOST industrial towns and cities, has always been a place of considerable migration. It grew out of the movement of population from the countryside and from Ireland; and then, in the fifty years after the First World War, a quarter of its population left – going south or to North America and Australia. In the summer, some of these people come back to the town for a visit: mill girls who went with hopeful fiancés to Canada try to locate those they were at school with, give interviews to the local paper, saying they wish Britain well and hope that our oil flows plentifully. Many able people left during the Depression. Few of those who went to university since 1945 have returned, having been absorbed into professional structures that are national, not local. The reason why Blackburn existed in the first place – textiles – is now served by about 10,000 immigrants from India, Pakistan and East Africa, who still work in the dwindling textile industry, maintain public services and small shops.

For a long time Blackburn has seemed a socially depressed place, wanting in purpose, looking for the meaning it once derived from its rôle in producing goods. And during the past few years, that new purpose has been slowly defining itself. It is as though people felt that the immigrants from Asia have somehow usurped the old working-class identity. They are in mainly working-class occupations, they live in the houses lately deserted by the old mill workers. They have a strong sense of neighbourhood and of family. And this usurped identity is strengthened by strong religious and cultural traditions which they have brought with them.

When I was last in Blackburn, I visited a mill where the foundation stone had been laid by the Textile Prosperity Queen of 1949. Even thirty years ago, that must have sounded a little archaic; and, since that time, the traditional function of the town has been eroded even more swiftly. Many people attribute those changes to the immigrants who have come, with different customs and beliefs, to make their holy places in terraced houses that were once the homes of weavers. The opportunity for self-definition against the immigrants has given many of the townspeople a new and galvanic sense of excitement that has been absent since the war. But because it is a negative definition, it expresses itself in images of violence and destruction. A whole generation has grown up, sheltered from any edge of conflict by relatively full employment and more money than has ever been seen before in this town. Many young men feel that they have always lived under the emasculating influence of an oppressively maternalistic and caring society, which they resent as much as their fathers resented the cruel disciplines of poverty. They have been denied access to what they see as traditional male rôles, and they are now reaching out for something they have been robbed of – a need to fight. For many years violence has been contained. It has been random and unco-ordinated, expressed in football punch-ups and the enormous amount of under-age drinking. One boy told me he had broken his ankle making Kung-fu kicks at a shop window; another said he had black belts in twelve martial arts. The reservoir of aggression fills like a cistern; and there is no outlet.

I spent a day with two eighteen-year-olds, Gary and Pete, both of whom have been almost continuously unemployed since they left school. Their life as unemployed young men is in many ways simply an extension of the life they led as schoolboys. For the last two years at school, they attended rarely, but spent their time in each other's houses while their parents were at work. 'We used to have a drink, have some girls in. My mum came in one afternoon, she were bad at work, and she found me in bed with this girl. She didn't mind though, she said I could be doing worse things.' 'Yeh, and he's being doing 'em ever since.'

Gary and Pete get up late in the morning, after their parents have gone out, brew some tea, read the *Sun*. They meet in the middle of the day in a pub, where they try to get people they know to buy them a drink. We go to a workmen's café, where dinners are being served. They ask for a cup of tea. The woman who is serving says, 'If it's only tea you want, will you let people waiting for their dinners sit down.' 'No, why should we?' They agree to have a piece of toast between them. 'Fucking old bag. That's what it's like in Blackburn, see?' When she brings dinner to the next table Gary says, 'You can tell she's got gonorrhoea by the way she walks.'

Two girls are playing the juke-box.

Gary says, 'Shut that fucking row off.'

'Why, what's the matter with you, don't you like music?'

'Not that sort.'

'What sort do you like then?'

'Come here and I'll show you.' One of the girls comes over to him. He says, 'Can you play the horn?'

She says, 'Not yours. I've seen better on a neutered cat.'

They are joined by some of their mates as they walk through the town centre. Pete pretends to fuck a lamp-post; and when a woman stops to see what he's doing, he says, 'What's up, jealous are you?'

All their encounters with strangers are aggressive and diminishing. They try all the doors of the cars parked in side streets, and they throw anything that can be used as a missile – Coke cans, stones, bottles. Pete treads in some dogshit and says 'Pakis'. In the shopping precinct, they are noisy; they are surrounded by all the things they can't have.

By the middle of the afternoon the effect of the midday drink has worn off. Everything about them expresses enervation and

resented idleness. We sit on the grass and talk. Pete says, 'When I
was a kid I always wanted to be a soldier. I put a bit of cardboard
in the back wheel of my bike, and it was a jeep. I thought "That's
me, that's my destiny." Everywhere I went, I was always reviewing
my troops. I always wanted to be top dog, king of the castle, big
noise. You want to feel you're somebody, prove yourself.'
GARY: 'My Grand-dad was in the war. He met a guy who walked
right across Russia to find his wife. His comrade died in his
arms, and he said he went so stiff with rigor mortis, he had to cut
his hands off with a knife to get free. People want action. What
happens if there's a plane crash or a car accident? People want
to see something happen.'
JS: 'What would you like to see happen?'
GARY: 'Personally, I'd like a lot of money. A lot. Get a
motorbike, a house, clothes, all the women I want, not have to
worry about signing on twice a week.'
JS: 'What about work?'
PETE: 'No thanks.'
JS: 'What would you like to see happen politically?'
PETE: 'I don't care. Get rid of the Pakis.'
JS: 'Why?'
PETE: 'They get everything. I've nothing against them in
Pakistan. Don't want them here. I think everybody should be in
their own country. The way I look at it, you're white, you should
be proud of it. What did we do for all these countries, they then
turn round and kick you in the teeth.'
GARY: 'They run this country. You know what it'll be next?
They'll arrange marriages for us with all these Paki women
wrapped up in Lurex. You'll have to by law.'

You can sense that people are becoming united in a way that no
one can remember since the war. The nostalgia for the national
unity of wartime joins with the memories of working-class
solidarity against poverty. It's like fighting the bosses and mill-
owners all over again, but this time the mill-owners wear the
guise of do-gooders, media lefties and race-relations officials.
They are all those who have been unable to achieve with
humanity what their masters formerly tried to do with harshness
– stifle and deny the feelings of people. Those who are now
expressing themselves so intemperately against the immigrants
feel themselves to be victims, but their sense of oppression is

located with the class that 'gives' them education, social services, entertainment, goods: the agents of maternalistic capitalism.

The wretchedness of Gary and Pete is only a more extreme form of something that afflicts a whole generation of the working-class young: a sense of futility, a lack of function and purpose. And the only hope which our society can hold out is the promise of more money, more access to goods; as though this were an answer to people who are required to give nothing of themselves, to commit themselves to nothing, to create nothing. The outrages against immigrants, the anger and resentment have all the elements of a deformed crusade. In fact, the model for the growth of the parties of the far Right echoes the struggles which the old talk of when they were fighting for socialism: the need to be secretive, the sense of persecution, the feeling of mission, the profound emotional attachment to a cause. I visited one house in Blackburn where there was a meeting of the National Party; a council house on the outskirts of town. The wife of the party official was busying herself making tea and coffee, and enjoying her rôle, the sense of importance. At one point she said, 'It's just like the old days.' And it later emerged that she had been brought up in a socialist household, and her father had held Labour Party meetings in the front room.

A student from Blackburn said, 'All the years we were growing up, we were told, by the media, by schoolteachers, by politicians, that we mustn't think of class any more. There is no such thing as being working class or middle class, we're all just individuals. I think we are now paying the price for that consistent assault on working-class values. If you undermine them to that extent, what is there left to define yourself by, if not race? I don't think that was the intention, I think the idea was to weaken the labour movement, by inviting people to think of themselves as consumers, as individualistic; but there's always got to be some sense of social purpose, and this is why you've got this travesty of it now. It's not quite what they bargained for, but it's logical.'

Blackburn has changed in the eight years since I spent six months there. It has changed conspicuously. It is a far cleaner and a more attractive place than it has ever been. Much unfit housing has been cleared; the improvement areas have varied the uniformity of the streets and created open spaces in the terraces which let in air and sunshine.

But if living conditions have changed remarkably, the atmosphere, too, is different. Some of those things which people were happy to claim for themselves eight years ago – our 'British' qualities of tolerance and sympathy, or our 'Northern' friendliness and hospitality – are suddenly no longer mentioned in a place so obviously full of tension and suspicion. People do not welcome strangers. There is no longer the easy intimacy in public places. Now you are asked who you are, what your business is; above all what you want.

The day I arrived in Blackburn, I sat on a bench on the Boulevard. (The Boulevard is a kind of open-air bus station between the railway station and the cathedral.) I sit next to a woman in her thirties, carefully made up, with thickly-pencilled eyebrows and butterfly-shaped glasses. She wears a lot of powder, but her face glistens in the intense heat. Her hair is swept back and cascades over her shoulder. She is wearing a short white skirt, white blouse and white sandals. I ask her how she feels about race.

'Race, what race? I'm not interested in racing.'

'No, I mean the trouble there's been in town.'

'Trouble? Oh, has there? I haven't heard of it.'

'The immigrants and the National Party.' (In May 1976 two National Party district councillors were elected in Blackburn.)

'Oh don't talk to me about that. I've just been to Blackpool, there's thousands of them. You can't go anywhere. It never used to be like that. I had to go into five restaurants before I could find anywhere to eat, and even then there was some of them there. I'm very particular.'

Her speech is very clipped and careful, and she is uneasy. Until now, she has not looked at me directly, only glancing sideways, and sitting with her legs crossed and her hands clasped round her knees. Suddenly her eyes dart over my arms and face.

'Why do you want to know what I think?'

'Uh?'

'Are you English?'

'Yes.'

'Are you sure?'

'Of course I'm sure.'

'Your skin's a bit dark, isn't it?' There is a sudden challenge and authority in her voice.

'What's that got to do with it?'

'There's too many of them. Look at that lot. They could turn nasty.' Obligingly, a group of Indian teenagers passes in front of us, oblivious of her scrutiny. 'They go about in gangs. Why aren't they working? What could you do if they attacked you? You need lessons in judo. Can you do judo?'

'No.'

'I hate them.'

A man of about sixty walks past. He is white; he wears a string vest and khaki drill trousers. His face is creased and sunburnt. He looks at her.

'Look at him. The way he's looking at me. I hate men like that. It's disgusting!' She catches his eye. He is about to light a cigarette, but turns, and predictably, comes to sit on the bench between me and the woman. She tries to place her white polythene carrier bag on the seat. 'This is somebody's seat.' He ignores her. She makes a sound of annoyance and walks off.

Two days later, I am on a stationary bus, waiting to go to one of the large council estates on the edge of the town. The bus fills up. A woman of about fifty, in a bright summer dress, carrying shopping, comes upstairs. She takes one of the few remaining seats, next to an elderly Indian with a fringe of white beard. She places her shopping in her lap, and glances several times at the Indian, who does not return her glance, but looks straight ahead. It is suffocatingly hot. The sun glares through the glass, the seats are sticky and uncomfortable, the cigarette smoke stagnates. The woman suddenly gets up noisily and goes to sit in the last vacant seat, next to a workman of about fifty-five. She leans over to him and says, 'Filthy bugger, he was moving his leg right close up to me.' He doesn't respond, but closes his eyes. She looks round for someone else to talk to. It is too hot. People want to get home from work. She says, to no one in particular, 'And they're still letting them in.' For a moment all the processes of misunderstanding and ill will are visible. I want to say something about the consequences of immigration without wives and dependants, but it isn't the place for such a discussion.

In spite of the weather, there are few white people on the doorsteps. Most of the front doors are closed, the curtains drawn in the front rooms, paintwork beading and blistering in the sun. On the shady side of the street, an old woman sits on the threshold in a wheelchair. Inside, the passage is cool and dim, and an old chenille curtain is draped over the stair entry. She is fanning herself with the evening paper. 'I feel self-conscious, sitting here,' she says, almost apologetically, 'only I can't walk, you see. It's the only way I can get some air.' Sitting on the doorstep is something proper only to immigrants now.

When I was in Blackburn eight years ago, I heard many stories about immigrants (nearly always referred to as Pakistanis, despite the fact that there is a minority of Pakistanis among the town's immigrants). Many of these were told in such a way as to illustrate the privileged and protected status of immigrants, the preferential treatment they receive at the hands of officials, their arrogance towards the indigenous population of Blackburn. Although there was at that time a growing sense of grievance, the stories were related half-humorously: the eagerness of social security clerks to give money for colour TV sets; the familiar tale of the man who thinks he hears rats in the space between the bedrooms and the roof of his house, and who investigates to find Pakistanis sleeping in the rafters along the whole street; the man drawing £200 a week for three wives and fifty children. These same stories are being told, and in precisely the same terms. They are being transmitted as though they were new, and, I was assured, were happening as recently as last month. How can these stories have persisted so tenaciously, and still be passed on with such relish and solemn assurances of their truth? It seems that they have become part of a public repertoire; and they directly parallel the recurring stories that came out of the hardship and poverty of the past.

But there is a difference today. These stories have reached a new section of the population which had not heard them a few years ago; people who were then unaffected by or neutral in their attitude towards immigration. Those who were either vaguely tolerant, or simply not interested, are compelled by the clamour of scandalous gossip and folklore to take a stand, and the stand they take tends to the more noisy and persuasive side. Meanwhile, from the centre of distribution of oral information – a strangely elusive place – issues a flow of progressively more violent and shocking news, a fuelling of the anger which has to be renewed constantly as time goes by. It is like a pulse of feeling which spreads out, affecting new sections of the population, but,

as it spreads, it necessarily loses some of its impetus; and
this is why it has to be diffused in an aggravated form. For
instance, it is currently being said that the immigrants 'all carry
knives'; and, more frighteningly, that they are arming. 'It makes
you want to apply for a permit to get a rifle. Only they'd refuse
us. They can get them, though. I know that's true. And what do
they want them for, that's what I want to know. It's not to send
them home, because it's not as if they were a hunting country, is
it?' said a woman in her twenties. 'Of course, they're forming
vigilante groups. That means there'll be somebody beaten up
before long.' The most vehement expression of anger is not
generally in the immigrant areas themselves, but on the fringes,
where people talk of 'an invasion', and on the council estates. 'I
know what I'd do, I'd put 'em all in a ship and sink it.'
'Everybody says Amin is a buffoon, but he managed to kick 'em
all out, which is more than we've done.' A man who gave me a
lift into town said, as we approached an Indian at the roadside,
'This is where I hope my brakes fail.'

An official of the Indian Workers' Association described how
a series of events in the town had contributed at a local level to
the increased anti-immigrant feeling that has been observed
nationally. First of all, plans to build a mosque produced a
demonstration by the National Party and a counter-
demonstration by the Muslims. Then the designation of the
Brookhouse Action area as an improvement area caused much
anger, because the grants available to householders were seen as
further benefits going to 'immigrants' rather than houses, and
furnished more 'proof' of their privileged status. But more
macabre was the refusal of the grave-diggers to bury the Muslim
dead without coffins. This kindled a fierce antique argument
about miasma and disease seeping out of the earth. There were
rumours of outbreaks at the Infirmary of typhoid, cholera,
TB, 'only it all gets hushed up'. Many visitors to Blackburn have
noted an isolated, old-fashioned atmosphere. My feeling is that
it is in the forefront of the movement in popular consciousness
which is now taking place.

The networks of working-class communication have
remained impenetrable, impervious even to the effects of the
media. In such an atmosphere, no story has need of
corroboration. The most fanciful assertions nourish a need to
believe the worst. There is nowhere else for the anger to go now

but into practice. On the side of the racialist there is mythology and magic, a ghoulish dimension of graveyard poetry which cannot be countered by common sense or good will. The rhetoric of the Left sounds tired and unconvincing by contrast, and the arguments for conciliation seem powerless against the surge of 'truths' exchanged in pubs, on the shop floor, among families and friends. The voice of reason is easily drowned by the rumour that white people are shortly to be forbidden to go along Whalley Range at night, by the assertion that by 1989 there will be 29 million black people living in this country, and by the clamour of individuals offering members of the Government the chance to live where they do for a week, and see how they like it then. The scenario for wholesale repatriation has been worked out. 'We don't want violence. We can live in harmony till it's time for them to go back. It would be easy. There's plenty of disused army camps, air strips where they could be kept comfortably. . . .' The idea of repatriation has taken strong hold. It is all felt to be pleasingly simple. There is little idea of the disruption and violence, the immensely destructive power that such a process could unleash. Many I spoke to seemed to think they would be sitting quite serenely watching *Coronation Street* and eating their tea while their next-door neighbours were being deported.

But the pain of these working-class communities is real and deep; and it hasn't been recognized by those who claim to care for working people – the Labour Party or the trades unions. The only thing they can see that is wrong is an absence of money, lack of resources; and it isn't an adequate palliative for the pain, even if it could be achieved. Increasing prosperity is insufficient unless there is some corresponding sense of being affirmed and validated in what people can give or achieve. People will always remain inconsolable when they are denied a sense of purpose; and rightly so. The resentment against black people only conceals the true source of the wound that has afflicted Blackburn.

In the Jahingir Café, with its formica-topped tables and Subbuteo and pinball machines, I talked with Prem, an Indian bus driver. Around us, young Indians are playing cards. A boy with long hair, a green corduroy jacket and a rosebud in his buttonhole says, 'This is where I was brought up, and this is where I'm staying.' Prem fought with the British army in the

war. He is eloquent about the need for conciliation, the
importance of living together. He says he has many English
friends, good neighbours. He is committed to the idea of one
race, the human race. But he is not optimistic. 'The labour
movement is the one hope of transcending racial differences. I
don't see any of the others in this country have the power to
resist racialism, I don't think your religious institutions have
enough influence over the people. I don't know about the
labour movement, is the leadership strong enough?' He likens
the situation to pre-Hitler Germany, a comment I was to hear
from many immigrants. Prem is aware of the rumour and gossip
that flow among the whites; and to counter this, there is already
emerging a folklore about 'atrocities' against Asians. He told
me of a girl who had allegedly been raped by two white youths,
but could not go to the police, because the shame of appearing
in court and disclosing the details of what had been done to her
would have brought a disgrace on her that could not have been
redeemed by bringing her attackers to justice.

Outside the café, the police patrol in twos. Earlier in the week,
a stone had come through the café window. 'We have no faith in
the police.' I was told that Asian girls coming from the cinema
on Sunday had been told by a certain policeman, 'We'll have
you, one by one, before we're finished.' On the other hand, a
National Party official said that it was well known that the police
in Blackburn are 'the most Left-wing in the country'.

As Prem talked, he became more impassioned, and some of
his real feelings began to show – the equivalent of the real
feelings that so many white people have few inhibitions about
displaying. 'If you want to deport us, who will do all the dirty
jobs we do? Who will work as hard as we do? What is your
country now, anyway? Look at its currency, it is worthless. You
couldn't keep your empire, you are in debt. You think that a few
barrels of oil are your salvation. You are the laughing-stock of
the world. English people don't want to work. What a mess you
are in. Your whole world has crumbled. You need us, but you
hate us because we still have a lot of things we believe in. We
have our holy places still. What do yours mean to you? We don't
send our old people to die in hospitals because we haven't the
patience to look after them at home.

'People come up to me and say "Why do you have a bigger
house, a better car than I do?" And the reason is that I have

been working six or seven days a week for ten years. I save money. White people are only thinking how soon they can spend it. If overtime comes, he says, "Oh, fuck the overtime, I want my weekend to go out and enjoy myself." Well, you can't have everything. I tell them I have denied myself to save money, and they don't like it.'

In fact, they like it so little that a number of immigrants had their windows broken throughout 1976 and 1977. An elderly man, who allowed the young children of a neighbour into his house to watch television, had his windows smashed one night. I spoke to an Indian shopkeeper, who had recently moved into a previously all-white area. His windows were broken on the first day he moved in, and were subsequently broken three times after they'd been repaired.

All this is not to say there is no feeling against racialism in the town. On the contrary. Those who support Action Against Racialism are articulate and organized, while the Asian Youth Organization has been formed by some young people to urge a more militant stand upon some of the more cautious community leaders. But it is simply that the surge of feeling is stronger in the other direction, and can call upon depths of disappointment and bitterness that have been there for generations.

I spoke to one of the leaders of the Asian Youth Organization. 'The young people are not sheep. We won't be pushed around. We have been brought up here, we have got our O- and A-levels, we're not going to beg to be allowed to stay. This is our home. We are here; there is no question. We have to show people that we have not come to take away their homes or their jobs, but that if there are no homes and jobs, that is the fault of the Government, of the system, and not of the immigrants. I am spending all my time at meetings and demonstrations. I don't particularly want to spend all my time like this, but I feel I have no choice. You have to do it, you have to fight all the lies and propaganda against us. I've only been married two years, I've a little child, I have to make sure the world he is growing up into will be safe for him. I am missing my wife. I go to work, and then I'm off to meetings in Bolton, Wolverhampton, Manchester, I get exhausted, I sleep on people's floors. When I get home, my wife feels bad because I've been away, I'm tired, and instead of comforting each other, we have an argument. You think I want to live like that? I don't want to. I want to get on with my own life, like everybody else. But you can't, not while all the things that have been happening here still carry on.'

Late evening. A woman of about fifty is standing in a doorway along Bank Top with a West Indian of about the same age. The woman has blond hair, with a blue muslin scarf to keep it in place. She wears a fur-trimmed coat, and knee-length boots that pucker around the ankle, which seems incongruous in the warm evening. She says to him, 'I love you, Mick.' 'Mack,' he corrects her. 'Yeh, I love you, Mick.' The women who have just come from Bingo look at her but don't say anything. 'Where shall we go now?' she asks. He doesn't reply. After a few minutes she says, 'I do love you, Mick.' 'Mack,' he says.

On the day I arrived in Blackburn, there was a report in the evening paper that a white man whose windows had been broken four times and who then advertised his house for sale 'to whites only', had had his house entered and his furniture slashed in the night.

I visited the house, in a small neat terrace on the edge of the main migrant area. The woman tells me that it all began when she and her husband were attacked on their way home late one evening, after a visit to relatives. Their attackers had been 'four Pakistanis', a vigilante group. She had been punched and badly bruised. She was with her three children, all under five. On the morning before I visited, they had got up and found the three-piece suite in the living room slashed and the baby's cot broken. Some money had disappeared. She showed me the furniture: the red moquette had been cut symmetrically and diagonally across the back and the seats. She had been to Social Security for a replacement for the stolen money, but had been told that anything she was given would have to be considered only as a loan. 'If I'd had a black face they wouldn't have said that.' She said that the Pakistanis had heard that the house was for sale, and had come and offered £1,500 less than she wanted for it. She had refused; and that was when the windows had been broken. They had been repaired; but it happened again. She then put up a *For Sale to Whites Only* notice. The windows had been smashed again. 'So to calm things down, we took the notice down.' Her husband is giving up his job to stay at home and guard the house. She said she had no idea why they should have been singled out; I heard of no other white person's house that had been attacked. I asked if she knew anyone in the National Party. No, but her father might be able to help. I 'phoned him and arranged to go and see him. When I got there, there was an official of the National Party at the house.

Nearly all the young people I spoke to talked of Blackburn as though it were on the point of becoming uninhabitable. Many still want to emigrate: Canada, New Zealand, South Africa. But the idea of mass migration to North America or Australia is really folk memory. And the greatest migration has already occurred: the journey inwards, away from the communal commitment of the struggle for a better life.

Many people, especially politicians and academics, say they are pleased to see the decay of the old working-class communities, because with them mass poverty has also disappeared. Such people see regret as simple nostalgia, empty romanticism. But with that poverty, something else was discarded – the sense of a shared human predicament. Such a loss has nothing to do with nostalgia; it remains a grievous one in these orphaned and purposeless places.

A friend of mine, who was brought up in Blackburn, shares this feeling. 'Even when I was at grammar school, every dinner time I used to get two buses to go to the mill where my mother worked, and I'd sit by the loom where she was working. And as I went back up the cobbled streets to get the bus back to school, I remember being very clearly aware of the division between the world of school and the familiar comforting world that the streets and mills represented. I knew which I preferred; although it's left me with a legacy of guilt I can't get rid of, and a feeling of being ill-equipped to deal with the life I now have, middle-class life. I always identified very strongly with the working class. I think they evolved certain institutions and relationships which were those of a class embattled against the world, a corporate defence against society. . . . Only when I go home now, I find it remote and dislocated.'

3

COVENTRY

COVENTRY IS ESSENTIALLY a twentieth-century working-class city. It has doubled its population four times since 1900. It has often been described as a Klondike, boom city, frontier town. Throughout the '30s, it offered hope to many people from declining industrial areas. To us in Northampton after the war, with our decaying craft of shoe-making, it seemed a place of vitality and excitement: it would secure a future in engineering and manufacture which the older industrial towns could no longer provide. It is functional and efficient. The church spires which pierce the flat geometrical skyline suggest aspiration and reward that have long been secularized in the precincts and enclosures for shoppers.

George Hodgkinson is eighty-five.* Formerly a member of the Independent Labour Party, he was one of the founders of the shop stewards movement. He was in local government for the thirty years that Labour retained power in Coventry.

'The chief reason for the emergence of the shop stewards in the First World War was that we felt a need to safeguard the humanity of work people at a time of great pressure. We were concerned that a man should be more than a tool, a cipher, a number. A man expresses his soul in his daily work. Work shouldn't be just a question of making a living; it is also a question of sharing, of comrades, of making life worth living. Capitalism has devitalized the human spirit. It still does so. Only the Labour Party seems to have lost heart. So many young people have gone into pressure groups, Age Concern, charities: no force in them, just sentiment.

'I think there's a lot of disappointment, distress even, because of the Labour Party's failure to fulfil its promises. These promises are always interpreted as meaning material prosperity – lots more money, in crude terms, and this is a view which the Labour Party has been pleased to go along with. I think that

* See George Hodgkinson's excellent autobiography, *Sent to Coventry* (Maxwell & Co., 1970).

misrepresents what the Labour Party did promise. It promised a different kind of society, and it hasn't happened. Well, strictly speaking it has happened, it is different, only it's the wrong sort of difference. The kind of prosperity that the labour movement has managed to wrest from capitalism has been acquired at a terrible human cost.

'We've always worked together as a close-knit community. The blitz was a particular influence. We all had work to do, the fire-guard organization, emergency medical services, warden service. You were never sure tomorrow would come; but the uncertainty welded us together – it was uncertainty for all of us. It was an epic struggle. In the back of your mind was the awareness that you were fighting the evils of fascism. There were no rules to govern behaviour at that time because the situation was so unfamiliar. But people evolved a proud collective morality, a sense of common purpose. And that carried us into the post-war years. The devastation of the city gave us an opportunity. We were in ruins. We knew we had to rebuild boldly. I'm not sure what's happened to the dream we had, only the city shows the extent to which commercialism has submerged the need for social satisfactions.

'We acted, I think, from a sense of collective responsibility. Many of the councillors had religious, non-conformist backgrounds. That's now been lost. I always say that Christian in *Pilgrim's Progress* missed out, because he went to Heaven on his own. We were resolved that we should be actuated by a sense of this place, this community, not by notions of individualist glory. Good heavens, all the rhetoric you're bombarded with about incentives, rewards, carrots, what do they think people are? The soldiers didn't go to war for the 1/6d incentive of the pay. They went because their homeland was threatened, because Europe was threatened with darkness and barbarism through fascism.

'I think in many ways Coventry has a more solid base than many other places from which to resist the lure of racialism. We always had a tradition of internationalism. Philip Noel-Baker was one of our MPs; the sentiment of the universality of the human race goes very deep, I think. And if you go and listen to the voices of Coventry – Irish, Scottish, Tyneside, Welsh, Polish – they've come from everywhere. This is an immigrant town, it's something you can't get away from.

'This city pioneered comprehensive education and education welfare, including the mixing of handicapped children with the comprehensive school. We pioneered home helps, meals on wheels, analgesia for childbirth, smokeless zones; we were in the forefront of many humanitarian ideas.

'We're living through a time of great savagery. I think. You can see the crudeness of capitalism everywhere, its inhumanity. The population are becoming far more ignorant, politically. A majority of people are becoming less skilled. Where the nineteenth century required hands, the twentieth requires mouths, and consuming requires less skill than even the most elementary manual labour. Look at all these children with pocket calculators and all their other aids to idleness. It's a paradox, with the amount of money spent on education, people actually learn less. I don't say that calculators can't be useful, only what do you do with the energy released by not having to work out figures and sums? Somebody I know gave a lad who was working for him the job of writing down a list of customers' names in alphabetical order. After an hour, the kid was looking puzzled. "What's the matter?" he said. "What do you mean by alphabetical?"

'I came from Nottingham. I was born in Beeston in 1893. I started working with a dairyman at eleven-and-a-half. My mother had TB, and I saw her die; and being the oldest of four boys, I had to sort of mother the others when she was gone. I would have liked to stay at school. But experience tested my resources, and shaped me in a way that people who had an easier time never knew.

'My father had a job with the Beeston Boiler Company, and at thirteen I went to work with him there. They made radiators, pipes and valves. It was low-class engineering, which I knew wouldn't be any good to me, so I went to classes at Nottingham University in machine tools. It meant a walk of eight miles, three nights a week, but I was keen to improve my skills as a fitter and turner. It wasn't that I yearned to get on socially or become wealthy. It was the drive to more satisfying work.

'I courted a girl whose father was the branch secretary of the Amalgamated Society of Railway Servants. He was a steady liver, and he didn't drink. In 1911, there was a dispute, and their house was the centre of the union's operations. That was where I first saw something of the labour movement, and had my first

contact with socialist ideas. I'd always been to Wesleyan chapel,
and later I taught in a Quaker Sunday school. I always had a
fundamental faith that the body is the temple of the holy spirit,
and that all human beings must develop the ability to assess
certain decencies of behaviour; not necessarily right from
wrong in any absolute sense. I used to go to the Adult school on
Sunday mornings, a mixture of Bible study and social activities,
and that's where I picked up the rudiments of my socialism.
Christ had socialism in him. The Sermon on the Mount and the
Ten Commandments can only be put into practice, it seems to
me, within a context of socialism.

'In 1912 a friend of mine went up to Preston in Lancashire to
establish a factory. He worked for a Roman Catholic firm, and
they had contracts to fit and equip religious buildings in
Ireland, monasteries and churches. They bought pipes, valves
and radiators, and this friend decided to start making them on
his own account. He was a foundryman. He asked me to go up
to Preston to set up the machinery and fitting department;
which I did. He was linked with the Carey Baptist Chapel, and I
used to go with him. There we had a mock parliament, and that
was where I learned to speak in public. Of a Sunday we would
walk anything up to twenty miles, into the Ribble Valley. We
used to talk and exchange ideas. What a time it was of learning
and exchanging experience. I joined the ILP and the
engineering union in July 1913.

'When the war came, the Daimler Company in Coventry was
advertising for skilled turners. I was offered a job, so I packed
my things in August 1914, and set out for Coventry. All my
worldly possessions fitted into one suitcase. I went into
lodgings. Well, you hear stories about immigrants sleeping in
shifts in one bed. That's what I did, until I got married.

'It wasn't long before I was chairman of the union branch, the
Amalgamated Society of Engineers, and I became interested in
the shop stewards movement. It was *sub rosa* at that time. The shop
stewards had to report to the district secretary any infringements
by the company that might destroy the living standards of the
workers. There was intense pressure on the labour force,
because of the war. The skilled artisan felt threatened by the
recruitment of any Tom, Dick and Harry.

'In 1917 we finally got recognition for the shop stewards,
December 1917. We gained recognition because they were

afraid of disaffection in Coventry. It was just after the Russian Revolution, of course, so you can see why they conceded as much as they did. The conditions in wartime Coventry were chaotic and dangerous. The Daimler Company was making tank parts, aero engines, shells and ambulances, a seven-day week, overtime every day. Work was from six in the morning till eight at night, Saturday and Sunday till five-thirty. I had a job to get leave for Sunday afternoon to teach my Sunday school class. People were flocking into the city for munitions work, and there were no services for them – housing, schools, shops. There's no doubt that the shop stewards movement was a force for morale and social cohesion. When you consider how shop stewards have been vilified in the press in recent years, it is quite extraordinary. They are one of the few remaining influences on the labour force for morality and some kind of order.

'My political life was governed by a sense of decency and morality. I've always seen in life a moral purpose, even in a system that was crude and savage. You're a commodity in that system, and that hasn't changed since I was young.

'Of course there were offers of corruption when I was in power, but I never had any difficulty in resisting them. There was one man after the war who had a business, a shop that had been blitzed, and he had temporary premises in the city. He came to see me one day, to find out where he stood in the queue for new accommodation. He was a tailor and outfitter. I wasn't at home, but he left a book of cloth samples, you know, and a message that I was to choose some material for a suit and let him know. He wanted me to tell him of the leases that I knew were available; so you see, quite small things in themselves, but if you gave in – even though you might not think of it in those terms at all – it could all be used against you some day. That's what happens to a number of people in positions of power, they fall into temptation without realizing it almost.

'My own experiences of the poverty and deprivation of working people fired me with a resolve to fight for them. I'd seen a lot of the cruelty of working-class life. I remember when I was a lad, a work mate who saw me with a girl took it on himself to warn me about sex and its dangers. He wasn't married himself, a middle-aged man. He said, "You know that thing a girl has, well, it's used for more than just pissing out of." Sex instruction. Life was harsh: it reflected the conditions. My father did a

working week of fifty-three hours in the Beeston Boiler
Company. In the foundry, it was like being in hell with the lid
off.

'When I became a member of the union, the induction was
quite an ordeal. You didn't just go along and that was that. The
chairman of the branch made a solemn address. It was rather
uplifting: "Let charity and wisdom guide you in your efforts.
Remember that in aiding others, you are elevating yourself, and
that co-operation is the embodiment of both charity to others
and wisdom to yourself."

'Since I was young, the trades unions have become part of the
Establishment. Everything tends to support rather than contest
the basic ideas of capitalism, which hasn't changed. The brass
balls of the pawnbrokers' shops have been superseded by flashy
silver-plated shop fronts; but the principle is still the same. It
hasn't become more moral; but the labour movement is in
danger of being invaded by the morality of capitalism, which is
none at all.

'There is nothing that is energizing or satisfying in people's
work. There is regimentation, specialization, a lack of involvement in what they create. There is no stress on achievement. The
mass of the people are required to become less skilled, not
more. There is little of that sense of morality that activated
working-class people against the inhumanity of the system when
I was young. It is still inhuman. It serves money and not human
beings. It is the humanitarianism of the labour movement
which should provide a sense of continuity between the past and
the present. It will do in the end, I'm sure of that.'

The Coventry which George Hodgkinson fought for exists as a
physical place; only it is informed with values which had no
place in his concept of what a living city should be.

The precinct in the city centre and its shops are surrounded by
the ring road, so that it is a properly protected fortress, where
nothing distracts people's gaze from contemplation of the
merchandise. Despite ourselves, this imposes on us a terrible
process of emulation: the changeless lay-figures in the windows,
elongated nymphs and stylized metallic supermen fill our
consciousness with the images of their cruel perfection. In the
absence of any other morality, they impose the discipline of
their lasting promise: the possibility of endless renewal,

innovation, fantasy and release. They offer an escape from our flawed humanity. Through them we transcend selves determined by place or function. We are no longer in Coventry; we no longer work in an engineering works or an insurance office. We are detached, free, immortal. All we have to do, is become as much like them as possible, impassive, invulnerable. We have to forfeit something of our humanity.

This process involves the elimination of all those characteristics that betray our place-bound identity: accent, custom or habit belonging to the region, evidence of our social function – coaldust, flour, calloused hands. Our new identity consists of a cluster of instinctive wants, wrapped in a beautiful integument, which can be infinitely modified to follow current image; malleable always, ready to scent the most subtle changes in fashion and to adapt accordingly. Each new style exacts a pattern of appropriate behaviour, dictates reactions and feelings as a guide and model to the individual, who thus changes his identity as easily as his underwear. What is required from him is a passive pliancy, a readiness to offer himself to each new imprisoning image; and he is freed from the constraints of sameness and continuity. He comes to depend on the sources of the image-making; those through whose products he is borne away into a deepening fantasy. A whole culture is generated by it, where conflict rages around differences in styles and competing patterns of consumption, where warring modes and fashions give back an attenuated reflection of real human divisions, rooted, not in a clash of beliefs and ideals, but within a combat created only by the diversity of products of great corporations, whose empires shape and influence the lives of all of us. This process is no less exploitative than those in the past, which used human bodies as parts of a machine to make things they were denied access to; only now it is our function to destroy rather than to create things, to leave nothing of ourselves behind but quantities of ordure and ashes. We have no purpose but that of absorbing, ingesting. We are what we have, what we can buy, not what we create or do. We are the dependent passive recipients of what is done for us, to us, on our behalf. This process is sometimes described to us as freedom; but it is a freedom between consumer products which all tend to the same end.

The consciousness of many young people in Coventry, as

elsewhere, has been fashioned, not by work, not by place, not by kinship, but by a homogeneous culture of shops, images and *réclame*, a display from which they are invited to choose and to become. Such choices are doubtless individual ones; but they show the same results, have the same consequences everywhere; produce the same feelings, the same attitudes and responses – in Coventry as in Wigan, in South Wales as in Hackney. A freely chosen sameness?

In the precinct many young people meet on Saturday afternoons. They say they are bored. Everywhere they say the same thing. 'This town, this city is boring. The place where I was born and have lived offers me nothing.' The talk is of flight and escape. The desire of the young for change, the ancient impatience with the traditional and the received is channelled into fashion and image, offering an illusion of novelty in a static society. The impetus of the young towards idealism is colonized and neutralized, as they prowl around the shopping centres like the souls of the suicides outside Elysium. Beneath the poisoned yearnings and spoiled aspirations, there is real pain. Only it cannot be perceived as originating with the constant images of wholeness and perfection that unfurl before us, the beauty and inimitability of things, which we strive to be worthy of. The things themselves can't be wrong. Utopia is here, if you can pay for it. The cause of our dissatisfactions has to be lodged with those who prevent our access to them; our competitors and rivals; those who want to spoil things; those who disagree with us. And the young, with their unexampled beauty and health, cannot tolerate anything that is not as they are, or are trying to become.

On the upper deck of the piazza Scott and Kevin are looking down at the shoppers below. They are seventeen, both unemployed. They come down to the centre of the city twice a week to sign on at the Labour Exchange. That is their principal excursion of the week. Both wear blue jeans, white T shirt; both have a small earring in the left ear. They are neighbours on a council estate on the south side of the city.

'I worked in a factory for a little while for £12.90 a week. It wasn't worth it. I get £9 on the dole, and for that I don't have to do anything. I don't mind doing nothing. Who's going to work for £12.90, forty hours a week in a dirty smelly factory? . . . I go round his house, and we sit up late at night, talking. We talk about what we'd do if we had a lot of money. Maybe I go to bed about one o'clock, maybe two. We make plans for what we're going to do when we get rich. It's a tiring job that. I spend the mornings in bed. Get up about one o'clock, except on Mondays and Wednesdays, because we come down here then.'

'I've got four brothers. Sometimes they clip me round the ear, tell me to go out and get some work. Two of them work for the Corporation.'

'We live on a rough estate. There's nothing to do round there. I don't like it. There's this woman who has schoolkids in her house during the daytime. Somebody wrote on her window "Sheila is a slag".'

'We've just been round Woolworth's. There's a music centre there, we've been looking at it. Sixty-two quid, £20 down and £4 a month. I might be able to get my old man to give us the deposit, then I could manage £4 a month. I give my mum £3 a week out of my dole. That doesn't leave much. I'd like to buy records. I've just bought two, £1.40. I like Rock and Roll, I like Reggae. I might have to give these records away as presents. I don't know yet. I only give things away when I'm in a bad mood.'

'He gets ever so generous when he's feeling bad. He gave me a shirt. He gave me a lighter last night.'

'I found it. If I'm in a bad mood I get generous. I put my hand through a hedge last week, because I was fed up. Look.' He holds up his arm; a row of scars and scratches with dull barbs of congealed blood along them. 'It's because of my girl-friend. I've been with her two and a half weeks, and now she says she's going to throw me over. She makes me mad. She wants a good hiding. Girls like that, if you hit 'em.'

'She might hit you back. You find a lot of girls now that are really hard. My girl dug her nails in my neck the other week. They've got to prove how hard they are, show they're better than men. . . . Look, there's a picture of mine. Guess how old she is? . . . Thirteen. She's a real beauty, you'd think she was twenty. . . . All I want now is to get a job and get some money. . . . I'd like to do landscape gardening or carpentry. I don't know if I will. You have to have an apprenticeship, and I'm too old for that. My girl want to be an air hostess. She's got two more years at school. When she makes up her mind to do something, nothing will stop her.'

'My mum doesn't mind me not working, but the old man bawls at me sometimes. I think there's no hurry to get into work. I wish I'd taken a bit more trouble at school though. You don't think about it till it's too late. You're too busy dreaming about your future, and you're finding out about sex. I think most kids have their first experience of sex by the time they're thirteen or fourteen. You know about it a long time before that, but not many do before thirteen. Twelve, some girls. . . . But it means you're too busy to think about school.'

'We don't belong to any gang, we just go about on our own. But if there was a fight between Teds and Punks, I'd be on the Teds side. They're more original. The Punks think they can come in and rule everybody. . . . One kid I know, he had a chain from his nose to his ear. He got in a fight, and somebody grabbed the chain. It tore half his face off. . . . I know somebody who got his ear cut off. . . . I think they fight for something to do. I wouldn't want to, not to disfigure each other. It's their business.'

'Some nights if we're fed up, we do the ouija board. Late at night. We did it last night, but nothing happened. You can't always get through. If you're too tired or not serious, they know, and they won't answer when you call them. . . . I believe that life goes on after death. I don't know about religion. I know when my grand-dad died, my mum and dad got out the ouija board, and he said, "Take care of Dave." That was my little brother. His name was really Daren, but my grand-dad always called him Dave. Nobody else used that name, so it must have been him. We have had contact with people that have died. You can get people who've been murdered or hanged. . . . You can ask them what it's like being dead, only they won't answer you.'

'I think you come back on earth again. If you've got something you haven't finished, or if you die young, especially. There's a family near us, they say they've seen a ghost on the estate. It comes in their house and talks. They say they've got it on tape, but I don't know. I haven't heard it, it might be phony. . . . Nobody's ever recorded a ghost as far as I know, so how could you tell if it was genuine? It could be true. They say the estate is built on old farms and graveyards.'

On one of the circular slatted seats on the precinct, in the shadow of a plane tree, two girls of sixteen. It was two or three days after the death of Elvis Presley. One of the girls wears a black vest with a picture of Elvis embroidered in silver Lurex thread, and on the back ELVIS LIVES, also in Lurex. She said that she believed this to be true, literally. The pictures of his body in the casket, and the crowds filing in front of it were all false. It was just someone who looked like Elvis. It was all a hoax. Elvis was tired of living in the limelight, he didn't like all the publicity and the people who were ripping him off. What he wanted more than anything else was to go and live quietly somewhere. When she heard the news, she sat up all night embroidering a transfer of Elvis on her vest. She knows where he is, but wouldn't say. 'Do you know then?' 'I might do. I've got a good idea.' 'Oh?' 'Well, there's one of his songs that might give a clue. He was persecuted by his fans. . . . He didn't want to be seen to grow old. He went away so that he can grow old in peace and quiet, and leave us with a memory of him being eternally young. People will always remember him as he was. That's his act of kindness to us, and shows what a wonderful person he is. . . . I don't think he's dead. He isn't, he couldn't be. As a matter of fact, I'm saving up to go and see if he's where I think he is. It'll take me quite a long time, because I've got to go to the other side of the world. But if he's alive, I'll find him. I wouldn't tell a living soul where he is. I haven't even told her.'

A city centre pub, late evening. Orange leatherette benches, red wall lights, curlicues of wrought iron around the bar, tables of rough-hewn varnished wood. The folksy décor is at odds with the conversation of students.

'I think it's been proved that there are beings on other planets, like us, similar to us; not exactly the same, but not with two heads or anything like that. And they are trying to communicate with us, or they would do; but they know that if they do come down to earth, we'd probably attack them, because we wouldn't trust them. We are too earth-bound to hear them. I think they may well be finer beings than ourselves. Man is too destructive.'

'I'd love to visit other planets. I love travel. I don't mean to foreign countries, that's boring, and anyway I've seen a lot of them with my parents. I'd love to travel in space.'

'I sometimes have this idea that I came from elsewhere. I sometimes don't believe my parents are really my parents, you know. I think it's possible a person could be conceived by someone who came from space, simply using the body of someone on earth. . . . I know I'm not like other people. I get flashes of insight about what people are doing, illuminations; and I'm nearly always right.'

Ben is nineteen. He has a fragile face, fair hair and intense grey eyes. 'I believe in evil. I believe in the devil, because I think you can see evidence of him everywhere. I think the devil is winning in the world, and basically I want to be on the winning side. I mean, if you look at the slaughter and the hatred and the violence, it stands to reason that evil triumphs. We went to some church ruins, an old graveyard near Northampton, and we dug up some bones, and asked Satan to be our witness. We sacrificed a black cat. I didn't like that very much. You're supposed to wash your hands in its blood, but I didn't fancy that. We made a pact with Satan to carry out his work on earth. . . . I can't tell you what I get in exchange. What I can tell you is that you get a much greater sense of freedom. You don't have so many petty restrictions on your life. You feel things more deeply, love and hate. If the time comes when I have to pay for it, well, I shall be ready. I do know of somebody who made a pact with Satan, and now he's quite a well-known singer. I believe he got success because he was prepared to bargain his life and soul for what he wanted.'

These beliefs are not poses. Fantasy is for many young people more than an idle indulgence; it is sometimes an attempt to interpret the world. If many of them are preoccupied with evil and violence, degradation and death, this is perhaps an inevitable response to a situation in which all negation has been suppressed, only goodness and concern made manifest, not only in the care of their parents for them, but in the spectacle of perfected things in which they have grown. Their parents, themselves often raised in poverty, vowed that they should want for nothing. But the good things that were showered upon them came, as it were, accompanied by certain undisclosed dis-advantages – the reverse of all the free gifts and rewards and prizes so stridently offered all the time – which are the morality of the market-place, the illusion of the conjuror/salesman, the commoditized feeling and diminished humanity. The lament, 'I gave them the best money could buy,' is heard everywhere from bewildered parents, whose children have deserted or rejected them, have got into trouble or failed to live up to ambitions cherished on their behalf. The children have grown up in security. They have been through schools in which liberal humanitarian values prevail. They have indeed had the best of everything. If their values seem harsh now, perhaps it is because our exaltation of things is harsh. The perfection of things denies them the right to any feeling that is not positive. Failure and negation are prohibited by the taboo which our sentimental and oversimplified view of childhood binds upon us; and those forbidden thoughts have gone into a spontaneous collective belief, barbaric and dangerous, which threatens all the time to invade the fragile equilibrium of our weakened respect for humanity. Violence, racism, nihilism threaten their revenge against the abject quietude, the vacant passivity of a generation brought up, not under the tutelage of parents and teachers, but under the cold amoralism of things.

During the time I was in Coventry there was a bread strike, as it was called. In fact, the bakery workers were banning overtime, which meant that there was a much reduced supply of bread to the shops. The result was that queues began to form outside bakers' shops whenever there was a rumour that bread was expected. Some of these rumours were false anyway; and some people decided to get there early in any case; and at times people queued for up to four hours. A lively sense of sharing developed, echoes of the blitz; nobody seemed to feel the discrepancy between the heroics of queuing and the event which had united them.

In one shop a woman who had queued for just over three hours got the last loaf in a small consignment of bread. The woman behind her was disappointed. She offered her a pound for it. The woman who had bought the bread didn't hesitate. Triumphantly, she exchanged the loaf for a pound note.

Another woman in the queue announced, indiscreetly, that she already had twelve large loaves in her deep freeze, but that she was still queuing for more. A man who overheard her said, 'Well, what are you doing here then? Why don't you give other people a chance? There's old-age pensioners in this queue.' 'Well,' she said indignantly, 'I've got small children. They're growing up, they need it.' It was a total explanation. Nobody contested her right to more bread. Somebody did say, 'What about rice or potatoes?' 'Oh no, they must have their daily bread.' Somehow that phrase seemed to sanctify what she was doing. She bought four loaves, and as she was departing, somebody joked, 'Mind you don't get mugged with all that bread on you.' Some of the women were quite old, some of them with sadly bandaged legs and varicose veins. There was something traditionally anxious and self-effacing about their patience, but at the same time, an excitement, as some ancient memory is rekindled of bread, struggle and survival. But for the most part, the queue seemed to represent the redundancy of the providing rôle of women, their helpless dependency, this frieze of women robbed of their function, already rehearsing the triumphs they would recount to their family when they got home in the evening.

On the south side of the city, past the 1930s Tudor houses, with names like Thistle Do, and overtaken now by motorways and the dust and mud of roads far busier than was anticipated when these houses were built, there is a small close of modern houses with open-plan gardens; bright borders of late summer flowers, newly planted willows and miniature conifers. At the back of the house, a garden full of vegetables, dahlias, runner beans. The garden slopes down to the river, and a cluster of poplars and aspens. There is a seat suspended on a metal frame, under a floral fringed awning. The air is full of wasps, the sky cloudless.

Bill Warman has recently retired after a life of work in the car industry.

'What has hit Coventry suddenly is the spectre that this boom town could become a distressed area overnight. Unemployment is the highest it's been here since before the First World War; above the national average in fact. It was never really hit by the Depression. I came here at that time to look for work. A lot of the money invested in Coventry is multi-national: it could be transferred elsewhere just like that. In fact, this is almost inevitable. Already half the jobs in the city depend on overseas capital. It used to be labour that had to be adaptable and mobile, but now capital can vanish almost overnight. Capitalism is weaker in this country than it was when it still had the Empire to buttress it; but the working-class movement has gone from strength to strength. There's nothing but advance for the working class. There is a danger from racialism as a backlash from the loss of empire, but it won't become a serious threat. There is a far greater understanding and political awareness than there was the '30s.

'When I moved here, the car industry was still seasonal work. Humber produced cars only for England. You expected to be slack or out of work in the winter. Of course conditions have improved. Workers will fight for safety in their place of work. Some workers are inbred with capitalist ideas; but at other times, they will rise against them and take a class-conscious stand. There's always been only a minority of people active in the labour movement. The movement does suffer from a certain loss, pessimism. You do get men opting out, sometimes on the insistence of their wives. You hear people say, "What've I got out of it?" – the what's-in-it-for-me individualistic argument.

'I don't think the desire for consumer goods is anti-socialist. Not at all. There has been a lot of rubbish talked about working people become middle class because they have a car or a house or a colour TV, or because they go abroad for their holidays. That's rubbish. People still owe their allegiance to their class. If there's a dispute, some injustice, things like that aren't going to win them over. That's superficial.'

JS: 'How would life be different under socialism?'

BILL WARMAN: 'Well, there'd be no need of the Stock Exchange, gambling with people's lives. All the parasitic fringe activities would go. Estate agents, for instance. Privileged education would be eliminated. The need to develop collective instincts would be fostered at school. Of course, a lot of the old ideas would still hang over. But look at the advance we've made this century. The power of imperialism over small nations has disappeared in my lifetime.

'I was chairman of the shop stewards' committee for fifteen years at Standard Triumph. I led them in the strike in 1956 against redundancy. That was what educated me. It was my university. The rôle of shop steward is nothing like anything you might read in the papers. Those people know nothing about it. As a shop steward, you're part social worker, part legal adviser. You'd be surprised at the needs we meet that are not answered by any of the official agencies, over and above our own function.

'Of course the working-class movement loses out to some degree through the education process. That's happening all the time. There's a constant hunt goes on to try and track down those who can be won over to the other side. Even some shop stewards go over sometimes. But on the other hand, today even the foremen are in unions. They move towards the working class rather than the working class going to them. There's a growing willingness on the part of people who used to think it was indecent to discuss salaries to go in for collective bargaining.

'Under socialism, people will have the right to live decently. I was in Berlin recently, and the contrast between East and West is amazing. West Berlin is full of sex shops, advertising; everything is garish and exploitative. East Berlin is more sober, cleaner. There are shops with enough in them: not the abundance you see in the West. There, the biggest commodity on sale is sex. As socialists, we have got to take people as they are. Human need is something to be answered, not something to be exploited. I think that's it, it's the unfettered plundering of even the highest, most worthy human needs that debases the West.

'I'm a revolutionary, because you can't get socialism through education. This has been the Labour Party's greatest error. Of course it's nothing new to encourage children to get on. That the individual benefits himself, and thereby benefits everybody else, is very deeply rooted in capitalist belief. We need to develop not the feeling that an individual has to get out of the working class in order to benefit them, but a feeling of pride in the working class themselves. You've got to keep winning the people again and again. It's a continuous process. You never win the battle. Individuals – if it had been up to individuals, Britain would have been socialist long ago.

'To be a shop steward you have to have a respect for your fellow workingmen; and I'm proud of the service I've given to my class. I never thought I knew all the answers. We always argued about everything, but always accepted majority decisions. I never wanted to be anything but working class. My ambitions aren't personal, they're those of my class. The working class is far more advanced today. Most of the old SDF were very narrow and economist in outlook; that way you can become very defeatist and pessimistic. In the early days it was difficult to raise politics in the union; they didn't think that was what they were there for.

'My father had only two years of schooling. He started work when he was ten. He lived on a farm, and he worked in the fields.

He used to be whipped by the man in charge of the plough. Once he was bitten by a horse as he tried to run away from the ploughman's lash. He was a Tory. He was for the King, religion and drink. Of his first marriage there were eight children. He married a gipsy woman; but only two of the children lived. I'm a child of his second marriage. I remember at the time of the First World War, having an argument with my father. He was talking about filthy Germans, atrocities they committed, echoing all the things he'd been instructed to say. I knew I couldn't accept that, even then. I knew my life wasn't going to be bound up with all that jingoism.

'I was lucky. I got an apprenticeship as a sheet metal worker, in South London. But after I'd finished that, I was unemployed. That's why I came to Coventry. You'll find a lot of people came here to escape from unemployment. This is a very skilled working town. It was fed by a lot of the more able people who left the depressed working-class areas. This means that it's relatively Left-wing. There was full employment here right throught the '6os. There were highly paid jobs. Of course in the last few years we've seen some of those strong basic industries in decline. Between the wars this city represented the new big industrial concentrations – cars, engineering, machine tools. This has always happened – the old locations slowly disappear, and new foci of industry appear.

'When I was young, working-class life was harsher, fifty-hour week and no unions: the problems of struggle were much greater then. Drinking and gambling were the only way out of it. There was always a need for escapism. My father used to gamble and my mother would have to go without wages some weeks. You don't often find that today. You must have faith in the working class. You're never going to get anywhere without them. The trouble with the Labour Party is that it says to the working class, "Look what we've done for you." It expects gratitude. It looks on its achievements in a static way, as though it was a once-for-all situation. But the working class moves on. Life continues, change, there's fluidity. The Labour Party has been overtaken by inertia because it doesn't know where to go next. But the way to look at it is that nothing has been achieved without the working class. It isn't a question of gratitude.'

The flow of people into Coventry over the years was absorbed.

But like most towns that have grown rapidly, there is always a residual population, mainly unattached men, who live in hostels and lodgings. Some of these move around the precinct during the day time, lie on the grass in the adjacent areas; sometimes ragged, dirty, corroded by the extinction of hope.

A man sits alone on one of the wooden seats. Although the other seats are crowded he keeps his to himself. He is perhaps sixty-five. He wears a greasy herringbone coat in spite of the warmth. His flannel trousers are shiny with grime. He wears on one foot a boot without a proper sole, and on the other a woman's sandal tied with string around swollen black toes. He carries a rucksack, which he has placed beside him on the bench. His face is red, and the sun shines on a glitter of silver stubble. His eyes are pale blue and water incessantly, so that two channels of rheum have made parallel grooves in his face. Around him there is an intermittent smell, sour and fetid.

'I came from Glasgow in 1935. I've been everywhere. I came to Coventry for work. I shouldn't think anybody'd come here for any other reason. I worked for Standard, I worked on the buildings. I helped build this precinct, that's why I always sit here. It's partly my work that you can see. I'm proud of it. All these people going about their lives, they don't know that without me they wouldn't be able to go into these lovely shops and sit here. . . . I've tried to tell them, some of them. They think I haven't got all my marbles, or if they're women, they think I'm going to molest them. I've lived rough. For five years I never slept in a bed. I'm lucky, I've got quite a keen brain. I've been all over the British Isles. I'm in the Salvation Army now. Social Security pay them direct, and I get £4.60 a week. I have a couple of glasses of beer at dinner time. I don't go out at night. We had one fellow there, he got beaten up by two girls. Girls. They broke his arm. What kind of a world is it?

'I never wanted to settle down. I got married. I left home to look for work, but in those days that was the only way to get rid of your wife. You went on the tramp. Christ, I hated her. In those days it was easier, you were accepted as a tramp. You were recognized, people left you alone. People would give you bread. There were barns and hayricks you could sleep in. You could do odd jobs. It's not like that now. I see these poor bastards lying in the gutters, you see them in the winter wrapped up in newspapers; human parcels they are, in doorways, anywhere for a bit of shelter; human parcels.

'The only thing I regret is my daughter. She wouldn't know me if she saw me. I've thought about her since I got older. She'd be forty-four now. I often wonder what her life is. I'm all right, I had my freedom. I wouldn't have given that up for anything. Sometimes I feel shame. I'm ashamed that I shan't have anyone to close my eyes for me. That is a terrible thing. If I was going to give anybody any advice – which I'm not, nobody would ever listen to me – I'd say, "Don't give up your freedom, but don't finish up so that nobody cares whether you live or die." I heard once about a man who was killed, or he died, I don't know. And nobody ever found out who he was or where he came from. They buried him in a pauper's grave, with a wooden cross on it. It said, "To the memory of an unknown man." I've seen it. That's my epitaph.'

It is a sunny September evening in the public gardens. Some canna lilies glow blood-red in the late sunshine; the insects hang almost motionless in the caramel breath of a lavender bush. Most people have gone home from work. A man in lovat-green flannels and jacket sits doing the crossword in the *Coventry Evening Telegraph*. 'Just finished?' he asks. 'I finished three years ago. Time, oh time, it does hang heavy. I was a capstan operator for twenty-five years. I did a lot of jobs before that. The one I liked best, it was loading scrap metal on to a lorry with my bare hands. I did that for two years, it made me feel fit, good for anything. You'd be surprised how beautiful scrap metal can be. Shavings of steel, iron, little pieces of copper or zinc, all heaped up. I enjoyed that.

'Well, today's been a good day. I've an old people's ticket. I went to Birmingham. I had a couple of pints and a sandwich. I don't want to go home, there's nobody there when I get there. I'm a bachelor. I live in a little flat. It wants a lot doing to it, but I haven't the money. The worst thing about retirement is not the things you know you can't have, but the things that are tantalizingly just out of reach. . . . I think the best thing you can have in life is a friend, a really intimate friend, a real pal; somebody you can tell everything to. Believe me, that is the best thing in the world to me. Whenever I've had someone I can trust, someone who won't' – he opens and closes his hand to indicate gossip – 'you know. There is nothing better, more comforting. But the terrible thing as you get older, you see your acquaintances and friends fading away. You think, I wonder what happened to such a body? I haven't seen so-and-so for a long time; and then you meet someone who tells you they've gone. You wonder when it'll be your turn. Today's been a good day, but I'd like to have had somebody to share it with. I've enjoyed it, but on a rainy day, what can you do?

'Loneliness is a terrible thing. I never wanted to come here. Coventry. I'm from Blackburn. I always wanted to go on the stage, but of course you were a pansy in Blackburn, the minute you mentioned owt like that. But I did do ballroom dancing. I went to London. I never became brilliant, but I was starting up my school when the war broke out. I was sent here, directed labour you see. There was no place for the sort of thing I wanted to do in wartime. Well, it's all right. I've had some good times here. I don't think it really matters where you are, as long as you've got a friend, only it's not so easy here. They're all for their wives, you see.'

For the first time he looks at me. Suddenly he is overcome by shame; the fear that he has said too much. Hurriedly he folds his newspaper, replaces his glasses in the blue case which he snaps shut. Defensively, he zips up his woollen cardigan, although the evening is warm.

A street cleaner, sitting in the sun in the middle of the day. He offered me some coffee from his thermos flask. 'The missis always makes coffee in the morning. Don't want to pay their fancy prices. She's a good old gal. You hear some of them talking about their wives. I wouldn't say anything, but I wouldn't talk like that about mine. . . . You won't find many people like me in Coventry, I was born here. It's not a bad job. I take home about £55 a week, there's only the two of us at home. It's not so good this time of the year, now up till Christmas, till all the leaves have come off the trees. Some people treat you as if you were part of the street, they look through you. I see all the stuff people throw down, some of them won't look at me because they know I'm the one got to clear up after them. You see the terrible waste that goes on, food, chicken and chips, bread, buns, fruit, the stuff people throw away, my missis and I lived on worse when we were

young. I'm not exaggerating. After the weekend it's the worst,
you find all these smashed bottles, chips and wrappers, I reckon
the kids go round on Saturday night just smashing things up.
Nothing better to do. We've gone soft, whatever way you look at
it. I reckon this country's finished. We're pushed around by
anybody. I've had most of my life, I don't care. The only ones
I'm sorry for as them as come after. They've got to live with the
mess. I think there'll be bloodshed before they've finished. You
can't run a country the way this is without it all falls to bits in the
end.'

Work is the most immediate way of relating to people in
Coventry.

Many commute to Birmingham, like Derek Jenkins. He
works in a car factory in the outskirts of the city. The buildings
are rambling and cover several acres, but the main entrance is
through a building dating from the 1930s, with a curved gravel
drive, flagpoles and lawns; it seems to have been modelled on
the design of a country house. You enter a ceremonial hall, with
tiled floor and an enormous ornamental balustrade in dark
polished wood. You almost expect to be welcomed by a hostess
with marcelled hair, offered a cocktail and told there's someone
dying to meet you.

The first thing that strikes you in the machine shop is the sense
of space, and the relative absence of people. Individuals are
concealed behind the bulk of machines, constructs of great
complexity, which carry out jobs formerly entrusted to five or
ten or even twenty workmen. The workers now mostly tend the
machines: perhaps clamping and unclamping the core of the
engine which has come from the foundry into a position where a
series of automatic drills descends and penetrates the metal,
throwing up a rain of silver. Everywhere the machines dwarf
people, diminishing the rôle, usurping the function of men.
In some places the machines work independently: a brutish
intelligence of metal and grease automatically sucks in thick
whorls of wire and spits out a rhythmic succession of bolts,
complete with head and screw. The whole shop, with its concrete
floor and roof of dingy smudged glass, is strewn with swarf and
flakes of metal, a constant precipitation of waste in this different
climate, where the air is full of the narcotic influence of solvents
and thinners, and the addictive power of trichlorethylene is a

risk to all those who work with it – one of the processes was so
addictive, that when men were taken off it they had symptoms of
withdrawal and hostility. There are admonitions all over the
walls to wear protective gear for eyes and ears. Some wear ear
muffs against the noise, so that they look like disc jockeys, or
people attuned to some secret music of their own. Some men
with wads of cotton over the mouth are spraying the engines.
They are like crude surgeons or butchers, wading through a
sticky discoloured blood. Even at night, when they spit or blow
their nose, the blue paint will still have managed to penetrate the
thick wadding and enter their body. There are swirls of metallic
detritus all over the place, silver flakes in oily pools of
iridescence; and everywhere a milky liquid is used in the
frequent washing processes. Overhead, pneumatic and
hydraulic power tools hang from their rubber tubing like some
vast disembowelling. The machines are like deformed, but
infinitely more powerful, extensions of humanity; in the same
way that people seem to exist like shrunken appendages of the
vibrating, grinding inexhaustible power of the machines: image
and origin of a joyless symbiosis, which is a metaphor
elaborated in the wider society outside work. In some parts of
the shop, the machines seem to have vanquished the people
completely. It is as though the invasion from space has already
occurred; but it is the invasion from inner space, our own
inventions, made in West Germany or Zanesville, Ohio. While
they work, many people have no one to communicate with, even
if it were possible to hear what is said; so that some men are
immured within three walls of different kinds of metal, pulsing
and breathing in its smooth ultramarine casing. At the far end of
the shop, the machines are tested. They are conveyed on a series
of pulleys, so that they hang from the roof like trophies: the
finished product of this sequence of operations.

Everything in this capital-intensive place speaks of disregard
for people. The mess and recreation areas are recesses in the
shops themselves, barely separated from the work areas, with
rudimentary tables and seating provision, like an improvised
picnic. All round the shop are kiosks which open at break times
for the sale of food; but many people still prefer to take
something from home; something touchingly human in the soft
white bread, the colour of tomatoes and green apples in a
Tupperware box. The mess area contains padlocked lockers.

Some chalked graffiti have been scratched more or less ineffectually into the relentless metal: *Muppet Aggro, Here Lies Black Jim RIP*.

Some of the shops cover such a large area that you can hardly see from one end to the other, because over them there hangs a bluish and fumy metallic haze. Trucks carrying components keep up a constant traffic within the alleyways between the machines, their track marked out by continuous yellow lines; the trucks disappear through gates of rubber and once transparent plastic, the texture of toenails, scored and discoloured by the comings and goings of the trucks. As the gates part, even the glimpse of sunshine and piles of silver clouds seem to have been contaminated by the metal.

The tracks themselves, where the engines are assembled, are in great hangars. They move continuously, but at a speed precisely calculated to give the workers the time needed to carry out their respective tasks. The tracks are a series of metal plates, with, every few yards, a curved metal stem on which an engine is attached so that it looks like a spiky iron flower. As the tracks move, the engines are pieced together, cylinders inserted, wheels and nuts tightened, so that by the time they arrive at the end of the track, the process is complete. The men weave in and out of the inexorable progression of the tracks, a ballet of automated precision. Sometimes they seem mechanical too, as though they themselves had somehow been engendered by the tireless rhythm of the metal. It is a curious sensation, the long sequence of metal plates, edging forward with their identical plinths of cast iron passing in rows like metallic soldiery. Humanity appears weak and vulnerable in the presence of this relentless exactitude. At times it feels as oppressive as being in the bowels of a vast living creature, swallowed alive among the intestinal bulges of pipes and boilers around the roof and walls. Engines, tubes and valves seem to indicate a remote and extra-human intelligence which maintains perfect control over its clumsy and diminished servants. It is a place where only metaphor and simile can be used to mediate that implacable coldness of things which extinguish human responses, which, by contrast, are as feeble as candle flames.

Most of the shops are in red-brick buildings, with arched skylights dimmed by a growth of moss on the reinforced glass. The metallic emissions from the machinery are illuminated by a

shadowless artificial day, so that the real daylight beyond looks
grey and indistinct. Some of the buildings were built as 'shadow'
factories during the war, to look like housing. Between the
various buildings there are asphalt driveways and concrete
yards, some of them piled with scrap or retrieved components
from worn-out cars. At the entrance to each shop there are the
wooden pockets for clocking-in cards, and the kind of clocks
you see only in factories, with spindly roman numerals and a fat
minute hand like the ace of spades. Most of the men work in
overalls or brown smocks; but some of the younger ones keep
their own working clothes, ancient sports coats and jeans,
stained with oil and grease but symbols of a slight retention of
control over something of themselves. Many workers bear the
stigmata of the metal: splinters fester in the skin, dust of the
metal stains the grooves of the flesh with a lead grey.

If the toolmakers are the least subservient to the machines –
they have the prestige of repairing and maintaining them – those
who work in the foundry suffer the worst working conditions of
all.

First of all the foundry is at a lower level than the other
buildings. The rainwater and factory liquids drain downhill and
mix with oil, so that to get to the foundry you have to cross a
sticky expanse of indigo mud. You pass through some
rubberized doors into the foundry. You are sucked into what
feels like a vortex of heat and fumes. The machinery throbs and
vibrates with such force that you have the impression of having
been absorbed into the machine itself. Here, the hot-box cores
for the moulds are made of sand and linseed oil. They are coated
with a kind of terra cotta glazing, and hardened in huge ovens so
that they will withstand the heat of molten metal. The hot boxes
emit an uneven flame, tongues of sulphurous yellow and blue
illuminate men's faces and bodies in the darkness. Everything
seems to be in movement: rollers, trays, the great cylinders of
the hot boxes with the rotating planes of metal on which stand
the cores. It feels impossible not to get caught up in it; so
inevitable in fact, that you are almost compelled to throw
yourself into the violent heaving machinery before it consumes
you. The worst place of all is the furnace, where the blocks of
metal are melted and poured into the moulds to produce what
will be the basic carcase of the engine. Buckets of liquid metal

are suspended from cables, giving off a shimmer of scorching heat and fume. This is the climax of the process. The great bulbous cylinders of the furnaces discharge choking heat and vapour, and the men, lighted by glowing metal, flame and incandescence, are like figures in a medieval allegory, condemned to eternal torment. Some of the men don't even wear protective clothing; their bare bodies look frail against the destructive power of heat and machinery. The light from the metal hurts the eyes with its unwavering glare. A trap door opens in the floor, a studded metal flap like a manhole cover, and a man emerges from a cloud of steam and vapour: below him you see a whole submerged stratum of pipes and pistons. Just when you imagine you have seen the worst places in which men should have to work, you catch a glimpse of an even greater ill-contained fury of pulsating metal and heat. The smell of linseed and molten metal, fumes and gas totally fill the mind and senses. The newly moulded engines are deposited on to the plates where they will cool, a white incandescence that slowly subsides into a sulky scarlet glow and then into a dull and blackened hardness. When the cooling process is complete, the metal looks tarnished and lifeless; and it is polished and cleaned before it is sent to the machine shop.

Much of the machinery in the foundry is old; some more modern pieces have been added, ice-blue metal boxes and bright red switches only emphasize the more cumbrous bloated machinery of the past. One man said, 'I've worked here for thirty-one years, and it looks the same today as it did in 1946.' The foundry is the only place in the factory where labour is still needed even when Birmingham suffers from 7 per cent unemployment.

'If you read in the paper that so many men have walked out, it'll probably be because the fans or the extractors have stopped working. You can see what it's like in here even when they're all going full blast. You think what it's like when they all pack up. Only you won't see that mentioned in the press, you won't find any description of the conditions we're working in. The press wants people to think we're a lazy lot of bastards. Well, let them. Perhaps they might come and see for themselves. They might get a shock.'

During the break, some men are playing cards. They prefer to stay in the foundry rather than go outside. 'You ask these blokes whether they'd rather have a cleaner or safer working place or an extra fiver a week.'

JS: 'Don't you care about the conditions?'

'I don't care. It's my life. I can look after myself.'

JS: 'But you can't control the amount of fumes you breathe in.'

'I've got to die sometime. Life's a gamble. You have to take risks. I take a risk every time I step outside my front door. Every time I light a cigarette.'

I spoke to a man who travelled every day from Watford. 'Why do you do it?' 'I have to. I want to give the best to my wife and children. I was driving a van, 42 quid a week. That's no good to me. The wife has to stay in Watford, her mother's housebound.' 'How is what you do giving the best to your wife and children?' 'Well, it isn't, but what else is there? You fucking tell me.'

Humanity is twice subordinated to the product: once in the process of manufacture, and again when it takes its exalted place in the cold glitter of our idolatry of things.

In a corner of the machine shop is the chief shop stewards' room: a high bare place, distempered yellow, and furnished with some discarded chairs and gunmetal grey desks from the offices. 'It's true, there has been a certain loss of contact between the floor and the shop stewards. For instance, there is a fair amount of racial feeling; only they tend to modify what they think in front of us.' The shop stewards do exercise a moral authority over those they represent. Far from being the wreckers they are sometimes depicted to be, they have at times an almost priest-like function, advising, supporting, representing. 'There is a lot of positive feeling in people, only this society doesn't bring it out. We've got an appeal at the moment for a scanner for the hospital, we had a sponsored parachute jump, people are only too pleased to take part. Society took over caring, and individuals have abandoned it. I think the welfare state is a wonderful concept, but like anything else it gets warped under capitalism: it's an excuse for everybody to neglect everybody else. We have had opportunities to change society radically, but we've lost them. They'll come again, and we must be ready next time. My wife could learn to do the job I do in ten minutes, and I'm supposed to be semi-skilled.'

Pete is twenty-two, the youngest shop steward in Birmingham.

Born in a caravan, one of a large Irish family, he was always cast in the rôle of troublemaker when he was at school, and duly fulfilled it; a rôle that was exacerbated by his obvious intelligence. He did manage to get an apprenticeship with a small firm as a toolmaker. He signed his indentures, as did his employer, but they were not properly registered, and were therefore never valid. He didn't realize this until a few months before his apprenticeship was due to finish; and then he observed that his employer was finding fault with his work all the time. 'Even the most trivial things. It was as though he was trying to convince me that I was no good. He was just waiting for me to make a mistake. Well, if somebody is that determined, they'll get you anyway, sooner or later. One day, after an exam that finished at dinner time I went to the pub instead of going straight back to work. That was it. I was sacked. So that spoilt everything. I went abroad, went round Europe for a year. I came back, spent a year on the dole. I couldn't get a job. In the end I was lucky. I got a job through a mate of mine at this factory. I don't intend to stay there. I'm studying while I'm there. There are ways out, but only if you're sufficiently motivated. I think work is a valuable discipline, a training ground. It can be tough. If you've got some sensitivity it can be hard. Everything is done to squeeze out anybody who has the chance to get out from the working class. You have to resist that to some extent, because everybody who gets out impoverishes the working class a little more. To me, the miracle is that even after the working class has been bled of so much talent, there are still so many people who are dedicated and caring. There are about 350,000 shop stewards in industry altogether. They're not all on the Left, by any means, but however you look at it, that's a pretty impressive force of people.'

Derek Jenkins has been at the factory for eighteen years.

'Being a car worker is becoming less and less important to me now. I feel I'm thinking of it increasingly as part of my past. I like to think that has been the first half of my working life. I've got other things I want to do with the other half, and if I don't do it for myself, nobody else will. You have to find the will to do that inside yourself, and then have confidence in it. It isn't easy for working people to do that. Most people let themselves get hooked on dreams of something external happening to them – chance, luck. They do the pools, dream of the big win, fate rescuing them from their own lives.

'I've never been happy there. I always resented getting up in the morning to go to that place, giving so much time, so much of myself; going to work in the dark and cold. As soon as you get off the bus you can smell the factory. It's the foundry, a smoky sort of vapour. They process the smoke now, because so many of the residents of the area complained. They filter it now and scent it with a disinfectant. So now it discharges scented soot instead of filthy soot, and the people seem satisfied.

'They say you get used to working in a place. I never have. It gets familiar, but that's not the same. You file in there with all the others, a sort of suspended resentment, because after all those years you can't go on hating it at that pitch. You can tell by people's posture what their attitude is, a lack of spirit, resignation. You clock in, and then, until the next bell, you're an extension of a machine spindle. Clocking in is an act of surrender. The rack full of cards: you place yours, and that's the symbolic moment.

'Work starts at seven-thirty. You get into your overalls, boots, goggles, masks, gloves, hats, barrier creams, and you advance like a Dalek to your machine. The thing that keeps you human is the companionship, although even the possibility of that has been reduced in some jobs. The assembly and sub-assembly jobs engender more friendship than the machine shop, for instance, because in those there is still a sense of collective working. In the machine shop, you have an isolated function, with only a few thousand pounds' worth of equipment for companionship. If you're on the tracks, your work dovetails into that of other people. On the track, you have to notify the floater if you want to take five, and he'll take over your job. They always have a certain number of floaters on the tracks who have to be able to replace anybody, so they have to have a number of skills. There's something irresistible about the tracks, always on the move; you see men bent over this piece of metal, bowing down, on their knees sometimes, contorting themselves round it. The metal governs their lives, they have to adapt themselves to it.

'I'm on measured day work, and it's just a question of beating the clock. You have a quota, scientifically established and agreed, which you have to get through. My job is making manifolds for the cylinder head in the engine and I have to achieve four an hour. If you under-achieve, you have to account for yourself; but there's no medals for over-achievement. Everything is established by custom and practice; there's no rule book. The machine I work at, it's a radial driller, single spindle; and there's no one in the factory old enough to know where it came from. It had nothing to do with cars. It's probably over seventy years old. The concept of the machine dates from when they had old belt drives, overhead power shafts.

'There's a tea-break at 9.50. The kiosks are open, and you see people start to take the shape of human beings again. The factory blots out the senses. There can't be much communication, hearing is about 90 per cent impaired. In the machine shop you can't talk because of the noise and the distance of people from each other. All sense of feeling is muffled, people are insulated from each other.

'After that, the next landmark isn't till dinner time. Then human patterns of acquaintanceship and communication get re-established. We have a messing area, which is a comparatively recent concession. There are benches, tables and lockers, it's almost like a club room. You get people listening to the radio for the horses, playing cards, reading. Some go to the canteen. There's only half an hour and it goes by like five minutes. The pause isn't long enough for you to get into a relaxed frame of mind. We did have three-quarters of an hour, but we chose to make it shorter to take a quarter of an hour off the end of the day.

'The afternoon is more relaxed. Most of the work is out of the way by the end of the morning. By then I should think about three-quarters of the day's work is finished. You start off with a relentless burst of energy, and that exhausts itself, and you can anticipate the rest of the day more comfortably. There's a ten-minute break at 2.50. The company tried to negotiate this out, to finish even earlier, but the stewards insisted it should stay, if only to deprive the surgery of any more accident cases – obviously in the afternoon people are more tired and less attentive to safety. The stewards do get it in the neck if they don't go all-out for the maximum amount of money; but sometimes factors other than the wallet have to take precedence.

'After three o'clock you can pinch a minute or two before

going back to work; and then it's tidying up, finishing off, leaving the place in order for the next shift. Overtime comes in dribs and drabs, it isn't general at the moment. It's rather uneven. You go suddenly from overtime back to forty hours or even on to short time. I can't say there's much joy when four o'clock comes. Most people feel too knackered. They just want to get home.

'That's the routine, with the punctuation you expect. Of course there is a lot of unplanned disruption to that routine. If there's a breakdown, you have to find the setter if it's a tool breakdown, or get the foreman to send a requisition order. Work has to stop while the millwright, or whoever it is, is sent for. The toolroom are the elect of the factory. Then there might have to be water tests on the machines, something may go wrong with the suds pump or the gutters round the machine might overflow. There might be an argument about whether the windows should be open or shut, or the heating on or off; small things maybe, but in that atmosphere of excruciating tedium, any diversion is welcome. Then the viewers come round, inspectors.

'Although the days follow an identical pattern, each day is subjectively different. There's a cycle in the week, just as there is within the day. Friday, for instance, is a strange day. The administrative staff and clerks are tidying up for the week, getting out quotas and statistics, the manual workers are preparing for the weekend. Friday night is a night out for a lot of the lads. Friday is a happy day: finish at three instead of four, it's a seven-hour day. Quite a few go for a jug at dinner time, there's a feeling of end-of-the-week elation. A weekend in prospect seems somehow longer than it really is. But because the time at the weekend is your own, it expands in anticipation. You get an illusion of freedom.

'Monday is the reverse. I know it's a cliché about Monday, but if you experience it, you feel it afresh every week, the self-control needed, the constraint of having to get up for work. People are more grey, more subdued on Mondays. Thursday is pay day, so that has its own feel about it. Wednesday is a sort of half-way day, you're pleased to have reached the mid point of the week. Of course you accept the logic of work, the values of the work place, you have no option, you wouldn't survive otherwise. For instance, there are certain jobs that have to be done in every section. There's a built-in allowance for absenteeism; but absenteeism is generally above the level which is allowed for. This means that every morning certain numbers of people don't know exactly what work they're going to do. This is what's known as having a flexible labour force – it means you've got to be able to adapt to do the job of anybody who isn't there. The result of this is that if I start on the machine which is my rightful job, I'm relieved to be doing my own familiar work, but if I have to replace someone who is sick, I feel less pleased. On my own job I can fit in a certain amount of reading in the course of the day, but if I'm doing somebody else's it absorbs all my time.

'My own job gives a certain amount of time to me as a shop steward. There are complaints to look into, a foreman may come and ask if it's all right to move someone. I'm the safety representative, so people who'd be under other stewards normally gravitate to me if safety's the issue. Each of these problems may be the cause of a minor or major dispute. If you just read the press, you might have the impression that armies of workers are always just waiting to walk out because of something trivial. That isn't my experience. There's nearly always been something nagging for a long time, and what sparks off a dispute might be only a displacement of something much deeper. Somehow human emotions are very close to the surface in situations which are so denying to humanity; a resentment is always smouldering which is sometimes scarcely conscious. Well, it's bound to come out in some way. You don't have to wring the last drop of physical strength out of a man to be exploiting him. The conditions of work might look better than they were. They are better, no doubt. But that doesn't mean that, therefore, everything is all right. Capitalism has been cleaned up, the PR men have all been busy. Does that mean we should all go to work with cheery grateful smiles on our faces?

'Conflict and dispute are absolutely inherent in the whole process. You try, as a shop steward, to nip trivial conflict in the bud. Let me give you an example of the kind of thing that happens. It shows how small things get magnified, and if they aren't seen to, grow into something serious.

'Fred was sixty-three, and he was working with a Worksave, that's a small electric truck with a forklift on the back. It is pedestrian-operated. Well, the floor is concrete and pitted with holes, and Fred felt they were getting deeper. His truck carried

eighteen engine blocks, that is a ton, on each load. The two
wheels on the truck are close together, so if a wheel falls into one
of the holes, the steering arm turns violently, and you could
have your stomach severely wrenched. Fred complained first of
all to his local foreman, then to his own steward. Then he tried
to draw in the other truck operators to attract someone's
attention to the danger. He complained to me. I asked him what
he'd achieved so far. He said, "Nothing." People had been to
look at them, and then gone away again. Nothing had been
done. In my rôle as safety representative, I went to see the block
manager. I got fobbed off. I thought, Well, they've had enough
notice, and therefore it's time to get definitive action. I asked the
manager when he thought it could be dealt with. He said,
"Forty-eight hours." Nothing. I went back again. I said if the
holes were not filled in within the next twenty-four hours
there'd be a stoppage, or he'd be getting a claim for
compensation for an accident. It still wasn't sorted out. Next
day Fred came and said, "Shall I start work?" I said, "Yes, but
steer right round the holes, even if it takes longer and you make
yourself unpopular. If anyone challenges you, you can tell them
to come and have a word with me." He went to his truck, picked
the weight up, went to move off. The wheel went down a hole,
and the handle pulled him over and his stomach was wrenched.
We left the truck where it was and stopped the line. Fred was
taken to the surgery, and I went to see the manager. I said, "I
told you five days ago you'd have either a stoppage or a claim.
You ought to have seen to it, because now you've got both."
The holes were filled in within four hours. Fred never worked
again. He got a few hundred pounds in compensation.'
JS: 'How do you see the rôle of shop steward?'
DEREK JENKINS: 'Well, for the most part, he is a mouthpiece of
the men, but then he is also a leader. These two aspects might
seem contradictory. The shop steward is only as strong as the
men he represents. To get stronger, he has to work on their
militancy, and that's where the leadership comes in. You must
have your own aims and ideals, your own sense of what you
should do; but at the same time you're subservient to the
members. Perhaps I should say you clarify for them some of the
implications of decisions made collectively, you explain and
expound ideas. But as soon as you put your own ideals above
theirs, you begin to fade out as a steward. Not many who have

been stewards go back on the section; they tend to leave the factory or take promotion. It's a very subtle game. You're on a tightrope. Your position as shop steward puts you into a different relationship to people from the one you have as an operative. It's a lonely job in some ways: they relate to you in your rôle rather than personally. It can be lonely, because people come to you to complain most of the time, either when the complaint is justified, or simply because they feel in a complaining mood. You don't see people at their best. You see them when they're vulnerable or aggressive – it quite often comes to the same thing, of course. You have to ask yourself what you can do as a shop steward rather than as a human being; not that those two things are incompatible, but it is imprisoning, the concept the men have of you. There is a lot of interaction between the steward and the others, but a lot of it is at an official level. You can't develop a personal relationship with everybody. You represent fifty men; and then I'm safety rep. for about a hundred. Officially, the shop steward should be only the second line of complaint. A man should see his foreman first, but this doesn't always happen. It depends on the accessibility of the individual. Then there are things which you have to complain about on the men's behalf: for instance, if the fans aren't working. That can be dangerous, but it's not the kind of thing that individuals tend to notice.

'When I look back to when I first started in the factory, I find it hard to believe that the person I was then has anything to do with the way I feel now. In fact there is very little connection between them. I was totally entrenched in the factory world. I'm not now. Looking at it now, it seems inevitable that there should be some collapse or breakdown. I underwent a great personal change. I don't believe in the old values I had, and the new ones are slowly squeezing me out of the factory. The way I was living, I used to work nights because of the pressures on me, the need to live in a certain way; in the end, far from achieving what I thought I wanted, it affected my marriage and eventually destroyed it. After that, I started looking more critically at things. I don't say that consciousness can only come to you through some traumatic experience like that, the shock of having your whole world shattered; but that's what happened in my case. I'd always been fairly radical, but in a far less conscious way; until then it was just something I sensed and felt. But after

that, I started thinking more deeply about other things. Now I
no longer want to live in the factory situation. I want to be able
to relate to people on a deeper, closer level than I can at work
now. I think it is the fear of change that inhibits many people
from taking a more radical view of their rôle and position. It's
not that people are happy the way things are; on the whole
they're not, the way they talk about their lives. But they're afraid
that change must mean loss. Typical conservative attitude. But
the sort of passive resentment at work, this also enters into other
areas of their life. It can poison their relationships at home, their
marriage. A lot of people really have faith in the big win, the
providential escape, they actually believe in it. But fear is the
strongest factor, the feeling that they are individually isolated,
the worry that there aren't millions of others who feel the same.
If the change actually occurred, they wouldn't see anything in
the same light again, ever. You don't, you can't go back. I've felt
it. Everything has a new perspective, a new shape. The thing is,
the excitement of change is tremendous. I think that is the
tragedy of a lot of working people. The fear of loss of familiar
things outweighs the appeal of wanting to understand and
dominate your environment, through becoming conscious of it.
If that does happen, you don't have to rely on a sullen kind of
small triumph over authority, nicking something here, taking a
few minutes off there, getting something for nothing somewhere
else; cheating and fiddling are paltry satisfactions compared
with the feeling of power you get – not power over other people,
but over your own destiny – when you begin to figure out what it
is all about.

   'I left school at fifteen-and-a-half. My father was in the
Marines. He worked in this factory himself when it was a much
smaller concern, so it was more or less the thing for me to do to
come and work here when I left school. The first two years I
didn't mind, because there was conscription, and I knew I'd get
called up. I went in the RAF, and stayed there five years. That
was largely a waste of time. When I came home I went back to
the factory. It seemed a harmless thing to do: you go there
temporarily, but that is a terrible trap. You stay a bit longer, you
tell yourself you've got all the time in the world. You might look
round for something else, but then before you know where you
are, you're married and you have a wife and children to support.
And time, that had seemed your friend, becomes a deadly

enemy, has you in its power. Not only that; but once you've worked in a factory, you start to have a past, and this then determines your future. It's another weight that adds to the pressure to keep you where you are.

'I wouldn't recommend a personal crisis to everyone. I mean, the same thing embitters some people. It can squeeze the humanity out of them. I've been lucky. For me it released all sorts of abilities I never knew I had. I'm doing an Open University course at the moment. I wouldn't have dared do that before; especially working full time, being a shop steward and managing to spend time with the family as well.

'I earn £68 a week, gross.* I take home £52 a week. Out of that food takes about £25 a week for the five of us. I'm lucky with the house: I bought it sixteen years ago, so my mortgage repayment is very low – only £25 a month. Otherwise I don't know what I'd do. My gross pay is slightly below the national average. So much for the greedy car workers I'm always reading about. The stereotype developed in the 1950s and it has stuck. The media know nothing and care less. Full household expenses take up about £30 a week. We haven't had a holiday for years. There are the two older children and the baby. After heating and lighting, that leaves about £12–£14 a week for clothing, travel, all incidentals, any excursions, children's needs, furniture, household goods. I don't think you could say we lead an extravagant life. Quite the reverse. When you think of the work I do, I make eighty manifolds a week. They're worth £50 each, when you've allowed for the cost of the raw materials. That means they're worth £4,000 a week. Now if I'm getting £68, I can only wonder where the other £3,932 goes. A week.'

4

LONDON AND BEYOND

HACKNEY IS THE kind of area that people want to get out of; and it has already suffered too many departures. It bears the demoralizing stigma of a place from which most of those who could go have already gone. It isn't simply that there is a waiting

* In October 1977.

list of more than 12,000 families for council accommodation. It is a testimony and a defining edge to the success of the thousands who have made their way and moved on. Their success would be meaningless if Hackney were an agreeable place in which to live; and this is why, however much compensatory money is poured in, it must still remain as a place of deterrence. It isn't really a community now, and many of those who live there do so grudgingly and without commitment. A residue of despair and anger stays with those who are forced to remain.

In some parts of the borough, there is to be seen a sad wreckage of people who, in summer, spend their day out of doors, in the open spaces and parks, in precincts and courtyards; and they talk freely about their lives, a sometimes almost incoherent recital of pain and loss. People brought up in communal poverty have lived to see that poverty retreat, leaving them with nothing but a private grief which they seem not quite to know what to do with. So they share it, as they once shared everything; only now, they have to offer it to indifferent strangers.

Sometimes it seems to me that the air is full of the telling of secrets, the admission of long-suppressed shame and disgrace, confessions and avowals, the concealment of which is no longer necessary. People offer each other their lives; not to those who care, but to people met by chance in a pub corner or a park bench. The narrative is of course partly a process of unburdening, a sad reflection that so many of us lack people in whom we can confide; but it is also an obscure attempt to expiate. The telling of secrets is somehow a kind of reparation, a need to expunge guilt. The need for secrecy in the past implied deference to a sort of morality, however oppressive it may have been; and the ease with which everything can be told now suggests that those values have quite gone: the guilt comes from a dark feeling that we have acquiesced in their passing without any replacement.

A children's playground on the Kingsmead Estate. There is a paddling pool, a sandpit and some grey metal climbing frames. The mothers sit under the shelter of a kind of wooden pagoda, watching their children. An older woman sits apart from the others. She doesn't even look at me before she starts to speak.

'I come here sometimes and look at the kids. I think of my own. I brought them up on my own, boy and a girl. We lived in

Nisbet House. It was terrible how I struggled to work for them. I got up at six every morning for fifteen years to clean out the pub shithouses. Every morning they disgusted me. Then I worked in a school canteen, I had a machine at home. I did anything to get money. My husband committed suicide after the war. It just unbalanced him. He was never strong, but that was the finish of him. He was in a prisoner-of-war camp in Japan. He wasn't the man who went away, I knew it the day he came home. It was like living with somebody else. I had two husbands; the same man, but two husbands. He cut his throat in the end, and left me with two babies. Sheila was only three months old, Alan eighteen months. I hated him when he came back; something had gone from him. When the war started, we'd only been married six months. He was lovely then. I used to wish he hadn't come back at all. I found him with his throat cut. A Saturday afternoon. I can still see the blood after thirty years.

'I went to live with my mother for a little while, then I got the flat down here, and this is where they grew up. I'd've done anything for them, my kids. I tell you, you wouldn't believe what I did for them. I worked in a pub. I wasn't bad-looking; some of the men used to fancy their chance with me. I made them pay, I wasn't ashamed of it. I never got mixed up with them, any of them, even when they wanted me to go and live with them. One of them broke into my mum's flat one night, I went for him with a carving knife.

'I gave my kids everything. I protected them. Pair of swine they've turned out an' all, God forgive me for saying it. I made a vow I wouldn't let them suffer. . . . He started getting mixed up with drugs. He was a wanderer. I got him set up in a little shop, clothes, got his stock, paid a year's rent. He gave half of it away to his friends, he laid in bed all morning. In a year 4,000 quid's worth of stuff had gone down the drain. He went abroad, I didn't hear from him for over a year. He could've been dead. I could have been dead. And Sheila, she married a bloke worked in the Electricity Board, they went to live in Manchester. She's got a lovely house, only she don't like anybody in it, especially me. Why are they like this? It makes me bitter. I wish to God I'd never stayed by them. I should've gone off and looked after myself a bit more. I've got a sister, I see her twice a week. She's a widow, all she can talk about is, "My poor old Wal, what a terrible life he had." They didn't. They had no kids, they were

off having holidays in Italy before anybody else even heard of
such things. Selfish. She don't know what suffering is. But I do. I
have done all my life. Even now, I don't know the people who
live round me. People's changed.'

Summer afternoon in Victoria Park. A row of green metal
benches overlooking the flower beds. The sky has clouded over,
and, little by little, the people who have been sitting out get up
and depart, buttoning their coats and pulling cardigans closer
round them. An old woman with an ancient greasy hat and a
hatpin, and a fur tippet, lingers in the rising wind. She turns
away as eddies of dust are swept from the dry earth in the
flowerbeds. 'I was out all day yesterday, twelve o'clock till nine
at night. I brought me dinner and me tea, and I was here all day.
I'm going home now. I'd got me tea for today, only it's turned
colder. . . . I lost my husband in January. I can't get over it. . . .
We done everything together, forty-seven years. He always
brought me a cup of tea and biscuits in bed every morning all
them years. I woke up one morning and said, "Hey, come on,
where's me tea and biscuits?" I poked him in the back, but he
was dead. I can't believe it. I'll go home and watch the television,
I still talk to him sometimes, I forget he's not there. I like to
watch *Crossroads*, *Coronation Street*. I like a Western. Not love
stories. I had enough love to last me. I've had seven children,
and none of them ever come near me unless they want
something. Now I've got nothing I don't see them at all. I come
from a big family myself. I don't know where they are. I
shouldn't know where to look for them. Reckon I'd have to dig
for most of 'em.'

A bus stop in Queensbridge Road. A woman, perhaps in her
late fifties, with a bundle of washing in a blue plastic bag. She
looks thin and gaunt. Her hair, dyed black, is swept in a beehive
style, a fashion of perhaps twenty years ago.

'I'm going to my sister's in Leytonstone, if this bus ever
comes.' If London Transport will be kind enough to take me
there. I go to her most days. She's out to work, but it makes a
change for me. I can't stand it here. I'm on the fourteenth floor.
I do the tidying up for her, meet my grand-daughter out of
school, then it's time to come home. Home, I only sleep here. I
get so lonely, I dread the evenings. I'm a widow. Two years ago I
lost my husband. He went to Spain, lorry driver. I was expecting
him home on the Sunday evening. The doorbell went. I

thought, That's him, forgot his key. Two policemen stood there.
They said he'd been killed. A drunk driver mounted the
pavement where he was standing, just talking, and he was killed
outright. It cost me £800 to go out there and fetch his body
home, I'm still in debt to the family. They rallied round, and
between them they lent me the money. I had to pay £10 for
customs clearance. And than they brought him to the
international mortuary in Bayswater. He laid there ten days. At
£10 a day. I knew nothing about that till I got a bill for £100.
And there was no insurance, nothing I could claim. I don't
know how I lived through it. I tried to commit suicide twice, I
was going to throw myself over the balcony. I was in hospital
nine months. I'm still on tablets, even now. I still daren't go and
look over the balcony. I'm just beginning to get out for the first
time. Only I can't settle to anything. Restless. I'd like to move.
I've been offered several places by the council, but I don't like
any of them. . . . I went away for the Jubilee, I couldn't stand it
here. I went to see my son in Northampton. He's buying his own
house, Development Corporation house. They've a lovely
shopping centre there. I like that. There's nothing round here
now, it's not Hackney any more. All the people we used to know,
they've all gone. All these that are here now, I don't know where
they come from, who they are. They move into these blocks, they
don't pay the rent, three months later they've done a moonlight.
I liked it the way it was. These flats used to be lovely. When I
moved in. That's been seven years ago. But since then, they've
just gone to pieces. I don't know why people don't look after the
places they live in, but they don't. It's them that's got to live
there.'

People offer up their lives, without reticence, to strangers.
Griefs and fears are divulged as a matter of the most casual
conversation – a sad autism of isolation and hopelessness,
which can be interrupted by something as trivial as the arrival of
a bus. When the bus came, we didn't even sit together. An older
woman sat beside her, and before I got off, I heard some of the
same story being told again. Our pain, our solitude, even our
deepest relationships are like everything else in our lives – fit
only for throwaway small talk. They are of a piece with our
absence of function, our wasted energies, our exploited
vulnerabilities. All the official rhetoric about a caring society
and the worth of the individual really refers to our value only as

consuming units, as disgraced and powerless atoms of humanity offered a spurious healing through the products and fantasies of capitalism for the profit of someone.

It is early evening in a deserted pub which is intended for crowds: Tammy Wynette on the juke-box, an expanse of carpet, red leatherette seats, many of which have been slashed; red lights, dusty wrought iron and a smell of yesterday's smoke and beer. In this pub, those who are reluctant to go home after work linger into the evening: those who have no one to go home to, those who want to delay the encounter with a failing relationship or the clamour of children. A scaffolder in his late thirties is sitting on his own at the bar; he is drinking quickly. On his fingers are tattooed LOVE and HATE. On the back of his left hand there is a tattoo of a wreath.

'See that? That's for this girl I was going with. No, she's not dead, but she might as well be. She was a waitress in a hotel in the West End, Irish girl. She worked late, she worked so fucking late she should have been a millionaire. So I followed her one day, and she was going to this flat, and I found her stuffed so full of black flesh there was sparks coming from her arsehole. I could've broken her fucking neck. I wouldn't share a woman with anybody. I'm proud of my body, she didn't know when she was well off. I've always done judo, karate, weight-lifting. I think your body is a machine and you ought to look after it, same as you'd look after a motorbike or a car. . . . I'd just come out the army. I got a dishonourable discharge. Me and a couple of mates, we jumped this guy on our way back to camp. In court we said he was a queer, he made a suggestion to my mate Jimmy, asked him if he fancied some navy-cake. We hurt him a bit. He lost some teeth, maybe an eye or two.

'I think the army is the greatest life a man can have. When I came out of the army, everybody thought the army was a big joke. I couldn't believe it. It was like all the men in the world had had their bollocks twisted off, they were all poncing about and rippling their arses and wearing high heels. It's sick. It's sick to see men doing that.

'I was born just before the war. We lived in rooms in Silvertown. You could go on to the roof and you could see all these silver cones, searchlights, slicing through the sky, and then you heard a burst of ack-ack fire. My mother's brother was in the army; he came home on leave, it was the hero's return every time. We had his picture in uniform, in the living room. We had this big picture of the Virgin Mary, great big thing in a fancy frame, and this picture of Frank used to be stuck in the corner of the frame, right where her tits would have been if she hadn't been who she was. I always thought of him like the Sacred Heart. The last time he came home on leave, my old lady had a what do you call it? – a premonition. She asked him what he'd like for his last meal, before he went back, and he said, "Steak and chips." And she went to this butcher's shop and she kept him talking while I nicked a fucking great lump of steak off a tray. And we sat and watched Frank enjoy it while he ate the fucking lot. We never saw him again. His things, letters, kitbag, came back in a few months. I kept them in a cupboard. That cupboard was a fucking shrine to me.'

Mrs Hurst is thirty-four. She has three children: a boy twelve, girls of nine and seven. She has just divorced her second husband. She draws £40 a week from Social Security and £4.50 Child Benefit.* Rent for her maisonette, including rates, hot water and heating, comes to £14 a week. She works occasionally, mostly helping out people she knows, or short periods in cleaning jobs, usherette in a Lucky Seven Bingo hall, market stall. More often than not there is something to stretch the allowance from what she still calls 'the Assistance'.

She lives in a block of maisonettes, one of a series of blocks set at right angles to each other and fronted by areas of grass. The façade of each block presents an expanse of glass and blue brick, gently sloping, to form a pyramidal shape. Access to the maisonettes is via deep concrete chasms of the stairwells. Inside, the long narrow corridors are flanked by a series of wood and reinforced glass doors with metal fittings. Small children drive up and down the corridors on tricycles or skateboards, occasionally colliding with a pram or running into the back of someone's legs.

During the daytime, the blocks are amost deserted. A few women – those who have very young babies or who are too sick to work – stand in the doorways in house-coats and fleecy slippers, collecting and diffusing information from milkmen, creditors, social workers. The men who are out of work do not

* In November 1977.

stay around the flats. There are few tenants on this estate of retirement age.

It isn't until half past three that the first children come home. Those who have no key gather in the stairwells and forecourts. Soon after five o'clock, a tide of women from the fur, dress and leather factories engulfs the main road. They are met by a movement of children from the opposite direction, so that it looks like an eager reunion of people after a long separation. But it is brief and interrogative. 'What have you got?' 'What can I have?' 'Will you give me 10p?' The children run off towards the shops, while the women are enfolded by the high silent walls of the stairways. They cast a glance at the sentinels in the doorways who haven't been to work, and wonder perhaps where they got the money from for the new three-piece suite or the canopied fourposter that was being moved in last week.

The children spend their 10 or 20p in a few minutes. Only two of them are allowed in the shop at any time, as a precaution against shoplifting. They buy crisps, Coke, chocolate, chips, pie-mash.

Later, the men return. Most still use public transport; a few are on bicycles, and some park their cars, in defiance of a council order, on the muddy and already disfigured green. By six-thirty, there is a light on in almost every flat. The block was built in 1970, and is not insulated against noise; and the warring sounds from each living place are the only protection each family has against its neighbours. From the corridors you can hear television, a transistor, records, children crying, couples quarrelling, dogs barking; all the sounds of people long accustomed to each other, reconstituting their relationship at the end of a day.

The front of each block is broken only by the rubbish-chute — a huge metal container, impregnable as a tank, and described by the council in its *No Parking* notice as a 'refuse chamber'. Every day it overflows with waste: bottles and jars, of milk, sauce, salad cream, pickles, jam; tins of beans, fish, Fray Bentos steak pies, fruit, spaghetti rings, Spam, vegetables; hardened slices of bread fanning from their waxed paper, silver foil trays from the take-away, egg boxes, plastic containers, dispensers of foams, creams, oils and polish; nappies, tights, old clothing — torn jeans, overalls, dresses, odd shoes recently out of fashion; pieces of broken furniture — legs of coffee tables; transistors, broken cassettes, toys and dolls, gnawed and broken bones, rejected ornaments and pictures – a seascape or a little boy with glassy tears. Outside the block there are some abandoned cars, the chassis robbed of anything that could be used or sold. The road glitters with broken glass, splinters from shattered wind-screens, shards of brown beer bottles. The stairways of the flats are disturbed by constant minor whirlwinds of dust and crisp packets, lolly sticks, sweet wrappings, Kleenex, fag ends, bus tickets, pieces of newspaper, the dented silver cylinders of Coke and Cresta cans.

The dereliction outside is only a more extreme form of processes that are going on inside. Mrs Hurst's youngest child sits on the floor in a litter of broken plastic, dismembered dolls, ducks and elephants, moulded plastic trucks and cars; wheels, guns and spent caps, soldiers and tanks, the broken skeleton of a Chopper, comics, racing cars, rubber swords, cowboy outfits, board games, defaced books, broken pencils, leaky felt-tips, playing cards, dominoes. A bird twitters in its cage. They had tropical fish, but someone forgot to feed them; they have had hamsters, gerbils, mice, but none of them lasted long. Alsatians and Labradors roam the greens outside; they suffer endless torment from children, until they finally bite somebody and have to be put down.

Almost everything in these new flats has already been used up; has met a more or less violent end. The flats are littered with the debris of articles bought in appeasement of children, while the adults pursue their own dreams, contained in the promises of a life of leisure and romance, clothes, beaches and holidays, hi-fis, cassettes, furniture, light fittings, jewellery, ornaments; the kaleidoscope of prizes, rewards and consolations.

The ice-cream vans follow each other in daily procession round the estate, with their discordant snatches of abbreviated tunes. In the evenings, teenagers – boys with pierced ears and girls impassive as china dolls on high shoes – stand in the light from shop windows, waiting endlessly; waiting for something to happen or fashion to change.

In these places, a hypothecated future has caught up with many of the still young couples; the mortgaged time to come has arrived, eroded and diminished with having been too long anticipated and prematurely enjoyed.

Mrs Hurst, like many of the people who live here, is a victim.

She is not so much a victim of poverty, as of contamination from an ideology of a corrupting and dehumanized affluence. She and her children, while among the poorest, do not want for food or clothing. They have shelter and warmth. Neither do they lack entertainment or pleasure. Mrs Hurst feels the inadequacy of the rôle thrust upon her; but the only expression of that feeling which is allowed an outlet is through restlessness and longing that are not only unsatisfied, but not even defined. She hates the place where she lives. She says she has no friends among the people around her. She feels she can trust no one. She wants something better. She hates the blacks because they appear to get everything while she gets nothing. Her aspirations can go in only one direction – into things, and the money to obtain them. In this quest, other people, all other people, even at times her children, are only obstacles in her way.

The discontent, caused as much by her passive dependency on things as by an absence of them, and made keener by the lack of any energizing involvement in her own life, can imagine no other palliative than an even greater dependency than exists already. Mrs Hurst has no choice but to hope for a widening of those narrow and restricting choices that are at the root of the dissatisfaction and the unhappiness. It was from Mrs Hurst that I first heard 'All the layabouts and scroungers, you know what they want to do, bring back the workhouses.' Her anguish at her own lack of function and purpose is nowhere recognized.

This is where the violent society is born. Childhood becomes an apprenticeship in the destruction of things. It is an irony more than linguistic that the word consumption, which not many years ago would have meant to the people in Hackney terror at the erosion of the human body from within, should have come to serve as a quite neutral term to describe the way we live now, the laying waste of our own artefacts. We are dying of a different sort of consumption. Things are torn apart, while we seek to extract their perfect essence; a process of gutting, of ripping open; and the perishability of the product and the desperation of the human being meet at a hollow core of emptiness and frustration. These streets carry away the remains of these sterile encounters; constantly cleaned rivers of waste, a labour of Hercules for the dustcarts, street cleaners, cleansing vans and the carts of those who live off waste products.

In an economy which depends so heavily upon the rapid

erosion of the value of the things it creates, it is not easy to set limits to the destructive forces unleashed by that process. Other areas of social life become deeply penetrated by the values that underlie the cycle of creation, distribution and consumption. The individual as competitive consumer is violent by his very existence: it is a legitimation, the apotheosis of a need to destroy.

And the morbid and introspective fury with which we fall upon things is not contained – particularly when they are the object of all our hopes and aspirations; but spills out against other people, aggression and violence against an abject and universally disparaged humanity, which is seen as the only real impediment to our access to a fuller, more real life.

When material well-being – something it is well within our capacity to assure everyone – is indivisible from a system of values which exalts things and diminishes people, it seems of itself to legitimate anger and violence. Despite this, we are always being exhorted to believe that only more of this, on the same terms, will solve our problems.

In a society in which Mrs Hurst was offered a rôle and function, she would not consider herself poor. Here, she can be nothing else, because we have no reason for living other than the goad to get richer. If Mrs Hurst were no longer poor, what would that make of everybody else; all of us, the social workers and the concerned administrators, as well as the go-getters and the self-avowed rich? The spectre of poverty paraded on behalf of Mrs Hurst serves first of all as a means of justifying the pursuit of redundant personal wealth everywhere else; it legitimates the values of extravagance, waste and self-indulgence by which we measure the success of our lives. More than this: it links even the contesting and the concerned to the *status quo*, locked as they are in sclerotic attitudes to a poor who have vanished, attitudes that have little to do with the real problems that confront us. By floating the idea of what poverty is, by evading definitions, by setting it free and calling it relative, its perpetuation is ensured; and thereby a justification is created for an eternity of striving beyond satiation for everybody else, a sterile process of rewards and incentives increasingly dislocated from any feeling of human achievement, which in the end become their own object, a potlatch of superfluity, a celebration of our own capacity to consume. And this is offered to us as an ideal, the best prospect we have for social cohesion, peace and stability. The triumph of these values is our model for the future, the most positive hope that can be held out to us if growth and expansion can be achieved. This, we are told, is what we can expect, if the optimists are right. This in itself seems to me to be an eloquent enough argument for radical change, without even considering the possibility of what might happen in the event of this tawdry prize eluding us.

Jim is in his early thirties; he drives a refrigerated container lorry, distributing dairy products from France to various parts of the British Isles. He is restless, unattached. On the rare occasions when he is at home, he stays with his mother in a flat in Stoke Newington.

'I spend hours on the road, a lot of them alone. I always pick up hitch-hikers if they're on their own. You can see them standing on the edge of the roads leading to the motorways, kids running away. You can always tell them, there's a look about them, hope, it's really pathetic. Some of them are really young, I wouldn't give them a lift if I thought they were too young, but you can't always tell. They're full of what they're going to do when they get to London or wherever, their heads are just full of dreams.

'I don't mind my job, it keeps me alert, occupied. I was going to say it stops me thinking about things, but that's not right. It makes me think about everything under the sun; I ought to say it saves me from having to work out what I'm going to do about them.

'Nothing is quite what it seems to be. We live in a society of packaging, gift-wrapping. It promises you things it can't deliver. It's a deceiver. It's a bit like all the women I've had over the years, it's whoring developed to a fine art. Nothing it gives you has anything of the value it's supposed to have. I'm not against materialism, far from it. I like comfort and I like to enjoy myself. Only the heaps of junk we make. Why do so many thousand people die on the road every year, and so many more end up mutilated? Believe me, I've seen them on the autoroutes, such a waste of lives on the roads. Is it because the judgment of an individual isn't perfect? Yes, but it's also because the craft they travel in are so fragile. There's no doubt you could cut road deaths drastically if the cars were made so that they didn't fall to pieces after three or four years. Only what would we do if everybody had a car that lasted for years, and nobody needed a new one every five minutes? It's for the sake of the market, not for people; and everybody who works on that, the whole work force is a part of it, accepts it as a normal way to live. It's like everything else – there's the fashion industry telling you to throw away everything you've got and start again. . . . You think everything's changing, it's dynamic, only it isn't, it's stagnant. You get the illusion of progress through superficial things. It's like the latest craze, the newest sensation – they're all the same in the end. It makes no real difference to your life. When I'm on the road, I listen to the radio a lot, French and Belgian and Dutch and German, and even though I can't understand them, they're all the same as ours. All the songs are full of love and happiness and euphoria; all the ads use voices that are excited and hysterical and urgent. But the people you meet, they're all full of misery and grumbles and hate.

'People talk about standard of living. It isn't really that, that only describes the way you live, a way of life determined by capitalist distribution of resources. They talk about it as though it were life itself. It isn't. It's just that nobody has the courage to say that all the things we regard as so important are just drugs. Things that fall to bits, objects that fail to deliver the promise they're sold with. I'm not pessimistic. People can only go on being deceived for so long. They will demand a change in the end. It's not that people shouldn't have a decent living; only this isn't it, the way things are made and marketed: it's the deceiver's smile, the whore's leer. I'm not afraid of change. What have we got to lose, except the pre-packed cancer-bearing chemicals we use instead of food?'

In the kitchen of a flat in a new eight-storey block, three women sit with the door of the gas oven open, drinking tea and enjoying each other's company in the late winter afternoon. The only light in the room is from the bluish light from the stove and the fading light of the sunset against the windows. Condensation runs down the glass, rusting the metal frames and dampening the atmosphere.

'I'm scared to let the kids come home on their own, these dark nights, especially. There's been a man talking to some of them at the school gates. In a green van.'

'Yeah, I've heard that. Terrible. Just let him lay a finger on any of my kids, and see what he gets.'

'I'd slit him from his throat to his crutch if he done anything to one of mine.'

'Well we've got one in the block opposite us. He'd been showing himself to kids. Some of the blokes went round and gave him a good hiding.'

'Christ girl, what a waste. I wish it'd been me.'

'No, it ain't funny, Jean.'

One of the items on the news had been about whooping cough and how it is on the increase. All the women realized that they had not had their children immunized. Although the risk to their children's life is far greater from whooping cough than assaults, the chance of it being infinitely greater, what concerns them is something you can ascribe malevolence to, not the fact that disease is a far greater killer. When the children come in, flushed and cold and laughing, they have crossed two dangerous roads. Impersonal forces of destruction are not interesting. It is only against humanity that they can define themselves. As soon as the children come in, they are given money to go to the shop. They run out of the door and into the courtyard, past the graffitti which say *Gary is a cunt*, *NF OK* and *Wogs Out*, into the bright shop that is in part a kind of canteen, where they buy Coke and crisps and chocolate. And the women in the flat can resume their talk, the compelling gossip about who is out to cheat, damage or destroy them; and at the same time, they gain a little more respite from the clamour of the children. It is a scene of caricature, but with a bitter and sad undertone: that the sweetness of being together should be so imbued with menace and violence. They comply with their diminished mothering rôle, but at the same time wait for something disastrous to occur as a result of it; but then, they can only imagine attacking people, not the situation that has brought them to this.

A factory in a once industrial part of London. Now there are acres of factories for sale, rows of agents' placards. Some of the ruined buildings and neglected sites have been taken over and used for warehousing; geometrical new hangars are full of cosmetics, wine, stationery, imported consumer goods, and only a handful of people are employed to guard and distribute them.

The factory of Plastic Alloys International is an agglom-
eration of buildings, assembled piecemeal – sheds, prefabs,
wooden huts, brick barrack-like structures, and even incor-
porating an old Gothic chapel. It is late afternoon on a
December day, raining hard. The spaces and yards between the
various buildings are muddy and waterlogged. Powerful electric
lamps over the buildings shine on rain-soaked walls and
dripping eaves, the silver splash of rain into puddles that are
discoloured by the powder from the rubber compounds, which
is everywhere: a fine white dust that forms into milky rubbery
pools all over the factory yards. Inside, people are protected
from the white powder by visors, ear muffs, boiler suits. In the
yards there are black polythene bags full of the finished products
– piping for washing machines, grommets, bungs, rubber rings,
hot-water bottles, pharmaceutical rubberware, rubber fitments
for cars, household appliances.

Grace Ryan, in her forties, has worked for the company for
twenty-six years.

'The women here are on piece-work. In some ways, the men
have it better now, because they are on a target system, which
means that although some of them may have to work harder
than others, the wages are basically the same. But with the
women on piece-work, it's graded, with 100 supposed to be the
average; only it isn't really, it takes years to achieve that. You
start at 80 and it goes up to 120 maximum. The target system is
less of a rat-race, it's more of a collective situation, everybody's
together. In the women's department, we move from job to job.
It makes for a slight variation in the monotony, but we turn out
so many different kinds of product that it can take years to reach
a performance of 100. We can't get a majority reaching it, so that
means it isn't average. The women stand and their job is to push
a fly press, or else they work at the Norton machines. They are
like robots. You see their foot on the treadle, or their hand
moving to and fro, they look like an extension of their machine.
And the point about this work is that there is no sharing, you are
isolated, alone with your machine. Just you and it. And the noise
level is very high, so in fact you can't really communicate with
anybody. You are in a self-contained competitive tension, trying
to make as many of these things as you can. The machines make
work easier, but they separate workers from each other. Since I
started conditions have improved; that is, they've changed.

Where once a lot of people might have been needed to do a job which one machine does now, at least they used to share in a single activity, and this did a lot for communication, for pooling your resources, for having a laugh – human contact. These machines put a stop to some of that. Everything is safer, but the job is hardly more pleasant. In fact, human contact is harder to achieve. You produce more, you get more money; but that isn't exactly a guarantee of happiness, if the way people talk is anything to go by.

'We are gradually working towards equal pay. A lot of the men don't like it. Their ego is hurt. It seems to them to be denigrating their male superiority. Their pride is wounded when they see women, who've always had such a subordinate rôle, suddenly capable of earning as much as they do. It hits at their traditional rôle as breadwinner, it undermines them. This has happened to a lot of men in recent years; they feel that the rise of women has been at their expense. Sometimes you think there's bound to be a backlash; they'll have to get tough, prove they're still men; want to go and fight a war.

'I've worked here since 1951. I come in at eight o'clock, clock in, go into my department, change my shoes, put my overall on, look at the book to see what job I'm on today. We rotate, you see – like machines – so that we're on different machines. At the moment I'm working an old-fashioned cropping machine, it crops out 1 bung at a time, whereas some of the new machines will crop out 16 or 25 at a time. Then they have to go for inspection, and then they go to be washed and packed. All the products are rubber or synthetic rubber. A square of rubber comes to me, a heat it's called, I cut it in half, wet it and put it under my single cutter, crop it out by pressing a foot pedal; it falls down a chute and into a bin, which fills up as you go through the morning. The machine I'm on is seventy years old. There was an old lady who was here, and she was using the same machine during the First World War; although, to be fair, they are modernizing now and installing a lot of new machines which are more efficient. And that is it. That is my work. We have a tea-break from 10.25 to 10.45, dinner from 1.00 to 1.30, although most have an hour for dinner. I finish at four.

'Piece-work makes workers selfish. A lot of them would work right through the dinner hour and the tea-breaks. You have to see that doesn't happen, because it would make a difference to the piece-work grades. They don't like it. Or perhaps if the machine guard falls off and has to be fitted, they'd rather work without the guard, you have to stop them. That's the incentive, you see, to risk your safety, to jeopardize other people's work levels. It encourages you to compete with the machine. If you're not careful you find yourself becoming like the machine. You imitate it, cold unfeeling lumps of metal. The tea-breaks are precious anyway. They're really our chance for a bit of comradeship. There is a social club which I do go to but most people's idea of a night out is not to go back to their place of work. They feel they spend enough time there, without going back if they don't have to.

'People are conned into thinking money is everything. There's no doubt that piece-work makes a slave of you. You're tied to the machine just as if you were chained to it. You think of nothing else but the number you can crop out during the day. If I say it tends to dehumanize you, it is only a tendency, because I think that the really marvellous thing is that we do really resist, somewhere inside us, our humanity is stronger than the power of any machines; but sometimes it's touch and go. It makes you not want to think of anything else. If you do eight hours a day on slogging repetitive work, well you go on doing it in your sleep. All people want to talk about when they come in to work is, Did you see this or that on TV? Who won how much at Bingo? You know what it is – the machine makes you passive and lethargic in your mind. You suspend your life while you're at work, and then an awful lot of your leisure is like a repeat performance of work, part of the same process. I'm sometimes afraid that the leisure revolution is going to be a tranquillized half-life. Already a lot of people are never really awake; not awake to the real possibilities, the way life could be.

'You hear some of them say, "I'm voting National Front next time." You have to argue with them. I say, "Yes, it's blacks today, it'll be trade unionists tomorrow." I brought them one of the National Front manifestos to show them. There was one woman, she waved a newspaper under my nose about a gang of kids from Brixton who'd terrorized people on the tube. I looked at it and said, "There's nothing here about them being black." She said, "Oh yes they are. Brixton. It speaks for itself." Anyway, next day it actually said in the paper they were white. So I took it in and showed her. She said, "Huh." She wouldn't

accept it. She didn't want to believe it. You can't argue with
reason. There's a wish to see what they want to see, and nothing
will shake it, unless you can show them that you believe with as
much passion as they do. I think they do feel a bit guilty about it.
In a way, they're asking you to put them right. They say these
things to provoke you, but it's because they need a bit of
passion, commitment, leadership.

'Being a shop steward is more than just bettering people's
conditions. You get all sorts of human problems brought to
you. One woman brought me all her tax problems. My own are
in chaos, but you don't say that, you try and sort it out together.
If people are unsympathetic to anybody else's problem, I always
say, "Her problem today will be yours tomorrow." That works,
usually. Most things are things that could happen to anybody.
We're none of us proof against illness and bereavement, anxiety
about our children. You have to keep some collective feeling. I
have to be part lawyer, part social worker, part diplomat, part
big sister.

'The part of my job I like least is having to get the foreman to
sign dockets for bad work. There's such competition between
the different departments in the factory. They all buy material
from each other, on paper at least, so there's always this feeling
about which department is making the most profit. Then there's
competition between the different companies in the group.
We've been taken over in fact, last month, by a bigger company
that has a reputation as an asset-stripper. I don't know what the
outcome of that will be. You look round at what's happened to
industry in London – take-over, close-down, sell the land. It's
more profitable not to produce anything now than to make
things. We just sit and wait.

'I feel sorry for some of the young Asian girls who work here.
They see the white girls coming in with nice clothes and things
they would like. But of course, they give their money just as they
earn it, to their parents. I think that's a shame. One girl I know
has to go home and do all the family washing, because she is the
only daughter; and all that on top of a day's work. Sometimes
they come to me and say they want to leave home. I always advise
them to wait until they've got someone they can trust to share a
flat with; not just get up and go because of the pressures. The
way they live, it's about the same as working-class life was for us
in London fifty years ago. It seems a pity that we can't be a bit

more understanding, that we haven't learnt something from our own experience.

'I've always wanted to do something for people. I was brought up in a Barnardo's home. I left there at sixteen with a pat on the head, a Bible and a change of clothes, and that was it. I've always felt the need to do something useful. I was always in the Labour Party, and then the union. When I had a young family, I dropped out a bit, but I've taken it up again more recently. I regard the rôle of shop steward as working for better conditions as well as a decent rate of pay; to represent the workers' interests at all times, and be on their side; and if they are in the wrong to mitigate their offence. Of course, I sometimes find I'm out of sympathy with people on the shop floor. I argue with them, I never let things go. The Asians are now the chief target for prejudice. It used to be the West Indians. Before that the Poles, Lithuanians, before that the Irish.

'I think you've got to have some aim in life beyond just coming to work. You've got to look after the next person, to live through and for others as well as yourself. The world isn't poor is it, we could make enough to go round; the whole world I mean. Only the way it is now, some must have more than they need, and so others starve. Christ said "Love thy neighbour," and I agree with that; it's perhaps the only thing I do agree with him in. I think I put my faith in the labour movement, the possibility of changing people's lives and working conditions, bringing about a different kind of society. I've been disappointed with the Labour Party; maybe we have to change that now, give it back some of the idealism and caring it once had.

'As you can see, this factory is a really old-fashioned place. Its layout is messy; some of the working environment is really bad, especially where they mix the rubber compound. There's powder from the mill everywhere, the dust and the smell of it. Some of the men, those who've worked here a long time, their faces are grey, you just can't tell what may have happened over the years, breathing in that dust. A lot of them wear protective clothing, visors, they're lightweight, very good, but you can't help inhaling a certain amount. When they change out of their work clothes, the dust is thick on them. The worst thing about the department where I work is the noise, those Norton machines. They've offered us ear muffs, which isolate people

even more from each other. We have a system of lip-reading,
you get it in a lot of factories that are noisy. It makes you quite
loud-spoken, even though you don't realize it. For my week's
work I get £58.72 a week. That's going up to £66.43,* not a bad
increase, that's including some movement towards equal pay.

'People can't take any pleasure in their work. They live for
their life outside. I wouldn't say they begrudge time spent here –
you're in a state of suspension, waiting for when you can get
back to real life; only real life sometimes has a tendency to
reduce you to a bit of a robot too.'

Wet Monday afternoon in Hackney; the end of summer. An
even downpour floods the pavements and overflows the choked
drains. The litter that usually swirls around Dalston Junction is
waterlogged and decomposing. Lightning bleaches the
damaged nineteenth-century architecture of bricked-up
tenements and the old Dalston Empire; the sound of thunder is
lost in the traffic.

The Pensioners' Association meets in a disused shop, just
round the corner from the beaded Gothic gables of the Relief
Office and Dispensary, with *Males'* and *Females' Entrance* carved
into the corroded stone. In spite of the weather, there are about
twenty people in the room. Most of them agree that they look
forward to Mondays, because, with the weekend safely over,
there is a prospect of somewhere to go for the next five days.

The chairs are of green tubular metal, with plywood seats and
backs. There is a trestle table, behind which sit members of the
committee. Tea is served through a green-painted hatch; two
Marie biscuits in every saucer. It is chill in the room. There is a
smell of damp clothing; pools from wet umbrellas darken the
dusty floorboards.

The old have the function of offering a foil to the present.
They are expected to dwell upon the harshness and cruelty of the
conditions in which they were brought up; and this has the effect
of distancing their world from the one we inhabit. They
represent a time of poverty and oppression, which only throws
into relief our moment of enlightened caring. If they insist that
they did nevertheless triumph over circumstances, did enjoy
themselves and care for each other, this is a small indulgence
which can be allowed them from our position of total

* January 1978.

superiority. That something has perhaps been taken away from people who apparently had nothing, is a possibility we cannot seriously consider.

It is as though their purpose is to show us how lucky we are; to convince us that changes have indeed been profound and wholly beneficent. Behind memory and anecdote, it looks almost as if we no longer live under the same economic and social system.

At first, the old people respond in the way that is expected of them; stories of workhouse and want, sweat shops and the poor law.

'Talk about life being cheap in India, when I was young it was bloody cheap here. There was eight of us in my family, only three survived. When I was born, they got so used to 'em being dead, they said, "Oh he's dead," and they slung me at the bottom of the bed. My Auntie noticed I was breathing, so she picked me up and gave me to my mum. And I lived. In a way. So here I am.'

'The first job I got was in a warehouse near here. I got 10/- a week. Another kid came in, a year younger than me, said he wanted a job. Boss says, "How much money do you want?" "How much is he getting?" "Ten bob a week." "I'll do it for nine." Boss comes to me, "Get your coat on, you. You're out."'

They talk about their own past as though it had happened to somebody else. They talk of their younger selves as though these had died with their parents; in their tone is the regretful fondness of *in memoriam* notices. In their discourse recurs the duality you find everywhere: the harshness of conditions, but the consolations of the human associations; and when they come to talk of the present, it is the other way round – the bitterness is directed, not against conditions, but against people. With young people, the same dual consciousness is present – the wonder of things still leaves frustrations and dissatisfaction; but the possibility of human sharing is not seen as any answer to this – only more things.

'Your kids go away and leave you. Got no time for you. There's too many old people living on their own in Hackney.'

'We had an outing last week. Some of them wanted the coach to get home an hour earlier than it was scheduled. I couldn't make out why – there was nothing special on television. It turned out they are afraid of having to be out after dark.'

'It never used to be like that. You could walk in and out of anybody's house. Doors were left open night and day, and nobody came to any harm.'

'Well the reason my wife won't come here is because she was mugged. They pushed her over in the main road and left her lying there. And that was in broad daylight.'

'It's horrible round here now. It isn't Hackney now.'

'If I had the money, I'd get away from here as fast as I could.'

'Oh, I don't know. I couldn't change now. I'd never settle anywhere else.'

'It used to be lovely round here. I knew everybody round about where we lived. Now I don't know anybody. They're moving away every five minutes, breaking up, changing partners.'

'It'll get worse. It has got worse. The last ten years, it's rubbish that's here now. Problem families.'

'It's the *schwarzes*, I don't care what you say.'

I ask how many people have seen their children leave Hackney. Every hand goes up of those who have children.

JS: 'Why did they go?'

'We all struggled, we all lived in a terrible poverty, most of us that's here. We wanted something better for our children. We didn't want them to work in the terrible conditions we had to. So they went.'

'If it was so wonderful here years ago, why did we encourage them to get out? Seems to me we've brought it on ourselves.'

I asked what jobs their children have gone to do: work in Ford's at Dagenham, become a teacher in Manchester, work in an insurance office in Bristol, a shop in the West End; New Zealand as an engineer.

JS: 'But people don't have to leave Hackney to teach or be an engineer, do they?'

'You don't think of that at the time. They've got their own lives to lead.'

'A lot of them have lost that family feeling we had.'

'Yes, the difference between us and the kids today is that we had respect for other people. Respect and discipline.'

'Yes, respect for the rich and discipline to be poor. That was what the discipline was all about, make no mistake. I mean, it isn't a vocation, is it? You have to be trained to be poor, years and years of it; not having enough to eat, being under-nourished, your brain underemployed and your body idle. It's

years of living in a freezing tenement in Flower and Dean Street,
having to chip the ice off the windows in the morning, chip the
ice off the pisspot before you could empty it.'

'But you've got to have some discipline. And now there isn't
any at all.'

'Well, today, you couldn't bring your kids up the way we were
brought up, even if you wanted to.'

'It's all gone the other way now hasn't it?'

'They teach 'em now they can have anything they want.'

'This is it. Look at television. Get this, buy that, have the
other. They're not invitations, they're orders. Then the rest of
the time it's violence, shootings, robbings, murders. People
who say there isn't any connection, they're deluding
themselves.'

'That's where it comes from, all the violence. These kids,
they're brought up to believe that everything they want just
appears, by magic. They have everything poured into their lap.
Then at sixteen, they leave school—'

'Sixteen. Round where I live half of 'em pack up about the age
of twelve.'

'No, let me finish. They can't get a job, and even if they do it's
a dead end. Nine quid on the dole. They feel cheated. They feel
somebody's been telling them lies. They have; everybody has.
So they say, "Well, I will have what I want, I'll take it anyway."
That's why you get all these muggings and robberies. It's the
logic of the way we live.'

'I think it's television that's ruined people. People used to visit
each other when we were young. They used to talk, exchange
information about each others' lives. When our relatives came,
we'd talk for hours about friends and neighbours. But not now.
It's, "Shh, here's *Crossroads* coming on. *Coronation Street*." Good
God. People are a sight more interested in these bits of fiction
than they are in each other.'

'And then what do they talk about even when they do turn it
off? What's been on, what's coming on. It's a curse.'

'Well what else have I got to talk about, somebody like me? I
get out the pictures of our Ann's wedding, the photos of the
children. I've read her letters till they're falling to pieces. What
pleasure can you get out of your family when they're all that way
away? Half-way across the world.'

'Well, mine only live in Ilford, but they might as well be on the moon. Anything could happen to me. It has. I've got old and I'm on me own, and it don't seem as if they've noticed.'

Many of their sons and daughters had installed a telephone for them, because they can't get to see them as often as they would like; and what was offered as a comforting point of contact is seen as an avoidance of the duty of visiting. They wondered why it was that families have to be dispersed, simply for someone to go and work in a factory in Dagenham, a school in Manchester, an office in Bristol, or even to be unemployed in Birmingham. The private individual dramas turn out to be part of a process that is common to almost every working-class family. Social change, located externally, reaches down into the very depths of what we are accustomed to regard as our private lives. The processes which denied these old people basic necessities in their youth, and then released them into the pursuit of personal satisfactions in their old age – which for the most part elude them – come to be seen, not as obscure and puzzling dislocations in their lives, but as a continuity.

'You want your kids to have a better life. You don't want to see them in dirty unhealthy factories, you don't want them to stay in the working class.'

'Why don't you? I think that's it, what you just said. We don't want them to stay in the working class, because we've always had a feeling that being working class is inferior.'

'No, never. I'm proud of it.'

'Not deep down. That's where this society has got it all wrong. Working class is something to be ashamed of. Something to get out of. You associate it with being rough and ignorant. Now in a socialist society, working people wouldn't just want a diet of Bingo and television violence. Working-class life doesn't have to be like that.'

'No, but that's the way it is.'

'Only because we haven't developed a working-class alternative. Everything that's good and worthwhile is taken away from us, always has been.'

'Listen, I can remember in 1917, when the news of the Russian Revolution came through, a tremendous surge of hope went through working-class people everywhere. People down the East End wept with joy. A lot of us had relatives in Russia. We knew all about the pogroms and the persecution. But as the years went by, the stories we heard coming out of the Soviet

Union, we slowly saw the hope extinguished that had been kindled in us. If this is socialism, people said, we want no part of it.'

'No, but because socialism fails in one country, it doesn't mean socialism must fail everywhere. And if capitalism now wears a smiling face, that doesn't mean that capitalism has changed its nature.'

'Well, you've heard what people here have said this afternoon: "It's the young people, they don't do their duty to their family." Then you'll hear the young people say, "The old 'uns are a nuisance, they should be put out of their misery." Then you'll hear others say, "It's the coloureds, they've got all the best jobs," and in the next breath they're all supposed to be living on Social Security. Or it's the scroungers and layabouts. What is it that sets everybody against each other in this way? Fathers against sons, children against parents, neighbours against each other, black against white? That's the question we perhaps should ask. I have known people try to persuade their parents to commit suicide, so they should get the tenancy of a flat.'

'I don't care what you say. It was lovely before the coloureds came.'

'But why did they come? That's what we've been talking about. You've said why, yourself. We got our children out, because we didn't think it was lovely enough for them. We taught our children to despise it. Why should we expect respect from the poor sods who've nowhere else to live but the spaces where our children should have been? Somebody had to come and fill the gap, somebody had to do the rough jobs that weren't good enough for our children. If there's a lot of unemployment now, that isn't their fault.'

'Anyway, it was never very lovely round here. We fought slum landlords, we lived with bugs and TB, our children had rickets.'

'Yes, but everybody helped each other.'

'You had no choice.'

'How much more choice have we got, they way we are now? I wonder.'

It is expected of old people that they should lament the past. Their experience is widely called upon – in research, drama, publishing, the media – to reconstruct situations that are felt to belong to history: the kind of working-class life that has passed

and will never come again. They are an admonitory reminder of
what we have escaped. But behind this lament, there is often,
unnoticed, a depth of understanding and richness of perception
which have no place in the formal position reserved for them.
But any understanding they have is debased, because we leave
them no choice but to mouth the same antique and nostalgic
tune.

Their children have gone away; in many cases, in pursuit of
quite ordinary jobs. Do families have to be broken, old people
stranded, in order for their young to go and do repetitive factory
work in distant parts of the country? Sometimes, the whole
country seems to be in a state of aimless and functionless
mobility; in the stream of lights along the motorways on Friday
night, the endless chain of red rear lamps in the rain. What kind
of restlessness is this, that nobody stays where he is if he can help
it – everybody on the move, en route for somewhere else,
anxiously on his way to obscure destinations, rendezvous that
are uncertain?

Our sense of home-place has been destroyed, and the
relationships that might bind us there contaminated. If you visit
the children of these old people, their account of the migration
that has taken them to another borough, another city, a remote
part of the country, or the ends of the earth, is always the same:
it is essentially an escape story, a flight. The story is of how
impossible the parents are, how they inhibit the growth and
development of the young, how demanding they are, how
possessive and reluctant to let go. This process involves the
detachment of the working class from any sense of continuity
with the past. It is true that a life of poverty has nothing to do
with a life of self-expression and fantasy through things; but the
disjunction has damaged the deepest attachments of kinship.
The children are full of guilt and resentment; exasperated
'phone conversations end with mothers saying they can see no
reason for carrying on and think they'll end it all by putting their
head in the gas oven. 'Emotional blackmail,' they say uneasily;
and on the other hand, 'They have deserted me.' We are
powerless against the wound to our deepest human
relationships, we are unable to respond to each other's needs, to
heal and give comfort. And the machine that exacts this tribute
of us, this forfeit of some of the most fundamental aspects of

our humanity, is the same machine that tried to brutalize us through poverty in the only recent past.

Hackney; a compound of asphalt, cat's cradle of washing lines, red-brick balconies. The flats overlook Hackney Marshes and the beige-tiled towers of Leytonstone, a stretch of metallic canal, electricity pylons. To the east a flat bleak prospect, where the wind seems to travel vast distances, always strong and gusty in the spaces between the walls of brick. The flats echo with dogs and children; all human sound is intensified: a clash of laughter and misery, of anger and pain, made public because of the inward-facing structure of the flats. But it is a bitter and reluctant communality.

Cameron McIver and his wife Bettine try to remain aloof from the quarrels and friendships that are made and dissolved from day to day; but it isn't always possible. There is always someone who knows that he is on Social Security, and, because he can be seen in the street, assume it is paid gratuitously. He is on invalidity benefit, with a rare heart disease, and his life expectancy is short.

When he talks about his life, the migration from Trinidad eighteen years ago, the sense of pain, the transplant into a new place, the anxiety and insecurity, all remind me of my grandmother's stories of leaving her village in the 1870s and moving into the town in search of work and hope.

'My father was a bus driver in Trinidad. My mother died when I was young. There were eleven of us, eight lived. When my mother die, I go to me sister home. My brother leave Trinidad and come out to this country. Well, you hear all different rumour, how this country is going on, so he make a try. He come over here and was working with British Rail. In 1960 my brother write and ask me if I go out there.

'People say the place is good. You can earn a lot of money, you get a good job and can make ends meet. He was sending money back home to support the kids. And I arrive here 1960, December 25th, Christmas Day. When you get off the boat and look at England, well it was night, so you don't see much. When I wake up in the morning, my brother gone to work. I looked right round and through the window and outside was a big mist, and I started to cry and I realize that everybody just leave and

not say anything. I was fighting twenty minutes to light the
cooker, and I didn't know how was to light it you know, I didn't
know how to turn on the taps or if to use a match. . . . And I was
crying and I cry meself to sleep. And then my brother have a
friend working at British Rail, and he knock on the door and ask
what happen to me, didn't me brother make no breakfast for
me, and I tell him no, and I tell him I couldn't light the stove. . . .
And he carry me down to where he live and give me something
to eat. And when me sister-in-law get home she tell me I must
wash up the dishes and clean the rooms and get something to
eat, because they pay for me to come in this country. I was
seventeen.

'I stop one month in the house with my brother. I saw a big
hotel in the West End, I go in there and ask for a job. I was laying
table. I worked in the restaurant. The flat pay was £5, but to
come home with that I had to work rest day and Sundays. Well I
had to learn to lay table pretty quick, because it was the first time
I'm in big hotels, I never saw anything like that. Well, I started to
believe that when people are writing back to the West Indies and
say you can earn so much and so much, it is some bad rumour.

'When I work in this hotel for six months I give notice to
leave. And then the manageress take me to the governor because
she quite like me in a way, and they raised the flat pay to £7, so I
stay two years. Then one time the governor tell me to wash the
boiler, but when I went to wash it, the heat didn't turn off, it was
too hot; he tell me to wash it or go home. So when I finish work
at eleven o'clock I get my cards.

'When you leave home, you come to improve your position,
you don't think of all the other problems you will have.
Sometimes I used to be walking down the road late at night, and
a set of boy call me black this and black that. Things don't all
work out the way you think they will. One night I come out of
work, it was a bit foggy, and when I get out from the bus at the
Caledonian Road, there were some people in front of me that I
couldn't see. When I reach the crossing, I see a little light and I
make out it is a car. So I stand up at the kerb, and someone come
up behind me and say, "Could I have a fag?" But I was so
frightened, and I have a cigarette but I tell him that I have none;
and then I go to step off, and he stretch out a foot and I fall over.
. . . I get up and ask him what happen. Then the next other one
come up and I hear him break a bottle. And I see another one,

so I get up and start to run. . . . That happen to me twice since I come to this country. People call me a black bastard, it never worry me, because I get used to it. It used to worry me quite a lot at first, but going about I meet white blokes and they talk to me quite nice and I make friends with them.

'When I reach England I reach in the night, and in the morning when I wake up I see a set of building, my God, so high. . . . I think it'll be easy to get a job, because everywhere I see factories, so many factories about. It's only later I realize they're not factories, but houses. . . . The most difficult thing I couldn't stand the coldness. I had was to wear coat and cardigan and all them things. All the time. I used to ask myself question, Why should I have to put up with it? But it's to earn a living. At home I never worked. There was no work. All I do, you help in the fields. If they are cutting cane, they can give you a field to do, working on some estate. They might employ you like a yard boy, you go and feed the chickens, feed the cattle, donkey, horses and all them kind of thing. But it's not the same.

'When I worked in the hotel, it was real strange to me, especially when I see so many kind of people. I was quite shy. When I have to go and clear the table, I panic, because when I clear this table, I have to wipe it down, lay it again, and set the knives and forks right; then if anyone ask for something, tell the manageress what and what they want. I don't know what they are, some of the things they ask for, then I had was to carry it to the table, and I was quite shy, a set of people all looking at you and watching what you doing. . . . The people talk to me at the table, and they tell me I must talk a little more slow, because they can't always hear what I say.

'When I leave the hotel I was out of a job for three months. I keep searching, go to the Labour Exchange. They sent a man to see me where I was living, and they let me have £2.50 a week from the Labour. Then I get a job down Old Street, Clarinet Plastics, the place close down since. The first job they give me I had was to sweep the floor with a machine. I didn't want to idle since when I come in this country, anything I can get I take it. Then I get a higher job at the factory. I have a list, every morning a van come and pick up stuff from the factory, and I make him sign for it; and then the plastic come with the lorry; I open a chute and they slide it down the chute, I check none is missing. The plastic is blue, white, all different colours, because it is made into ladies' underwear, and I have to put them all on different shelves, all the colours separate.

'They pay you less when you first come into this country, because at home we don't have to spend money. Here, anything you want, you have to buy, where in Trinidad I don't have to buy nothing. I would like to go back, yes, but not in the position I am. I want to go back to the West Indies independent, in a better position, because if I go back in the West Indies tomorrow, I still have to start work on the same piece of land, we still have to work it up from the start. If I have a lot of money, yes, I go back. I'm lucky now, We live in a council flat. I live against a good neighbour.

'When the plastics factory close, I get a job in Wood Green. I see a job in the paper, plastic moulding. It say you could earn £50, £60, £100 a week, no flat rate, all piece work. You have to operate a machine; it was seven in the morning to seven at night, two weeks night, two weeks day. This was in 1968. The first payment I get was £11. When I receive £11, in the night I shed tears because I'd worked so hard. With overtime the highest I got was £17, that was operating three machines. So anyhow I go to the foreman, and he tell me you have to work to earn that big money, so the next week he put me on night on five machines, and then I get £41, but I can't get any more if I work to kill myself; so I left that job. It would have killed me. I couldn't keep up with it. When I reach home in the morning I couldn't eat or drink anything at all, all I do is sleep and work.

'What I see here, sometimes it shock me. In Trinidad, all the family look after each other. But an old man in the block where we live, he goes to hospital with cancer, and in the flat he left some hundred pounds he saved all his life. He comes out of hospital, but then he go back for an operation. They tell the wife it hopeless, they can do nothing else. They want to send him home, but the wife and the family say, "No, we can't have him home, there's no one to look after him." But what really happen, they thought he was going to die, so they take out all the money he saved and spend it already. When they thought he had a disease, they spent all the money, helped themselves to it, and now they are afraid he going to find out. Now is that the way to treat a dying old man?

'People here, they eat each other up. Money spoils things between families. It spoil us too. My brother, when he send for me, tell me I didn't have was to pay rent, because I help my father and brother back home. And my brother paid my passage, $336. But when I reach over here, he start to buy a car and all the like, so one evening when I come home from work, there is a note on the table, telling me that from now on I will have to pay a rent. And all the things he want to buy start to bring contention between us. Then he say I will have to pay back the money for my fare, so when he tell me this I start to cry, I say, "Well you make me a promise." He tell me how he had was to work hard for that money. Then one day I get a 'phone call at work, me sister-in-law telling me they moving. So when I go back to fetch me clothes, they gone, and I find they take my Post Office book and draw out the few pounds I saved at the Post Office. And then he went to work at Vauxhall, and they bought a house up at Stoke Newington. It's four years I don't see him now. And he write my brother and sisters and tell them things about me. He went home in the West Indies, and me father die, and he come back and never tells me nothing. He never even pass by to tell me me father die. He go past my house twice a day to work.

'This country, it gives me the money to live, but it takes away me brother.'

Mrs Hellence is from St Lucia. She came to live with her husband in a South London borough. She has six children, five boys and a girl. The oldest boy is in Borstal, the second at boarding school. Kenny, who is eleven, goes to a Special School. The youngest child, Leroy, has not yet started.

Her husband worked for a building company, installing lifts. He was killed in an accident at work, when a lift fell down a shaft. The firm denied negligence and refused compensation. The solicitor Mrs Hellence engaged failed to press the claim, until too long a period had elapsed for her to do so. With the help of a social worker, the solicitor himself was sued, and judgment having been found in favour of Mrs Hellence, she was awarded £4,500 damages.

She is still deeply depressed. She wavered between taking all the money at once and going back to St Lucia, and saving the money for the children as they grow older. She recognized that her children's prospects are better here, but she feels strongly for St Lucia and the idealized values which she attributes to it.

'One day I dig my garden, and if you have nothing, I give to you. Next day, your garden is full, so you give to me.'

At last, she agreed to open accounts in the Building Society for the children. The money that came to her was spent as it was paid. The flat where she lives is one of the largest single blocks in the borough, with a great concrete courtyard, a rent office in the middle, with garages and sheds all the way round; prohibitive notices prevent ball games, and an even older notice forbids access to hawkers and street musicians. The children use the courtyard as a playground, riding round on Chopper bikes and skateboards, and the closed stone yard amplifies every sound, so that it is always stridently noisy. The children play in the hallway and stairs on wet days, which are cavernous and strewn with litter. In summer, the courtyard is unbearably hot and glaring; in winter, when the sun is lower, patches of frost and ice linger all day, and when it is wet, there is a permanent growth of moss.

Inside the flat, there is very little furniture. Torn lino covers the floors. In one room there is a television and some wooden chairs. The television is the only undamaged object in the part of the flat the children use freely. The beds are always unmade, a pile of rough blankets and coats the only covering. There is one room which Mrs Hellence keeps locked; a sitting room with a bright carpet and some ornaments; a big glass fish and an azalea, a cold black leather suite and a glass cabinet. The children are kept out of here. Somehow, they destroy everything. Nothing lasts. They had a sofa, but the children jumped all over it and it fell to pieces. The older children come home and criticize their mother; this is deeply hurtful to her. She is anxious to propitiate them all the time, to forestall their resentment at what she feels is her own inability to provide all the things they want. The younger ones come home and describe the houses of other children, and want toys and treats. When Mrs Hellence talks of this, her eyes are full of tears of shame. She feels humiliated and guilty. If she had been able to give the older ones what they wanted, she believes that they would not have done wrong. They had demanded money at knife point from an Indian youth in a train; and it was as a result of this that Spencer is in Borstal. Mrs Hellence has a deep sense of failure, and a feeling that if she could provide more things for the children, everything would come right. If they had beautiful clothes, records, bikes, holidays, tape recorders, transistors, skateboards, money, there would be no problems. She watches the younger ones grow, and she is apprehensive. She feels them slipping from her control; and the only way she can gain their obedience is by promising increasingly lavish rewards. She is on a treadmill of anxiety and appeasement, spending on sweets and excursions and clothes and fashionable shoes. For her, parental caring is vested solely in granting her children access to all the things that the economy holds out as guarantees of compliance, control and satisfaction. She sees herself as a self-effacing intermediary in this process, and can see no other function for herself.

With other people she is impassive and dignified, and grieves constantly for her husband. She has no friends. When her husband died, there was a rumour in the house where she was then living, that she had been awarded £13,000. It was believed that the house belonged to her. This idea was supported by her neighbours, 'my own people', as she said, by the fact that she collected the rent and did a little cleaning for the woman who did own the house. She was met by demands from all sides for loans and gifts. Neighbours, acquaintances, even family from home wrote, saying that she should share her good fortune. 'Good fortune. I had lost my husband and didn't have a penny. The flat where we were was nice, because when he was working, my husband wanted to give nice things to the children. We did have the best flat in the house.' She took a job in a hospital, night cleaning, but the rumour that she had money pursued her even there; and it was said of her that she had taken the job only to persuade people that she had nothing. She left, and went to work in a toy factory, but the same thing happened. People shouted at her in the street, wrote abusive letters, shunned her.

The house where she was living was damaged by fire; and the other tenants told the authorities that the house belonged to Mrs Hellence. She was ordered to repair it and make it habitable. When she protested that it didn't belong to her, she was not believed. 'Because my people told the authorities, they believed them.' Her furniture and possessions were sold, and the house condemned. The real owner of the property had gone to Guyana and could not be contacted. Mrs Hellence went into emergency council accommodation, and was re-housed a year later to where she now lives. Nobody seems to have checked her story. She feels bitter towards the community, the housing authorities and the social workers in the area, and since then has led a reclusive and withdrawn life. She lives in constant fear that her children will force her into sudden and threatening contact with authority. The only way to avoid this, she feels, is to answer to all their needs and demands; which she tries to do, begging them at the same time to be good and think of their father.

With the money that was paid into her account every quarter, she bought things for the children; so many things that she soon became over-extended. There were letters from a firm from which she had bought some encyclopedias to help with their education, and a threat to prosecute if the amount outstanding was not paid at once. She bought new clothes so that they might attend the church Christmas party or a school outing; but the clothes were used up before she had finished paying for them. She said that the children saw money in her purse and could not understand that it was needed to buy food, to pay the rent. Michael is angry with her and punishes her when she cannot give him money. 'They think everybody has money, the only people who don't have money are dead people.' Selina had come in from a friend's house and said, 'Linda has special clothes to go to sleep in, why can't I?' Mrs Hellence had gone out immediately and bought a night dress and dressing gown.

The lesson which Mrs Hellence has learned from migration has been that in the caring for children, non-material concerns have been subordinated to the ability to buy things. She came from a society where children were brought up by coercion and by example – the disciplines of poverty. Her experience has been that of most of the indigenous working class in this country, but for her the transition has been abrupt and more shocking. She has discovered that caring has been wrenched from human emotions and vested in things, the provision of which absorbs all feeling and subsumes all sentiment.

Starting Afresh: Milton Keynes

It is more than ten years since the designation of the new city of Milton Keynes. In that time, the population has doubled, from 40,000 to 80,000. It is planned that the population will double again within the next eight years.

This means that about thirty people a day are arriving in Milton Keynes – over half of them from London – dispersed somewhere in its 22,000 acres, to start a new life in what has been

described as our appointment with the twenty-first century,
Britain's Los Angeles, a holiday camp, Dodge City.

The people who work on the city – architects, planners,
community workers, administrators – retain a strong sense of
commitment. The buildings of the Development Corporation
are full of people leaning purposefully over plans and drawing
boards, scale models, statistics, press releases and projects; all in
slightly futuristic offices furnished with pieces of tubular metal
and tinted Perspex, felt and hessian in discreet colours: beige,
oatmeal, coffee.

Everything has been thought of for the newcomers. It is, they
say, about the realities of disruption. People are visited before
they leave London, the likely problems as well as the advantages
of the move are discussed. There are arrivals officers for when
they move in, there is a community house where they can meet
people and make friends. There are community-development
teams. There is a resident artist, a resident writer; an extensive
information unit. Visitors have come from Saudi Arabia,
Argentina, Japan and even China.

Milton Keynes is about nothing if not the future. There is a
symmetrical network of roads, with fairly small estates
landscaped between the million or so trees that have been
planted since designation, 'no building higher than the tallest
tree.' The effect is of spacious skyscapes and gently wooded
countryside; so much so, that the living areas seem to be
embattled behind green ramparts. But as you walk through the
estates, the irony is that it is not so much the future that comes to
meet you as echoes from the past. One estate, Eaglestone, is like
a medieval village, with an irregular roofline clustered round a
green. You expect a group of angry peasants to appear at any
minute, dragging a protesting crone to the centre of the green,
where they will light a pyre and watch her burn from behind the
large picture windows that look on to the central space. Great
Linfield, on the other hand, near Wolverton, an old railway
town, takes its design from the old railway cottages, obsessed by
the memory of a nineteenth-century industrial suburb: it is like
living through the coming of the railways all over again, only in
a revised and idealized way; and you half expect to hear the
tread of studded boots on the road and see emaciated women in
shawls carrying bowls of dripping to each other's houses.
Beanhill, with its square corrugated metal cabins, painted black

and separated from each other by a metal grille, has something
of the frontier town, an empty and dusty horizon, against which
you can imagine only a figure with smoking guns, and a
saloonkeeper's woman with her hands on her hips. All the
estates are like this – redolent of somewhere else. The
architecture is a composite folk-memory of other places; and
the city of the future turns out to be something of an essay in
nostalgia. Everything is theatrical, has a borrowed identity.
There is a sense of masquerade and self-consciousness; flight,
evasion and fantasy are in the air. Milton Keynes throws into
sharper relief the way we live now. It would be asking too much
to expect Milton Keynes to transcend the society that produced
it; but it does illustrate the pain of absent purpose. Everything
has to pretend to be something else. It is as though we are all
involved in a tacit conspiracy not to tell ourselves what we really
think or feel. 'We cannot relate to each other directly at work.
The nearest you can get to it is a sort of joking relationship:
through cynicism and mockery, you just get a hint of repressed
affection. You can't approach anybody seriously at work, they
laugh at you if you try. What it is is a defence. A defence against
despair.'

   Jill and Kevin moved to Milton Keynes from Hackney
eighteen months ago. They lived on Beanhill, but have now got
a transfer to what they consider a better estate at Pear Tree
Bridge.

KEVIN: 'I don't like Beanhill. This is going to be the slums of
Milton Keynes. Where we're going is much nicer. If they offer
them for sale, I'll buy one of them.'

JILL: 'We came from Nisbet House in Homerton. You'd got no
chance of getting a place in Hackney. I hated it there. I couldn't
walk through Nisbet without getting accosted.'

KEVIN: 'We had a struggle. I got a job with a firm here, cooked-
meats firm. That's how I got the house. Only when I came to
take the job, they said it had gone. We got into debt, had the gas
cut off from September till March. The electric bill is £60 a
quarter, rent £54 a month, rates £4 a week. You need at least
£1,000 a year before you even start to eat. I've just invested in a
car, I've started minicabbing. I'm the cheapest minicab in
Milton Keynes. You've got to make your own life here. My
ambition is to be able to leave a home and a business for my son
to take over.'

JILL: 'I don't want just to live my life, without leaving anything behind me when I go. I want to feel I've achieved something.'

A neighbour calls with her three children, Stacy, Leslie and Lester. She says that she will stay in Milton Keynes for the children's sake, whatever she may feel about it herself.

'Well I've lived in a tower block. My husband was an alcoholic. He died of it after I left him. I couldn't take any more of it, not with the three children. They put me in temporary accommodation, bed and breakfast in a hotel in Camden. You couldn't stay in the hotel in the daytime, you had to wander the streets. And it was costing Camden £86 a week. So I came here to get a house, that was my only thought. I'd've gone anywhere to get a place. I had nothing when I moved in, I was on Social Security, £13 a week for me and three kids. But I've been lucky. I met a mate of Kevin's over a year ago, and he lives with us now. He has a good job and he takes care of us. So in that way, moving out here has been good for me.'

KEVIN: 'Yes, and this was a bloke who was never going to settle down, who said he always had itchy feet.'

JILL: 'Mind you, you can get fed up being stuck here in the daytime. The women get ever so friendly at first, and then they fall out with you. You get one, and you see her every day, she's in your house for a cup of tea, and then if you miss a day she says, "What's the matter with you, have you turned funny?" And then by that time she knows everything about you; and as soon as somebody new moves in, she's all over them, and tells them all your business. So when you meet a new person, she tells you what this other woman said about you, and there can be some right rows.'

KEVIN: 'There's not many round here that I want to get friendly with. There's a lot of things wrong with Milton Keynes. There's no hospital. A man had a heart attack in a pub last week, he was only twenty-six, and he was resuscitated three times and died again before the ambulance got there. And it's happened to a child as well. The doctor didn't get there to get the child to a hospital in time.'

The hospital is not planned until some time in the '80s, but work has already begun on the million square feet of retail space at the heart of the new city, which will have one of the largest shopping areas in Europe, climate-controlled arcades, extensively landscaped with trees, plants and shrubs.

I was told by a woman who left Kilburn two years ago, 'There's a lot of families break up when they come down here. That's what happened to me. There's so much pressure on you, the expense, the debts. The minute you move in, there's a stream of people knocking on your door, offering carpets, furniture, curtains. You feel you've got a new place, you must live up to it. It all looks ever so easy. Then the husband and wife start blaming each other when it all goes wrong. I'm not the only one. I go to Gingerbread, single-parent families; and I should think in the last few months, there's been four or five new members every time.'

In Milton Keynes I met a man who had been acquitted of a charge of rape in East London, and had come with his wife to find refuge from the curiosity and suspicion of neighbours. 'I came here to get away from people I knew; but one thing you can't get away from is the way that sex is pushed at you everywhere all the time. On the television, at work, even walking down the streets, everything yells at you Sex, sex, sex. They use it to sell almost everything. When I was in court, there was a lot of talk in the papers about rape, about men being great male brutes who went round screwing pure innocent girls. But it's not like that for me. . . . You don't want to give in to it, I've got a wife, I love her, only everybody's got sex on the brain, these girls they egg you on, then say stop. It's fucking hypocrisy. Everywhere, it's the great come-on, then smack, going all virtuous and moral over it. I used to go and visit my sister, and her little girl's four, and they used to dress her up in all this gear, and say, "Oh don't she look cute, isn't she sexy"; have her hair done, put earrings in her. That is what is really disgusting. The exploitation and then the hypocrisy. I'm all right here, where nobody knows me.'

Despite the almost maternalistic care which the Development Corporation expends on the people who move here, it is not the possibilities provided by the Corporation which shape people's values.

The show house on Fishermead is immaculately furnished with all the artefacts which determine the way we live: it is an idealized consumer capsule, to project people into the future, to compel us to live in the image of the better life. The woman who said that living in Milton Keynes was like being permanently on the Costa Brava wasn't being entirely complimentary. There is something of the contrived happiness of holiday camps, the hysterical ecstasy over quite ordinary products from the television commercials. The discipline to conform penetrates people's lives: the houses are new, they cry out for new curtains, new carpets, new furniture, almost for a remodelled and perfected human being. People sometimes feel they cannot live up to it. However free their choices, they have no control over the setting in which those choices are exercised. There is no place here for deviants or tramps. You would have to be very brave not to comply with the paradox of living privately in a profoundly conforming way. It is almost as though people's lives were turned inside out through the picture windows: everybody is living a spectacle, a piece of theatre, a charade of dehumanized inauthenticity, in which human beings are encouraged to assimilate themselves to the cold perfection of things.

There are no recesses, no secret places. The houses in Netherfield, silver metal cabins with a red-painted garage beneath each one, do not necessarily provide the freedoms which they suggest: they are gentle houses of correction, adjusting people to a new habitat, a changed environment. But there is a world of difference between starting a new life, and the sort of *tabula rasa* demanded of people here: in this place we become devoid of antecedents, we are without history, without anchorage in the past. 'It's paradise,' said one woman, 'compared to where I used to live.' If it is, the tree of knowledge has inedible fruit. It's the kind of place which the old workers in the railway sheds of Wolverton (now incorporated into the city) might have dreamed they were going to when they were dead.

But the stability of the secularized after-life depends on optimism, buoyancy and confidence. It is a product of growth and expansion, and for its long-term success requires an eternity of material improvement. Aspirations to improved material conditions have to be absorbed into a kind of metaphysic about striving for its own sake. The better life beckons; but it is never set against any definable good; and the slightest break in the flow of this sterile progression gives rise to a quite disproportionate surge of bewilderment and anger.

I talked to some girls who had just left school; sitting in the sun on the concrete benches of Bletchley shopping precinct, holding a bundle of forms and official papers, insurance cards and appointments to see the youth employment officer. 'What chance have we got? I've spent the whole week looking for jobs. It's the same wherever you go. You must have experience. How can you get experience if nobody will give you a job? We've been to all the shops round here. Even the factories don't want to know. I want to be a hairdresser, she wants to work with animals. I hate it here. Boring.'

'It's boring everywhere when you've got no money.'

'School-leaver has become a dirty word. Like lepers. They look at you as if you'd come from outer space.'

'I want to get away from here. It gives me the creeps.'

I spoke to a man who is an active supporter of the National Front. He said that one of the principal reasons why people are leaving London is because Milton Keynes has a negligible coloured population. He said there are a lot of sympathizers in Milton Keynes. 'It's one of the few places that isn't racially tainted.'

In these new towns, denied work that is stimulating or engaging, people are robbed of any social defining edge but that of race. Detached from a working-class past, isolated and functionless in these raw new places, people feel even more keenly the pain of the erasure of the old identity. And to be offered the possibility of expressing themselves through consumer goods seems sometimes a savourless alternative. It isn't that consumer capitalism causes violence or racism: it's simply that it denies people an alternative with which to fight these things. And the cynicism of the official who said, 'Everything is laid on for them; it's like painting by numbers,' betrays the lasting contempt it has for the people, despite the elaborate apparatus of maternalistic caring.

Part Four

WHAT CAN STILL BE DONE

1

A COMPREHENSIVE SCHOOL in a northern city. A glass office
looking out on to a rainswept playing field and a council estate
beyond. Dave Ransome is NUT representative. He teaches
chemistry and is twenty-seven. His parents were both active
trades unionists – his mother a weaver and his father an
engineer. But now, he says, they are rather defeated and
apathetic. In any case, they are both close to retirement. He feels
that he is continuing the tradition in which they fought. He is a
Labour candidate in the council elections in a neighbouring
authority, he is a delegate to the local Trades Council. His
parents always believed that the life of working-class people was
going to be transformed through education, and Dave sees his
life as being, in part, a practical embodiment of this belief.

Many Labour Party activists are like Dave now: second-
generation working class, at one remove from the reality of
working-class life. He says, 'We've got to change the image of
the Labour Party. It's too much identified with the cloth cap, the
industrial worker. We've got to get out and reach people in
some of the up-market posher areas, or we shall just become a
party of the ghetto, the enclaves of poverty. A lot of things we
worked for have been achieved. We've got to show we can cope
with the problems of the end of the twentieth century.
Otherwise, there is a danger people will think we're irrelevant.'

I've had this conversation, in one guise or another, many
times during the last year. We've got to change the image. We
must do a public-relations job on a party that developed to
protect the interests of the industrial worker, the poor, the
unprivileged; and it is now that image which they feel is their
greatest liability. To change the image has become far easier
than changing the reality; and in this, the Labour Party is truly
participating in the system which it accepts now and by which it
is accepted. The kind of human being which the Labour Party
served is disappearing, and will never reappear in that form
again.

Many Labour activists have brought with them into their
professional lives a concept of what being working class is like –

they have kept faith with the idealism of their parents, the morality of their struggle, things in themselves of great beauty and value – but these have become ossified in a conception that is already overlaid with memories, personal relationships, folk-memory of broken communities and family networks; and while this becomes their reason for continuing the struggle, the reality of working-class life is evolving all the time, and moving away from this increasingly idealized view. Within the space of a generation, the old working class has become an anachronism, a vestigial reminder of the way the majority of the population once lived. And these activists are increasingly isolated from the working class they still aim to serve. I can't count the number of times I've sat in pubs with groups of young and middle-aged Labour Party members, and listened to accounts of how their parents suffered – immensely moving stories of mill and factory and mine, the deforming of bodies and loss of limbs through pieces of unguarded machinery – the man who went home from work and placed his own severed hand on the table in front of his wife; the ingenuity with which the women contrived to feed large families; the grief of the mother who buried three of her children on the same day; the hope of a grandmother swinging her legs on the back of a carrier's cart that was bringing her into town for the first time; the arbitrary dismissals from work for singing, talking or being ill; the walk each day of eight or ten miles to work; the catalogue of obsolete tasks which people did in their rôle as parts of a vast machine making goods they would never enjoy access to; above all, faith in and the tireless work for a better life; of a counterfeit of which we are expected to be the grateful beneficiaries.

That world is remote from the way we live now, and is no longer the main influence on the consciousness of most people.

The improved conditions, which have influenced us, have involved a vast and unnecessary sacrifice in human terms; have been accompanied by anger and ugliness, a restless and aggressive violence, a deformity of all the values that once went into the struggle for humanitarian change. We were robbed of the possibility of that change; and changes that have occurred have been determined principally by the system which oppressed and impoverished us so recently; and as such they have been changes that have happened to us; we are passive recipients of what has been done to us, we are not agents in determining our own lives in our own context. The kind of hopes and dreams which some of the old workers cherished won't ever come again, not in that way. We shall not build socialism out of that stoicism and existential fortitude against the forces of death and destruction, which for so many of them became identical with the inexorable processes of capitalist processes in the nineteenth century. Then, our collective responses, our sense of a shared predicament extended to an almost metaphysical level: they became a metaphor about the consolations of being together in the face of certain bitter truths – the power of time to corrode and take away, our own brief consciousness and its extinction. It was out of those values that we were going to create a better life, not out of the denial of them which has been imposed on us in their place. It may be that the old working-class sub-culture was mainly a contained reflection of capitalist values; but it did hold certain elements profoundly opposed to those values, and it is the surrender of these which has characterized working-class life during the last generation or so. The whole sub-culture may have posed no threat to capitalist power then, but if we had been able to maintain it until the present time, it would be very radical indeed now. As it is, the changes that have occurred seem to tether working-class experience even more firmly to capitalist values. In this way, the growth of the trades unions, the anger and militancy of recent years, are not necessarily the radical phenomenon which the Left makes them out to be. While the destructive and nihilistic ideology of capitalism is so clearly reflected in the forces opposed to it, the possibility of radical change is blocked. It is precisely the pursuit of the delusions and fantasies which emanate from the great capitalist machine that so much of the ostensibly opposing power seems to be dedicated to. An alternative vision must contain something more worthwhile, more moral than a life of sterile having and getting, the barren fantasy of receiving and amassing rather than creating. A truly better life must be opposed to those things which now oppress us; and until the nature and extent of that oppression is properly located, the vision of an alternative remains senseless and irresponsible. As things are now, the reaction to any threat of loss or change in our infantile dependency on capitalism's providing power, is as likely to result in a victory for the far Right as anything else. In fact, the

National Front are consumer capitalism's revolutionaries, opposing something which is in itself damaging, inhuman and brutalizing with an alternative that outbids it in all those things. Humanity and morality have to be at the root of any alternative for it to be an alternative at all. The values of the old working-class subculture still have something to say to us, once the accretion of nostalgia and romanticism has been removed.

As it is, people have become more like things, and things endowed with human qualities; people become dispensable, disposable, interchangeable, arbitrary. It is absurd to imagine that we should expect the new sanitized market-place of consumer capitalism to yield the satisfactions which it previously couldn't. There is no replacement for human relationships, not even the caring agencies which we have evolved as a substitute for them, so that we may be released for a more total absorption in things. A vast pall of unhappiness hangs over these working-class communities, in the same way that smoke used to persist, winter and summer, in the old industrial areas; a sense of appalled shock lies over the shattered terraces and derelict cities. And it is more than images that will have to be changed before the Labour Party will begin to speak to people again with the passion it once knew.

2

THE COMBINE COMMITTEE at Lucas Aerospace developed as a response of the work force to the threat of redundancies. In the early '70s, the labour force was cut from 18,000 to 13,000. The mergers and take-overs of the '60s led to the emergence of massive corporations, which were increasing their profits while drastically reducing the work force. The workers at Lucas represented a wide range of skills and abilities, both manual and technological; over 2,000 engineers, designers, draughtsmen, and over 250 advanced machine tools; Europe's largest designer and manufacturer of aircrafts systems and equipment. The Combine Committee was formed originally to protect the right to work; and in early 1974 was strong enough to resist 800 planned redundancies. The Corporate Plan was drawn up, which proposed a range of alternative products which so skilled and competent a work force could undertake in the event of further redundancies in the aerospace industry, products that would also be socially useful. Mike Cooley explains the purpose of the plan with passion and eloquence:

'The most glaring discrepancy in our society is the gap between what technology could and actually does provide. In the winter when Concorde was brought into operation, 980 old people died of hypothermia in London alone. Car bodies are optimized so that cars are aerodynamically stable at 120 miles an hour, when there is a limit of 70 even on motorways; the average speed of rush-hour traffic in New York is 8 miles an hour; it was 11 miles an hour at the turn of the century. Messages can go round the world in a fraction of a second, but it takes longer for a letter to get from Washington to New York than it did in the days of the stage coach.

'The second thing is the misuse and waste of our most precious asset. There has been much concern about the waste of energy; but even more scandalous than this is the amount of human skill and creativity with $1\frac{1}{2}$ million people out of work. Given the state of London schools, the lengthening housing lists, the absence of hospital accommodation, does it make sense that 180,000 building workers should be suffering the degradation of the dole queue?

'Then there is the myth that automation, computers and robotic equipment are going to free human beings for more creative work. The opposite is true. Those things tend increasingly to take away the skills of men and vest them in machines. In Italy, in the most highly automated company in Europe, 18 per cent of the work force cannot face going in to work every day. In Sweden, in one factory the labour turnover in one year reached 52 per cent. In Sweden they have had to introduce protected work-places to shield people from the plant and machinery which was supposed to liberate them. At one factory in the United States, the cars coming off the assembly line were sabotaged by the workers. They destroyed what they were making; and one worker was quoted as saying, "If I couldn't improve the product, at least I could make it worse," a negative control over the machine and the labour process.

'Fourthly, there is a growing hostility to science and technology in schools and colleges and in society at large. Science is seen to be dehumanized as it is employed by the multi-

national companies, and idealistic young people feel
increasingly that they want no part of it.

'What we are not saying is that we wish to return to any
mythical good old days. Our criticisms are not a romantic
hankering after a pre-industrial age, when life was simple and
people led lives of Arcadian pleasures. Science and technology
must be harnessed to the needs of the people, not to profit.
Things must be made for use and not for sale.

'During the 1970s industrial combines have got bigger and
bigger. One industrialist was reported as having said he would
take human beings and squeeze them till the pips squeak. GEC
reduced its labour force from 260,000 to 190,000 in two years.
Lucas acquired parts of English Electric and we could see the
same process looming for us as for the GEC employees.
Workers were set against each other; but whether it was
described as managerial staff "being surplus to requirement",
technologists being "technologically displaced", or manual
workers becoming redundant, it all meant the same thing for
everyone – the dole queue.

'The Combine Committee was set up to resist this process.
The labour force had a high level of technological and manual
skills; the analytical power of the scientist was allied to the
common sense and understanding of the shop floor, to build up
a campaigning organization for the right to work. The factory
itself was occupied, a classic work-in, but, little by little, the
factory was starved of work, materials and replacements, and
the struggle became more ferocious and the resistance more
complete, including sabotage of machines and the removal of
machinery from the work-place. Some gas turbines were thrown
into the Grand Union Canal. But over time, morale declined,
and the lure of unemployment benefit eroded the struggle. We
felt we'd made a mistake. We looked at other places, like Upper
Clyde Shipbuilders: there, the work force had been reduced
from 11,000 to 6,000 and producing greater tonnage than
before – their victory had still involved a tremendous cost in
jobs. So we decided to extend the campaign for the right to
work on socially useful products. We wrote to 180 authorities,
universities, big companies, trades unions, and outlined the
skills and capabilities of the work force and asked them for
suggestions as to what socially valuable products such skills
could be applied to. All the institutions and individuals we

wrote to were involved, practically or academically, in the issue we raised. We asked a very specific thing: what could all these workers be making? They were utterly silenced by the concrete nature of our request. We had three useful replies. ASTMS wrote and said it sounded stimulating, and wished us well. TASS referred it to the appropriate sub-committee, and we're still waiting for a reply. So, that having failed, we did what we perhaps should have done in the first place: we asked the 14,000 work force. The people who spent their lives touching and handling the materials, using the substances from which the products are made, had not been consulted. We drew up a questionnaire – not one of those things which narrow your responses down to Yes or No to somebody else's proposal, but drawn up in a dialectical fashion; we appealed to people as producers and consumers, not to this illusion that somewhere there is a workforce and somewhere else people who buy the products. They were asked to think of work as being meaningful to home and community as well, and asked to consider products for use rather than for their value as commodities. In four weeks there were 150 suggestions. The equipment and skills could have been producing an enormous number of things that were meaningful; some immediate products, others long-term. Some could have been used in metropolitan areas, others would have been useful in the Third World, in a mutually non-exploitative fashion. We selected those that would be profitable and socially useful, and refined the suggestions to a range of six areas of production; many of them placed the workers into quite new inter-active relationships, designers with shop-floor workers, and so on.

'First of all, there was the field of medical equipment. The company already made heart-pacers and kidney machines. In fact, two years ago they tried to sell off this part of the company to a firm that we discovered was part of a larger medical-supplies combine that was already ripping off the National Health Service for drugs. If they had sold that part of the company to them, it would have meant we'd be buying back kidney machines at international prices, with all that implies. We knew that in 1977 3,000 people died because they had no access to machines to refine the body fluids, following kidney failure. In Birmingham, all patients suffering from kidney failure, if they were under fifteen or over forty-five, were allowed, in the words

of the medical authorities, "to go into a decline". In other
words, to die at their own pace. What the families of these
patients thought about it is not on record.

'So the kidney machines were redesigned. We are still working
on the creation of a machine which will be a portable unit, a bit
like a life-jacket; and there is no reason why this shouldn't be
successful eventually. As it is, the time required for dialysis has
been reduced now to fifteen hours a week, at three five-hour
sessions, and this can be done comfortably in the home.

'At our plant in Wolverhampton, the workers discovered that
there was no way for spina bifida patients to get around apart
from crawling on the floor; and they designed a vehicle they
called a hobcart. The suggestion was taken to the company, who
refused to produce it: they said it was "incompatible with their
product-range". In the end, it was built by young people in
Stoke Heath Borstal, and then delivered by them to the patients
who were going to use them. The designer – who is one of the
most able and best-known in the country – said he found this
more fulfilling than anything else he had designed. There are
profound satisfactions to be got from answering real human
need. In Burnley, they found out that 28 per cent of people who
die under anaesthetic do so because their blood congeals; and a
unit was constructed which would prevent the blood from
clotting, but keep it flowing round the body at the optimum
speed and temperature. At that time, the deputy chief designer
at Burnley had to go into hospital for a brain operation. It was
successful, and the pump that had been designed by the work
people was used during the operation. Yet there it remains, at
the stage of prototype.

'Thirty-two per cent of heart attacks which are fatal kill the
patient between the time of the attack and the time when he
reaches intensive care. A portable life-support unit was designed
for use in an ambulance, until he could be got into the main life-
support system.

'Medical products were only one range we looked at. There
were many others. For instance the use of alternative energy
sources, wind power. It takes more energy to keep New York
cool in summer than it does to heat it in winter, which is
obviously energy being wasted on a large scale. We suggested
research into a range of gaseous hydrogen fuel cells; and we
came up with a power pack for a car engine that would reduce

fuel consumption by 50 per cent and toxic emission by 80 per cent. It would be almost silent, and could be maintenance-free for fifteen years. This couldn't be designed or built, because it hits against the ethos of the car industry. The ultimate of this ethos can be seen at one well-known company, where an engine is currently being created that will be useless after 20,000 miles or two years, whichever comes first. We came up with a hybrid road-and-rail vehicle, which could be a coach on the roads, and also use the railway network; could negotiate a 1-in-6 incline, as against the 1-in-80 of ordinary railway stock. This could have enormous implications for the Third World, and even in Scotland within the United Kingdom. In Tanzania, the railway built by the Chinese cost £1,000,000 per track mile; with the vehicle we propose, it could cost no more than £20,000 per track mile.

'Those are just a few of the very detailed and elaborate proposals worked out; each one specific, with a carefully designed programme of research and development. Everything we did had a practical relation to society. For instance, the possibility of the combined road-and-rail vehicle had been tried in the USA in the '30s; a rubber tyre and a metal rim, which was all right on the railway tracks, but when it came to transfer from rail to road it would have driven on the rim. Se we sent a turner from Willesden to look at the Paris Metro, to see if he could suggest a way round the difficulty. Of course the company frequently sends people abroad, but usually it's the prerogative of the gin-and-tonic brigade, and they were afraid that a turner going to Paris might spoil the image. But who better? The worker has a tacit knowledge that comes from the application of his own skills. He knows how to ask elegantly simple questions and to assess the design without the mystification of immense calculations and theory; he knows a great deal about practical design from the materials he handles. He has knowledge in his hands and head. And in this case, as in so many others, there was a continuity in the processes between workers by hand and workers by brain, not a great gap from over-specialization and preoccupation with a single narrow area of activity. The design that was finally settled on was two separate flange metal wheels that could be raised and lowered, so that the metal wheels could guide the vehicle on the rails, and simply be raised when the vehicle transferred to the road. It was built at the North-East

London Polytechnic. All the parts were made at Lucas. Lucas has become so vast and cumbersome a concern that nobody really knows what is being made and what isn't being made there; but even they would have noticed if we'd tried to assemble it there, so this had to be carried out at the Polytechnic.

'But of course, anything that suggests any modification of the actual system which sells the motor car, will have a very difficult time indeed. The car being the basis of the economy of the West, a whole culture of fantasy has grown around it, which has several orders of reality of its own: first there is the ad-man's reality, cars as we said with peak velocity of 120 miles an hour when there is an actual limit of 70 and, in towns, far less than that. Then there is the presentation of the car as a liberating force; it is always shown in a natural setting, on the beach or in the countryside, which implies that you need to get away from all the rubbish that oppresses you for the rest of the time. Then of course there is the issue of work: people's lives are wasted on products that are throwaway products; people have to work on things which they know are not going to last, are inferior: what does that do to a man?

'Another area we looked at was that of telechiric devices, which imitate the motions of skilled workers, but do not objectivize it into machines. This is what has happened to many of our skills. They have been taken from the worker and placed in a machine. For instance, there is now a robot which sprays car bodies, and the underlying philosophy of it is to remove the skill from him. To spray a car, you need knowledge and experience of distances and shape to be able to do the job properly, spatial judgments; and these can be dispensed with. Knowledge that existed in the consciousness of the worker is now used for tool-making, with the result that not only is the surplus value of the product taken from him, but also skills that existed in the minds of men, and which are not replaced by others. This is the experience of Western technology; and for that matter of Eastern Europe as well. The liberation which this is alleged to bring about is no such thing. It is removing the creativity and skills of people, and leaving them as functionless dependents on the machine, mere appendages of machinery; doing single repetitive actions in the service of the machine. Look at what happened with farming, how with mechanization, vast numbers of people were released for work in productive industry; and the

WHAT CAN STILL BE DONE 253

manufacturing sector increased right up to the 1950s. Since then, manufacturing has been increasingly usurped by machines; and there was a corresponding growth of white-collar jobs. Now of course that too is becoming mechanized; there are machines that do the work of 500 typists; and this is where increasing structural unemployment is becoming the experience of the whole Western world. Even West Germany, perhaps the most successful of the Western economies, has currently over a million out of work. By the end of the century, it has been estimated that in this country unemployment could reach as many as six million. This isn't a problem that is going to go away, or even get less.

'The market mechanism denies us the right to our real needs; and among those needs, meaningful work is of primordial importance. We relate to society and to each other through what we do in our work, which is not the same as the grotesquely alienated tasks of the market economy. Work is one of the most precious learning processes that we have; and to deny people that is to deny them a basic right. Knowledge, the conceptual basis of work, is being taken from people. And this applies equally to intellectual workers, designers, creators; nothing is immune against the onslaught of a mechanized usurpation of our most valuable functions. This is to reduce the capacities of human beings, not to extend them. In the Allegro plant, all human activities have been allotted an official and precise time span: 1.62 minutes to go to the lavatory, 1.5 minutes for recovery after fatigue, 65 seconds for recovery after standing too long, 32 seconds for recuperation after too much monotonous work; and so it goes on, a grotesque litany. A French company has perfected a capsule, which is soundproof, for tired executives, with programmed music according to the needs of the person and his mood. It is a personalized padded cell.

'Technology is not neutral. It is ideologically applied, not to liberate, but to subordinate. Consider this advertisement for a drug called Serenid D, aimed at members of the medical profession.' Photograph of a woman against a high-rise block of flats. The caption reads 'You can't change her environment, but you can change her mood.' 'We are being told that we must be conditioned to change ourselves instead of our environment. That is no service to human beings. People created technology, people can use it for their benefit. The trade-union movement came into being to fight one kind of oppression. It should be in the vanguard in this struggle too.'

3

IN RECENT YEARS, much of the dissent which formerly found expression through the labour movement, has taken up a position outside of it. As the trades unions have appeared to become increasingly economistic in outlook, some of the moral issues have been taken up elsewhere: in the surge of community action in the late '60s, in radical charities, Shelter, MIND, Oxfam, Age Concern. The morality of Jessie Stevens and George Hodgkinson, however rich and complex the sources that nourished it, was a simple response of outrage at poverty and degradation in the lives of working people. With the abatement of the worst of that poverty – brought about on the terms of the system that caused it in the first place – much of the morality of the old socialists has been squeezed out and dispersed in competitive interest groups, where on the whole it fares no better. They are themselves vying with each other for the same money, either by an appeal to a dwindling reservoir of altruism, or by triggering guilt in people, which has become consumer capitalism's pallid version of morality in social and personal relationships alike; guilt is a sublimation, a folk-memory of what morality ought to be. In this way morality, both inside and outside the labour movement, is about money, or as it is sometimes euphemistically described 'resources'. It is the ultimate colonization, and it leads to acquiescence or cynicism or despair. One trade-union leader said, 'The most beautiful four letter word in the English language is MORE.' In this, the values of the trade-union leaders are at one with those of their masters. 'I don't think there is any limit to people's capacity to consume. You can never have too much comfort in life.' But the most usual response of trade-union leaders is to live off the moral capital of the past. 'Where my parents lived, I remember the dirt, going to bed dirty. We had a bath once a week. I don't want that for my children, they have a bath every day.' 'We had orange-box furniture, I can't feel very romantic about that. I don't think the changes in working-class life are anything to lament at all, people do get all emotional about it, but then people get emotional about all sorts of things. Where I come from, Temperance, if you please, saw people in a passion at one time.' 'Working-class culture? What was it, brass bands, a bit of singing, not much. I think it was a result of the geographical isolation of working-class communities, a lack of mobility. If there'd been a coal mine at Piccadilly Circus, I don't think there'd have been much working-class culture there, do you?'

But the need for a sense of purpose and commitment to something of moral worth is still there, often stronger and more deeply rooted in those who do not occupy positions of power than in those who are supposed to lead them.

A 1930s council house. Grey slate roof and raw red brick of an East Midlands town. The garden is well tended, but the last chrysanthemums have been touched by frost and their bronze colour has faded. Many of the adjacent gardens are wild and overgrown with dead grass and thistles. Next door some pram wheels and an old mattress have been overturned in the mud, and the curtains at the front windows have been pinned together with a safety pin.

Ken is in his late fifties, slight and balding. He always wears a tartan muffler, a sports coat with leather patches at the elbows, boots and grey flannels. In his garden there is a chicken run, made with old pieces of wood and rusty netting. The area where the hens walk is arrow-marked, and there are tiny feathers everywhere. The back garden is long and runs into some allotments at the bottom. Outside, there is a coal store and a shed, which is a workshop, where Ken mends his own shoes, makes things he needs, repairs pots and pans, assembles radios. There is a row of Savoy cabbages, almost blue in colour, some of them silvery from the trails of slugs. In the back porch some onions are drying, and a wooden box full of carrots and parsnips. In the cellar there are sacks of potatoes. The kitchen is plain, with a piece of coco matting, an old deal table and a comfortable armchair. The living room has an old-fashioned sofa in faded plum-coloured plush. There is a chenille curtain at the door and a draught-excluder. A coal fire burns in the hearth, and there is a patchwork rug in front of it. There is a row of family photographs on top of the upright piano. On the mantelpiece a clock from the 1930s and two orange-and-buff-coloured jugs, and two brass candlesticks.

'I've worked in factories all my life, and I'm nearly fifty-eight. That's forty-four years. I was a skilled man. I was apprenticed to a real craftsman, one of the finest in this town. I used to cut out the uppers of the shoes with a clicking knife. Most of it is done by machine now. I was made redundant twice, and I could see it coming a third time, so I left the boot and shoe. I didn't want to, only you could see what was happening – they were importing shoes from all over the place, bits of rubbish glued together, wouldn't last five minutes. That shocked us you know, because we'd always done quality work. They tell you your job can be done better by a machine, you know it's not true, but it still hurts. They try to make you feel it's your fault if you can't keep up with the machine. I wasn't going to be made inferior to a great lump of metal. Something goes from your life. It's not new, not in our industry anyway: ever since they tried to resist the Blake sole-sewer over a hundred years ago, men have tried to fight against their work skills being taken away. Only now it's gone so far, it seems there's just an élite of those who design and make the machines, and an army of machine-minders.

'I still like going to work, only now I enjoy the company of the people more than what I do. Working-class people are defeated before they start. They accept their subordination. Look at this estate. It's a horrible place. People don't notice where they live. I look at the kids coming out of these houses in the mornings, the boys as well as the girls. They really are beautiful people physically, they're healthy, clean and attractive. There were some poor little scraps around when I was a kid. But you watch them. They'll buy a can of Coke and then just throw it down in the street. They'll just drop everything they've done with, cigarette packets, bottles, paper, anything. Their own pride in themselves implies a contempt for everybody else. They seem unaware of other people. They don't know anything – yes, that's not true, they know everything; but they understand nothing. They're more sophisticated than we were, but they don't have a scrap of feeling for anything that doesn't affect them personally. They're hard.

'The working class hasn't maintained its opposition to capitalism, even in its own organizations. We've got capitalist trade unions now. Their aims and their masters' aims aren't so far apart now. You're not fighting society in a trade union now, you're not asking any questions; you're part of another bureaucratic machine.

'I've seen some terrible things in factories, cruel things. Doing piece-work, I've seen operatives injured at the bench, and nobody willing to leave off work for a minute to help them, for fear of losing a bit of pay. When the firemen were on strike, I saw one of them on television, he said, "Oh, yes, of course we have a conscience about people being burnt to death, but a conscience doesn't pay the mortgage." It's the juxtaposition of those two things – my mortgage, somebody else's death. Once you have to ask for money on those terms, well it's not my idea of a crusade. I don't blame them, they only echo the ideas their betters put there. But I wish I could hear some trade-union leaders say they'll fight to preserve the dignity of work, the value of a man being what he does. I'm not saying we don't all have a right to a decent living; only a decent living is impossible in the society we've got. You might have a rich living, you might be gorged on the fat of the land, but will it be decent? If everybody in the country had £1,000 a week, would that make it decent? I doubt it. We'd have a lot more of all the things we've got already; and what we've got is selfishness, a sense of futility and violence.

'In my lifetime I've seen working-class people become more cynical. People actually get through their lives without believing in anything. Now when I was young, the labour movement had a meaning; it had a moral content. It could challenge the morality of capitalism, and appeal to something in us that was generous and magnanimous. I've watched working-class pride and self-reliance and sharing get invaded by meanness and cruelty; the vices of our superiors in fact. I've seen us get polluted, morally, over the years. I don't mean like the Whitehouse brigade, it's much worse than that. What the working class had to oppose to capitalism is running pretty thin now.

'In 1945 I was a Communist. I'm not now. I'll tell you what made me a Communist then. My mother worked as a domestic servant up to the '30s, with a family that was quite well known in this town. And the old man took a liking to her. He got to be frail, he lived into his nineties. He was bedridden for the last ten years of his life. There was some affection between him and my mother, quite innocent of course. He was an old Tory, a very

humane man, and he always took an interest in my mother; he
was a bit of a father-figure, her own hadn't been up to much.
Even after she married and had a family of her own, she used to
go up every day and get a meal for the old boy. Every day of the
week, Sundays as well, oh, it went on several years, until in the
end he got too weak, and had to go into a nursing home. And
when he died, they said there was a lot of money. He'd got three
children himself, and at that time, two of them, daughters, were
still living in the town. When he died, these two daughters came
to our house one day. I was only a little kid. We lived in Myrtle
Street, little terraced house. These two women came in a motor
car, what a performance. The whole street turned out to look at
them. Like a visit from royalty. They said they wanted to speak to
my mother. She showed them into the parlour, and they were all
dressed up, lovely coats and veils. I can see my mother now. She
had her pinafore on when they arrived, and was holding a knife
she'd been peeling some vegetables with. She was trembling, she
could hardly get out what she wanted to say, a bit incoherent.
She wasn't normally like that, it was just the effect they had on
her. They told her they were contesting the old man's will,
taking legal advice. They said she'd preyed on him and
influenced him over his will, and they expected it would come to
a court case. Do you know how much the legacy was? It was
£750. I found out later that by the time everything was paid off,
he hadn't left so much anyway, and these women had spent it in
advance, sort of thing. I decided there and then that these
people were my enemies. Of course my mother gave up any
claims to the money without waiting for any further pressure on
her. She was terrified. She was rather a deferential sort of
person, came from the country. I do believe that she had no
thought of influencing the old man when she was looking after
him. She was a tenacious sort of person; for her it was the thing
to do to carry on what she thought of as a sort of commitment
after she was married.

'She died when I was thirteen. That was a terrible experience.
I'd got two sisters younger than myself. My dad went to pieces.
Our Eileen used to say he went to lots of pieces, any piece as'd
have him. I felt if I didn't keep the family together he would
never be able to. Mother was only forty-three. Bronchial
pneumonia. It flared up in a couple of days. It was quite
common in those days. There was always a crisis day, and if you

survived that, you were all right. . . . The mothers used to stop
their children from playing in the street when they knew there
was one of these crises going on. They'd put sacks down even,
straw. Everybody sort of went round on tip-toe till you knew one
way or the other. It's things like that; you can't imagine what
that means to somebody who's going through it, everybody sort
of shared the tragedy with you. . . . Anyway, two days later she
was dead, lying under a sheet. I did grieve for her. I reckon
losing her was what stopped me ever getting married. I don't
think I could risk another loss like that one. I didn't want to bear
it. I know that's wrong, it's a terrible thing to say, but there you
are.

'I've always kept something back. I'm out of my time, I'm a
working-class intellectual. When I was young there were a lot of
them, these men who'd taught themselves everything. I've been
lonely, I've never really taken part. I feel I see things clearly, but
I'm not a doer.

'In my lifetime I've seen the cleansing of capitalism. In the
'30s, you knew where the threat to your livelihood came from,
you could identify poverty and hunger easily enough, and you
knew what caused them. Well, when capitalism started to deliver
some of the goods, all that changed. Capitalism is the goose that
lays the golden eggs, and people are set one against the other in
competition for them. Only of course, there's no such thing as
golden eggs, it's an illusion.

'If our materialism was harnessed to serving people, that'd be
different. Only life itself would have to change, radically. You
see I'm a bit of a Puritan, and that's the worst thing you can be in
a society of throwaway products. When you hear people saying,
"We must get rid of this ingrained English puritanism" what
they mean is they want to sell you some gimmicky piece of
rubbish. They want us to live in the present, because that way
you can forget the past, and you can start to believe in happiness
on earth. I don't believe in that. I don't think it's possible. I
think you can be less miserable, but that wouldn't do for all the
advertisers and hucksters and salesmen: it's their business to sell
happiness, and we're there to buy it, and maybe wonder why it
doesn't work. They sell everything.

'It seems to me there's no guarantee that the working class
will throw off their oppressors; it's much more likely we'll start
on each other. I've seen the loss of that old working-class

solidarity, I've seen it supplanted by individualism, and people go along with it. More and more productivity deals to throw more and more people out of work, while bigger and bigger corporations take more and more control over your life. Products get more standardized, you get whole populations becoming more and more homogeneous, in a way that no socialist collectivism ever envisaged: you get total sameness, sameness of ideas, parroting prejudices – it's far more effective than if it had come from any State ideology. When I walk round the supermarkets, I wonder how many products come from the same company; how many basic needs have been taken over by all the monopolistic providers.

'The pull towards some sort of collective values is so strong that people are going to reach out for it anyway, however much you talk to them about the supremacy of the individual. That's why you get something like the National Front, the witch hunt: you can't offer anything else, so you get the community of death. Instead of fighting human suffering, you kill men and think you've actually conquered it.'

4

A GENERATION OF people who came from the working class have arrived since the last war at positions of prominence in the media, administration, the arts and professions like teaching and social work; and they have communicated an idea of the working class which, because of the authority with which they express it, is felt to be accurate and incontestable. Such people still carry about them a faint whiff of anarchy and heroics: to come from the working class was once considered a dangerous and significant journey. There has developed a sub-culture that is not working class, so much as a freemasonry of those who have come from it; a quite distinctive sensibility. People who belong to it recognize each other immediately. They have the air of exiles, of those who remember a distant country or a vanished age, like failing Edwardians, people who fled from Vienna in the '30s or St Petersburg after the Revolution. There is a tendency for such people to use their working-class experience as a kind of accomplishment; and they can be seen in any staff room, ageing *enfants terribles*, frightening the bourgeoisie, in the form of outraged schoolmistresses, who even now, will sometimes rise to the tired banter and the flagging posture.

The concept which these people have propagated has become ossified with time. It is often isolated from any contact with current working-class life. In practical terms, it often means little more than dwindling contact with scattered siblings and elderly parents; or else it is enacted in symbolic institutional ways, by those who teach in poor schools or who write novels and memoirs about a way of life which they have not directly experienced since childhood.

The views of such people are felt to be authoritative. They have a special title to speak on behalf of a class whose leaders they would certainly have been at a less mobile time. But those views are already an alloy of other elements: memory, guilt, fantasy and ideology are as likely to have influenced them as any sense of the changes that have occurred within working-class experience since those people knew it as children. But their idea is widely accepted as enduringly truthful.

It is perhaps conveyed most graphically in working-class writers, novels, autobiographies and plays; and, more recently, in television drama, especially the *Play for Today*. The result of this, which naturally involves writers expressing their own experience, and childhood experience at that, is that there is a time-lag between the 'reality' that is offered; with the consequence that the life of a generation earlier than the present is often believed to be an authentic reflection of contemporary experience. Perhaps the best example of this is *Coronation Street*, which, although clearly authentic, was an evocation of a way of life already in decline when it started. Its continued popularity is as myth, as much obscuring as illuminating changes in working-class life. The *Play for Today* in the '60s was a conjunction of writers evoking their past with the help of actors separated from their origins – a straining after authenticity which created some strange effects, like the broadening of local dialect to a degree beyond that to which it is actually heard in the place portrayed. These tendencies towards archaism have been reinforced by the obsession with period reconstructions: the General Strike, a Welsh coal-mining community, a meticulously detailed portrait of life in the East End or Tyneside, or in service, or during the war. The effect of this exposure of working-class life to mass audiences is to distance it even further from those whose lives it is supposed to reflect. People know that it all bears no relation to the way they live now, but they recognize their past, and the experience becomes consigned to history. Poverty and oppression, even the working-class struggle, are shown to belong, inaccessibly to the past. The events are frozen and remote from us. It is like walking through museums in the late nineteenth century, where every object was sealed in mahogany cases, labelled and exhibited, where it cannot be touched by the fingers or the breath of the people. Our own experience has been expropriated. The working class is something we have all come from, especially the workers.

When I was at university in the late '50s, we were always telling each other escape stories, in which we were all picaresque heroes of our own lives. No generation of eighteen-year-olds ever had such a long biography, as we described our avoidance of the worst fate we could imagine, which would have been to have to stay where we had been born, geographically and socially. This was in spite of the sympathy we professed for the people we came from. But apart from that, it was not so different from the awful tales which newly arrived petty bourgeois people might have told each other fifty years ago, people who had managed to pull themselves up by their own efforts from the sump of poverty and ignorance into which they had been born. We retained a notional sympathy with, and not horror of, the class we had come from. We regarded ourselves as mobile, and the rest of the working class as static. But we were going to vindicate them somehow, represent them, look after them, make sure they were not neglected as they had been in the past. We didn't see that the movement that had propelled us out of our class had profoundly altered them too.

Most local communities have observed an increase in interest in their past. Local libraries sell pictures and prints of places as they were; much community publishing like Centerprise, WEA classes, extra-mural adult-education classes have encouraged individuals to write about their own life experience. Many older people have been listened to and tape-recorded by historians in search of a new kind of authenticity. Older working-class people can talk of themselves when young as though they were talking about someone else. It is as though a whole generation had survived its own death, and can talk about their lives as though everything that had happened in them had occurred in a previous incarnation. And this is what has happened. The social beings they were have died; and they have lived through a social resurrection. Their experience is felt to be of no use to the lives they lead now; even less so to their children. It is being garnered up by social historians, artists, teachers, sociologists; and in the process it becomes fixed and hardened. This congealing of past experience acts as a powerful agent of control. It is a foil to the way we live now; a frightening spectre which has such force that it cows us into acceptance of all the negative changes that have accompanied the positive ones. It shows what a divide has been crossed, and demands uncritical acceptance of all that is now, even those things that are inimical to our comfort and well-being. It demonstrates to us the advances that have been made, how different our function is from that of ill-rewarded subsistence labour. Our society has become distanced from its own past by means of something more than the passage of time, which gives the impression of profound and radical change. We can look at the cruelties and degradation of a mere two generations ago from a position of a vast subsequent enlightenment; and this acts as an insulating barrier, a mystifying discontinuity between past and present: a hiccough in history. We believe that everything has changed for the better, and accept that we can't have improved material conditions without their accompaniment of violence, greed and loneliness; and the fact that it is still the same society is somehow obscured. If that society now takes on a more caring, maternalistic, giving aspect, its connection with the earlier denying ruthless past is no longer clear. The archaic impressions of the earlier time only buttress the idea of progress, improvement and beneficent change.

But the ossifying of the past working-class experience has another effect. Because those who are now the humanitarian liberal administrators, those in the caring professions and public service, saw poverty as the only element in capitalism which adversely affected people's lives, the new materialism over which they preside is sacrosanct. They are the benign and well-meaning givers, who believe that the greatest social reformer is prosperity, no matter on what terms it is achieved. And because the alleviation of poverty was a great humanitarian cause, they do not see when humanity is no longer served by what has become a cruel and undignified subservience to those things which were intended to release us from the tyranny of poverty.

When these people were crusading for reform, their ogre was the harsh employer, mill- or coal-owner, singing praise to his Maker on Sundays and degrading his work people the rest of the time; but today they are his equivalent (or at least his substitute), praising humanitarian values, and at the same time making the way easy for a new kind of brutalism and savagery. If theirs are the predominant values of the media, the official ideology of the welfare state, working-class people see in them the same hypocrisy they saw in the old employers; and the reaction against this is to be found in the cynicism and resentment, violence and dehumanized attitudes towards others. The scene is set for an ugly and deformed distortion of the working-class struggle; only this time, the oppressors are seen as the proponents of liberal values, and the villains aren't foremen, landlords and bosses, but blacks, deviants and Reds.

5

SOME RADICAL DISSENTING groups feel that the labour movement has been incorporated, however uneasily, into capitalism, and that the struggle now has to be taken up from a position outside the values and beliefs which are shared by capital and labour – the primordial importance of maximizing wealth, and arguing only about its distribution – an objective which has become superseded and dangerous in the societies of the West, confronted by a world of overpopulation, limited resources and the wider diffusion of nuclear weapons. Tom Burke, of Friends of the Earth, says:

'We don't have a manifesto, we are a pressure group. I want to change the world I live in because I live in it, and after all, we have a basic concern for survival. Perhaps the most important event in human history took place on 6 August 1945. The question now is actually the survival of the species. Hitherto, it has been a question of individual survival. Over the last hundred years, the fact is that over a wide range of societies, the State sees itself as responsible for the survival of individuals. That is a remarkable change, and goes very deep. I think you have to distinguish between the spread of change and the depth of it. For instance, I don't think that the dependency of people on consumer goods goes very deep: in a crisis, people would soon learn to do without certain things which they may at another time appear very attached to. I don't think the principal argument now is about poverty, or even necessarily about the ownership of the means of production; it is about survival. There has been a failure of the imagination on the Left. There seems to me no reason why socialism should necessarily always be in the vanguard; less still the working class. The Left is perhaps shackled by its historical analysis. I think there was a question Marx didn't ask, which was not about the ownership of the means of production, but the purpose of it. In a world of such amazing technological possibilities, it isn't just a question of making and distributing wealth, at least in the West; and that's where the imagination has failed – we've failed to think of anything to do with our powers; we have ability without ambition, resource without reason.

'We don't have a rhetoric or a programme, but I can indicate what I think we ought to do. They are not my ideas, but they are part of a current flow of feeling that belongs to all of us who feel like this; and we are of course international in our scope. I think that all our slogans would be gentle ones. We may sooner or later have to produce our ideas in written form, but at the moment we simply have an idea; in the same way that Marx had a powerful idea when he said, "From each according to his means, to each according to his needs." Perhaps an idea is more powerful in that form, while it has the ability to inspire and move people. We certainly see a lot of enthusiasm and optimism. What has to be restored to people are things like worth and dignity – words that are a bit embarrassing in the present atmosphere. I think one of the most important things to be resisted is the loss of a sense of place with people – the aimless mobility, the loss of the sense of community, the uprooted nature of our life is very oppressive. This has to be stressed, that the place where people are is not arbitrary but crucially important to them. People feel that everything is too momentous and complicated for them to be able to do anything; they have such a sense of their own unworthiness, quite unreasonably of course. Instead of people being dependent on great centralized systems of production and employment, it seems much more reasonable that everybody should have a bit of land, provide some of their own food and then work only three or four days a week. Be made more self-sufficient in every way; be given capital – rather than trying to reform people, we should start with what we've got. Give people solar-energy panels, rather than have them rent their energy from the State. There's nothing wrong with people owning their own home or having a chance to make money if they want to. But our powers are there to serve us not to ensnare us. The change has to begin in the developed world, you can't expect the Third World to take the lead in moderating demands.

'Our current model of affluence derives from a world view that has dominated Western civilization, and thus the whole (unconsulted) world for the last 400 years. It is a view that saw itself in a limitless world full of vacant spaces (the original inhabitants were by and large not counted) and untapped potential. It reached its culmination in the euphoric growth mania of the '50s and '60s – the era of conspicuous consumption and the throwaway society. That world view began to change, widely and fundamentally, in recent years. The quick and continuing succession of population explosion followed by environmental crisis, together with the increasingly apparent failure of growth to relieve poverty or to guarantee happiness, has shaken the confidence of such a view to its roots. The awareness that we live in a limited world which we share with increasing numbers of people has grown with encouraging speed. But at the moment the dominant mood is one of confusion, as people throughout the world struggle to come to terms with these changes. Perhaps it is at just such a moment that a new idea of wealth, appropriate to the times, is most essential to give direction to our policies. An idea which we can pursue with all the vigour, courage and ingenuity with which we have always pursued wealth, but hopefully, without many of the liabilities.

'The process of constructing a new idea of what is worth striving for has many starting points, and this is just one of them.

'The new wealth might count as affluent the person who possessed the necessary equipment to make the best use of natural energy flows to heat a home or warm water – the uses which account for the bulk of an individual's energy demand.

'The symbols of this kind of wealth would not be new cars, TV's or whatever, although they would be just as tangible and just as visible. They would be solar panels, insulated walls or a heat pump. The poor would be those who remained dependent on centralized energy-distribution services, vulnerable to interruption by malfunction, sabotage or strike, and even more vulnerable to interruption by inaccessible technocrats, themselves the victims of market forces beyond their control.

'The new rich would boast, not of how new their television was, but of how long it was expected to last, and how easy it would be to repair. Wealth might take the form of ownership, or at least access to enough land to grow a proportion of one's food. This would reduce the need to earn an ever larger income in order to pay for increasingly expensive food. Wealth would consist in having access to most goods and services within easy walking or cycling distance of home, thus reducing the need to spend more time earning more money to pay for more expensive transport services. A high income would be less a sign of wealth than of poverty, since it would indicate dependence on the provision by someone else of a job and a work place in order to earn the income to rent services. Wealth would consist in having more control over the decisions that affected well-being, and in having the time to exercise this control.

'The pursuit of such a model of wealth would inevitably bring about major changes in our society. The rôle of the State would change as it became less important as a provider of services, the relationship between a person and his job would change as the importance of non-financial transactions grew. Many institutions would become redundant and new ones would need to be developed.

'But it is likely that these changes would be no more, and quite probably a lot less dramatic and sudden than those engendered by the current idea of wealth – their impact on the physical fabric of the planet would almost certainly be less. The smaller scope of the decisions involved would make them much more reversible in the light of experience than is presently the case – you cannot spend £1,000 million on building a single fast-breeder reactor and then decide you have made a mistake and don't want it any more. Not that the pursuit of the new wealth will not have problems of its own, but those problems are more soluble in human terms than the continued pursuit of the old wealth.

'The most important feature of the kind of wealth I am describing is that it makes many fewer demands on scarce resources. It would make real the possibility of a more equitable distribution of wealth between rich and poor countries, which is the basis for any lasting solution to global problems. The advantage to the developed countries would be that standards of living could be more securely maintained without the constant threat that the corrosive competition for resources could precipitate a global conflict. For the developing countries it holds the prospect of achieving that satisfaction of basic needs which is the foundation stone of development.'

However true it may be that the leadership of the labour movement does not articulate such arguments, many individuals within it do; and at the same time feel the dehumanizing pressure of the way we live now. The will to radical change is there, but because the Left no longer recognizes the cause of the pain in working-class life, it is the far Right which makes the running. The National Front arises from a real anguish; which waits in vain for the words and the passion that the Left has set aside. It was ironic that an old man dying of cancer had more feeling in the way he spoke than almost anyone else I met during the twelve months I spent with the pain of these ruined working-class communities.

MR LLEWELLYN, retired miner: 'By pouring goods and money down children's throats, you get them to expect more of the same, you tie them more securely to the system. The only thing that develops is their appetite for more. We want to give them a better start than we had, God knows, but the only way we feel we can do this is to shovel into them as much as money can buy. Of course giving, material things, it's a good instinct. It's only our way of doing it that's wrong. Working for future generations is a good socialist principle, it's another idea that capitalism has pirated, deformed and sold back to us. It's counterfeit, because you're serving profit first, and children second. The kids we are bringing up are like blind mouths, mouths and stomachs, that isn't preparing for the future; well it is, but I shudder to think what kind of a future it is we're preparing. How can you expect children, subject to the influences of television, advertising, to parents who feel they can offer them nothing better than the commodities that are our pitiful substitute for caring – how can they conjure up a meaning for life out of thin air? Because that's what it all conceals – it's a painted mask which hides a lack of any real social purpose. It isn't enough. It must collapse sooner or later. We still behave as though what was at stake was some basic sense of survival. Our survival isn't really jeopardized, that's just to make more palatable the scandalous idea that the rich must get much richer if the poor are to get a little less poor, and this is the idea we've tried to export to the rest of the world. As a principle underlying society it's pitiful. The only way we shall in fact jeopardize our survival is in our failure to curb our greed and distribute what we have fairly and equitably. So we put off the idea of a better world on to our children. They'll put it right, they'll change everything. But how can they, when they've been brought up to expect their every wish to be granted, their every need to be met before they formulate it? It's a fairy-story world. People daren't curb their children, they're afraid of them. This has nothing to do with respect for the individual, but is a greedy and arrogant demand for space and self-importance for which there is no room in an overcrowded world. People are encouraged to believe that their every wish, however trivial, however unreasonable, should not be thwarted; and if it is, they become angry and violent. In a world of shrinking resources, to foster a selfish expansion of demands and wants in a whole society of spoilt children is to undermine the very future which you think you are bequeathing them. It is deeply unfair to the children. They deserve something better. It's all happened so fast. Children just tear things apart, gut them, suck the orange dry. I've seen that change in my lifetime. It seems to me that what we strove for when I was young, what we wanted was a decent distribution, humane and equitable; we came close to it, but somehow we got diverted from it, and instead we have this travesty of our ideal. Freedom of choice is something limited to a very narrow and petty range. You're not free to choose an alternative form of society. Choice can only be exercised within a system that creates needs in order to answer them; or rather, it creates the answers and then kindles the needs. It is in fact the freedom to be as we are. All basic human needs have been pre-empted, and the market all sewn up for their fulfilment – the fact that they are all marketable is perhaps the sorriest reflection of all.

'It is a sad thing, we have to start from scratch. All over again.

What we fought for in the old days has receded so far from us; even the issues have been forgotten. It seems a shame. I thought I would see socialism in my lifetime. It looked like it, even in 1945. We've got to start all over again. I shan't be here to do it; but there will be those who will.'

EPILOGUE: GOING HOME

WHEN I GO home, it is still to the central part of town, a place of closed-up houses, cracked pavements, fallen lintels, shreds of dingy curtain flapping through broken glass; a place for most people to pass through on their way from the shopping centre to the new suburbs.

In winter, the empty streets seem to express more strongly the absence of the boot-and-shoe workers they were built for. The houses, where the outworkers used to sit huddled over their iron lasts in the cold back rooms, look out onto a building site, where some new flats are going up, the Occultique shop, the Romanesque towers of a Methodist chapel, the ochre sandstone of a decayed eighteenth-century courtyard. After weeks of rain the brick is so red it seems to bleed into the dark afternoon. Some snowflakes trouble the eyes of the old women as they walk against the wind, holding their coats, pausing to marvel at the bitter weather, as though snow in January were the most unexpected thing in the world.

Many of the people I visit when I go home now are old. Some are relatives, others retired boot-and-shoe workers I have made friends with over the years, some are the parents of school friends who have left the town. Often I know what we will talk about, but it is reassuring to confirm that people's testimony is unchanged by absence or the years.

First of all I call on Mrs Wallace in her house that adjoins the former Regal picture palace. When I was at school her son was an object of great envy, because he could lie in bed and listen to the soundtrack of X films until half past ten every night; indeed, they had no choice. Mrs Wallace has always worked for the Labour Party; and although many of the things she fought for appear to have been fulfilled beyond anything she ever dreamed, she is still disturbed by a sense of apparently baseless disappointment. 'I go to the Unity Adult School twice a week now. They're Quakers. When I was young, it seemed that all we needed was to improve the material conditions of people's lives. But now I feel we need some spiritual alternative to the materialism of the world. The old Workers' Educational

Association used to be a very humanizing experience, but since the university took over, it's not the same. The WEA didn't deny the value of working-class life and feeling.' As she talks, something seems to focus itself more clearly: it was on the basis of that life and feeling that she fought for improved conditions; but that improvement, when it did come, was imposed from outside. Does it matter, she wonders, whether it should have been a concession or whether it should have been won on terms determined by the people themselves.

Then I go to see Mrs Ashley, now well into her eighties. She lives on the top floor of what are still called the new flats, although they've been there for twenty years. I am disappointed to find she is not at home, and I leave a bunch of freesias in the flap of the letterbox; at that height the wind rustles the paper and shakes the fragile flowers. I feel cheated. I want to hear again her account of her father's travels to Australia when it was still a penal settlement; her memories of the blisters on his craftsman's hands from having to break stones for the road. She herself started work at twelve as an errand girl for a shoe operative; she was observed by a foreman to be a good worker, and became a dresser of the uppers – shaping them and cleaning them with polish and chemicals so that they were ready for sale. Later, she dressed the shoes for display in shop windows in Regent Street: it was a skilled job to tie the laces properly and trim them with satin. She stood at a bench for forty-eight years. The firm where she worked made two fortunes out of the wars, while she worked a fifty-four-hour week. 'In the boot-and-shoe, it was well-known that TB wiped out whole families. Families were known as being "TB families", and you took care not to marry into them. I was going to be married, and my fiancé was wounded in the head in the battle of the Somme. There was hardly a worker in the factory who didn't lose somebody belonging to him when the news of the Somme came through.' Mrs Ashley was married at twenty-five, and widowed at twenty-eight. Her husband died of his wounds after three years of pain. 'I've worked for the union all my life. We had to form the branch secretly at first, because it wasn't allowed. We used to go at weekends into the countryside, into the peace of it, and talk about all the things we were going to do to change it all.'

I meet a boot-and-shoe worker who has just retired: the last morocco grainer in the town. He had just been down to the museum, to be recorded on tape, describing his craft. 'I retired in 1977. I did forty-six years as a grainer, and then for the last two years of my working life I was on a spraying machine, which was entirely unnatural to me. What's wrong with life today is the quality of everything you buy, and it all stems from the root source that work people have no pride in their work. Even those they call skilled, in the car industry, they're not skilled people in the sense of the word that we had to do seven years' apprenticeship, and buy our own tools of the trade. . . . But the things I've made, well I shall have left something behind me. In another twenty-five years, people still sitting on the chairs that I grained'll say "Well the chap as grained these lays up Milton Crematorium now". . . .

'When I think, it's a sad story, the last two years of my working life I earned more money on a secondary job, and I was thankful when I took my smock off and retired. I finished up on this machine that sprayed all kinds of leather, calf, buffalo calf, goat, where my job was to grain the skins, a highly skilled and hard job, a hand grainer. You had to have a lot of stamina. I was a morocco grainer: you don't put the grain on the leather, you lift the grain. The skins had to be prepared by dyeing and glazing; and before glazing it was tooth-rolled in a cross-section to make the grain smaller; and then the skins were dipped in a big tub of water and left to ferment overnight; and then we grained them eight ways. . . . You learn a rhythm with your body, you go one shank, two shank over the skin with your graining board, across the belly, and from the neck to the butt and from the butt to the neck, and then you hook them up; and when you looked at it you'd think, Well that's lovely. And besides graining goats, we had what we called skyvers, that was a very skilled process, you had to learn to grain the very thin skins, which were shaved right down practically to the grain, and they were used for making Bibles and prayerbooks. To finish the leather, on light skins you would use egg albumen and milk. I've got a wallet here that I made in 1935, and I gave it to my wife, and she still uses it as she has done for forty years. For black leather, we used to have to go along to Hornby's the butcher along St Edmund's Road, and get buckets of blood, and that's how you'd do the dark skins. They used to shine like diamonds when they'd been brushed.

'It was a hard job. Many a time I've come home from work, had my tea and laid on the sofa to recuperate, because it affected the stomach muscles. You got a lot of satisfaction from the work you achieved; what you resented was the fact that you never got sufficient reward for the lovely things you'd made. They used only the best skins, which came from Madras in India; and when I went there in 1941, it gave me quite a pleasure to see these goats running about, visiting the hog market in Calcutta, I never thought I'd ever actually visit our source of supply. When the war came, it was a luxury trade of course, and we couldn't get the skins, so I had to go on other work till I went in the forces. Before the war, there were sixteen of us doing my job; afterwards we started up again, four of us, but by 1975 I was the last one left. After all these years, it's sad to see this skill that I'd acquired from older people just disappear. I'd hoped my years of experience would be something I could pass on to younger people, but financial circumstances dictated that the firm simply stopped doing this graining, and the skill is lost. When you retire, you naturally are drawn to leather shops, and when you feel this leather, it's like a blind man feeling his way on something you've offered him – your fingers tell you more than your eyes do, and it's degrading to have to realize how the quality has deteriorated. My father used to be a hand finisher of handsewn shoes; and he lived to see his skill fail; and it's funny, I've lived to see the same thing happen to me.'

My mother's oldest sister is now nearly ninety-four. She lives with her daughter, herself almost seventy, in a damp rambling house, for which they still pay only 60p rent. The stairwell is dark and rancid; two of the bedrooms are uninhabitable, the walls covered with mildew and smelling of wet plaster. Aunt Alice will not move out of this squalid place, because it provides her with her only social contact, which is the pub on the corner. She sits, wearing her hat and pinafore, to protect her clothes from the housework she is no longer capable of. She looks intently at me for a moment, almost as if she has forgotten who I am. 'You're looking older, boy.' The early Victorian square clock – the only ornament in the cheerless uncarpeted room – has disappeared. 'Oh, yes. Nice young fellow came in and gave us £5 for it. We didn't half have a weekend.' Most of the furniture was originally discarded from our house; and since we never rejected anything unless it was already worn out, going to see Aunt Alice is like re-visiting my childhood, preserved as in memory, but not exempt from wear and decrepitude.

Mr Leet is the father of a school friend. He and his wife live in a cold house in a hollow down by the river, where the mist lingers and the heavy lorries make the whole house vibrate from five o'clock in the morning. They came to Northampton in 1939, but still feel they have never been accepted by the self-contained and distrustful shoe people.

'The night before I went away to join the army, I went into the local, the Duke of York's. I was standing there with another bloke, a Northampton chap, and we were talking about going away. The landlord had got just two packets of fags on his shelf, ten of Players and ten of Woodbines. He said, "Here you are lads, as you're going away, take these." And he chucked 'em over, and I happened to get the Players, and the other bloke got the Woodbines. Anyhow, next time I went in that pub, it was four and a half years later. Four and a half years. I'd been all through Italy and North Africa. There's an old boy, sitting on the bench. He looks up at me when I go in and says, "I know you, you're the one as got the Players. Our local lad only got the bloody Woodbines." I thought, That's it, that just about sums you up. Northampton.'

My mother's sister is seventy-eight. I ask her about her first job. 'Your gran went with me. I was thirteen in March, and I had to pass the Labour exam to leave school. Your mother used to go with you to get your first job, go round the factories asking if there is a vacancy anywhere. I started work four days before everybody was due to leave off for the Easter holiday. My wage was to be 4/6. They showed me to a bench, and showed me how to tie knots. You used to have to tie all the loose ends. The machinist put the upper together, put the toe caps and vamps on, and the threads that were left hanging had to be tied and cut low. I worked in the closing room; they used the kids for knot-tying, because their fingers were small and nimble. Anyway, on the Thursday they were finishing for Easter. A woman said to me, "If you haven't done all these shoes" – and there were stacks and stacks of them – "you'll have to come back on Good Friday and Easter Monday and work till you've finished. You'll be the only one in the factory." Of course I believed it. I hated it. There were rows of machines and benches. The machinery went round on belts, steam-powered, terrible din. Horrible smell, as soon as you opened the factory door it hit you. We had a foreman who could smell a bit of leather and know what tannery it had come from. . . . I hadn't been there many weeks, and I was hurrying to work and I met a woman I knew; she said, "You needn't worry my duck, they won't need you today, your factory's been burnt down in the night." I couldn't believe my luck. It didn't last long – next day your pap had a word with his foreman and he got me on there.'

Many people are drawn by compassion to the downtown areas: social workers, reporters from local papers, teachers. They feel anger at the blighted core of the town; sadness perhaps. But there is something more here than simply the poverty of the people who remain. The passing of the old shoe-making community represents for me something beyond a subjective feeling about the ruin and dispersal of my own extended family. Somehow, that community – closed and impoverished though it was – held within itself a possibility and a promise of an alternative future; nobody wanted to perpetuate those conditions. But that alternative has not been realized; on the contrary, it has been slowly extinguished by the events of the past thirty or forty years. The suppression of the possibility of *their* change was an act of violence against them and the way they lived and the hopes they cherished. Their change was eclipsed and deformed by the change that actually occurred. Their past, the past of the people who worked in these empty factories and wasting streets, sentimentalized now in teledramas and documentaries and memoirs, has been isolated from contemporary experience. The values by which they lived – the dour stoicism, the self-denial and austerity – so hardly imposed, have become an irrelevancy. The shoe-makers, with their scepticism and reserve, going to and from work on those old bone-shaking bicycles, tending their allotments and their half-dozen Rhode Island Reds, playing darts and dominoes in their frugal pubs, everything they did is redundant in a sense that extends far beyond their industrial function.

In the uninhabited houses a spray of winter jasmine stars the sky over an old outhouse door; the bright shafts of daffodil leaves have begun to pierce the earth in an exposed patch of backyard. But the people have seen themselves die, and, wonderingly, be born again, so that they might wander in a kind of after-life through the new Grosvenor shopping centre, where the stores are open to the marble malls, and a euphoric music mixes with man-made zephyrs that strike with cruel irony against the worn-out bodies and tired spirit; and only the wolf-head emblem of Alsatian guard-dogs and the warnings that merchandise in the shops is electronically protected by Senelco, remind them that they have not, literally, died and been sent to heaven.

The old people offer a fading contact with a tradition that did contest the terms on which we live, and did suggest an alternative, in a way which the new town of Barclaycard and Avon cosmetics and Texas Homecare cannot. The only grievance which the new town can imagine is a sterile cry of insufficiency, the assertion that all we need is more of everything we have already; a proposition which, if it is true, has no need of socialism for its realization. The decay of the old industrial structure, and the changed economy of this town – like that of most others – had painful and damaging effects on the work people; effects unrecognized by those charged with ushering in a kind of plenty that was the mirror image of the poverty it replaced; and to whom it never occurred that there could be anything wrong with it.

Much of the pain and unease that persist in working-class communities, in spite of all the improvements, seems to me to be an obscure recognition of this appalling reality: our spoiled capacity for change. All the anger directed against immigrants, scroungers, the young, criminals, shirkers, indiscipline, speaks of a sombre sense of diminished freedoms in spite of all the things that are said to be evidence of their enlargement. What has been done is irreversible. These old people, with their frugality and stoicism, have been discarded; and another kind of human being is required to fit the modified system of manufacture and distribution.

In the evening, there is a meeting of the Northampton Fabian Society; a room in the club of the East Midlands Electricity Board in the town centre. I recognize many of the forty or so people present: teachers, lecturers, administrators for the most part. Many of them do not live in the town, but in the suburbanized villages in the county.

We are talking about the future of our city centres. The borough architect shows some slides of Lucca and Dubrovnik, and talks of the need for a human scale; a town councillor talks about the quality of life and the need for a concert hall in the centre of Northampton. I say that I believe people have been shifted from the central areas and replaced by shopping centres because this reflects our worship of commodities over humanity. Several people say, 'Rubbish.' 'Do you want to go back to weaving our own shirts and cobbling our shoes?' they ask scornfully; or 'Do you want to go back to grinding poverty?' 'It's misplaced romanticism, or joyless puritanism.' No, I don't want to go back to anything. It is true that material improvement was our most urgent need, but what kind of material improvement; on whose terms? Why is it, I wondered, since I have been back home I have heard so many times from so many people that they dare not go out at night; why are even the most moderate and sensible people suddenly terrified of being attacked, mugged, robbed? Why is the talk everywhere of violence and threats and cruelty; of indifference and loneliness, of the loss of friends and breakdown of community? But these things were not seen as having anything to do with our search for improved living conditions. There's no connection, or if there is, it's not important: it's the price we pay. I say that until we can look at all these things as inseparable parts of the same process, the Left will remain defensive and enfeebled. The man who attacked me most vigorously was the son of a director of the firm in which Mrs Ashley had worked at a bench for forty-eight years. As a young man he had been appalled by poverty, TB and unemployment in the courts and terraces, which she had helped him open his eyes to in the '30s. He had changed his political allegiance as a result; and those images have remained with him since that time.

On Sunday morning I visit the new part of the expanded Northampton.

Ten o'clock outside a community centre on one of the estates; a white painted hut, marooned in a waste of January mud, like a prefabricated Noah's Ark. The sun is dazzling on the empty wet roads, a scribble of silver across the dead grass and smothered fields of the Northamptonshire countryside. In the distance, the estate, with its irregular roofline, looks as if it had been sleeping like this on Sunday mornings since the Middle Ages; only five years ago it was still farmland.

Soon after ten, about twenty-five people have gathered in the temporary centre. Somehow it feels colder inside than out of doors; people's breath hangs in the air, and condenses in a silver sheen on the cold windows. There is no doubt that all the people in the room would prefer to be at home, lying in, making breakfast, reading the papers. People do not turn out so early on Sunday morning unless they have good reason.

This is a meeting of the Rent Action Group. Their aim is to get the Development Corporation to reconsider a 17 per cent increase, and have been withholding the increase for several weeks. It is apparently a single-issue campaign; but, during the two-hour discussion, the issues shift from the next move in the campaign strategy, to a vital and passionate debate about the way we live now. Why are people forced to move out of London? Why is there so little work? Why is the work that exists so unfulfilling?

For most people who come to Northampton from London and elsewhere, the move is not an act of positive choice. It is the result of years of waiting for a house, despair at ever finding a decent living place. People are guided, directed, ultimately compelled to come here by the impossibility of finding adequate accommodation where they would like to stay. There is no reason for them to feel particularly well disposed towards the town in which they have settled; the transition can be brutal from the old pressures of overcrowding and squalor to the equally chill embrace of a better life, which is so often accompanied by loneliness and debt. Their past experience has been of shared accommodation, inadequate facilities, long hours sitting in bleak council offices, unending battles against seemingly indifferent officials. Often there have been scenes of anger at home, the break-up of marriages, separation, disturbance and discomfort. Many of the people I have met in new towns were fleeing from something – alcoholism, divorce, mental illness, bereavement. One man had been cleared of a charge of manslaughter, and wanted to make a fresh start; one young family had a new-born baby which had had to sleep in a shopping basket because there was no space in their single room for a cot.

The effect of communal action on people can be very positive and exciting. In Northampton they are finding that the functional paradise of instant estates bears very little relation to human needs. There is something missing from life; only people find it hard to define what it is. The promise of a new life remains unfulfilled. One man said, 'When the time comes for me to die, and I look back on my life, I want to be able to say something more than "And then in 1976 I went to Northampton to make meat pies and get into debt." It isn't enough.' Many people who have been moved from London to Northampton or Milton Keynes or Peterborough feel passive and purposeless; the process requires people to give nothing of themselves; creativity and practical abilities alike are untouched. It is only when groups form for a common purpose that some of that energy is released. People are finding again the power of concerted action; looking for a way to mend the sense of belonging that has been broken by uprooting people and flinging them arbitrarily across the countryside like seeds scattered on the wind. 'They want us in these little boxes, up to your ears in wall-to-wall carpet and debt, not knowing anybody outside your family, and listening every night to the gospel according to the TV.' The experience of doing something together unlocks possibilities that had remained hidden; which these new towns seem designed to keep hidden. One girl I spoke to said, 'You go into people's houses and they say "Shh, here's *Coronation Street* coming on"; and they talk about the people as if they were more real than the people who live next door. Well they're not my bloody friends and neighbours. Your real neighbour could be lying dead on the floor for all you know, and you sit there wondering what's going to happen in the next episode.'

A man in his forties, out of work: 'I'm a one-parent family; bringing up two boys on my own. My wife died. It was only chance that made me finish up in Northampton. And this is the attitude. People don't think of Northampton as their final destination – it's just another stage on the way. The only trouble is, nobody knows where to. My neighbour flitted last week. Left me the key, a houseful of stuff on HP. Invited me to help myself. People are leaving all the time. There's a woman a few doors away, she's on her own with young kids. She's been putting music on at six in the morning, full blast. So her neighbour sends for the police. Well to me, that's a cry for help, not a case for the police. But this is the attitude.

'When I was coming up here, they said, "This is the city of tomorrow." I took one look and said, "If this is the city of tomorrow, God help us by Thursday."'

Alex Gower came to Northampton from Newham. 'I was living with the wife in my father's Off-licence. There were ten of us living in the house. There was my sister with her husband and baby sleeping in one room. They'd put up a partition, so it made a sort of separate room for the baby, plywood partition. Well my wife and I had to sleep in the partitioned bit of the room, and they had to have the baby back in with them. You could just about get a bed into our part of the room, and that was it. I kept going to the Housing Office. The wife was ill; we had a letter from the hospital. Not enough points to get a place. All the time, they kept shoving these pamphlets at me, "Come to Milton Keynes," "Start a New Life in Northampton". They said if I could get a job up there I'd be guaranteed a house. I came up to Northampton: 1,600 unemployed. Wild-goose chase. In the end it was my wife who got a job as a telephonist here; that was how we got our house. Then a couple of days before we were due to move, I got offered a job at the same firm as Jean. They wrote and said that a bloke had got killed who was working there, and so his job was going: £44 a week before tax. I had to take it. I couldn't get a job in my trade. At the moment I'm doing semi-skilled engineering, metal-tubing inserts for the suspension in Ford and Renault cars. It was a non-union firm. We had to change that. They employ a lot of young kids, £28 starting at sixteen, that's all right, they think it's great, they only have to give their parents a fiver a week for their keep, then when they go out on Friday nights, they've got £20 to spend. But the maximum for an adult is £36 basic. By working a fifty-hour week, plus Phase One and Two, I can get £57 a week gross, about £40 to take home. Rent and rates are £11.24. Now they want a 17 per cent increase, when wage increases are limited to 10 per cent. I'm not paying that. What they're trying to do is put the rents sky-high, so everybody has no real choice but to buy their house. They don't want the bother of maintaining them, collecting rents. Force you into buying; then the finance companies and the banks have got you in their control, and you're off the back of the Development Corporation. That's what it's all about.'

People feel they were driven out of London by intolerable living conditions; and then, when they get to the new town, they find every penny they earn is spoken for in advance, before it even reaches their pocket. 'It's either rent increases or food, and I'm not starving my kids for the sake of the Development Corporation. Who elected them, anyway?' 'When I told them I wasn't paying the increase, they said the amenities provided by the Corporation had to be paid for. I said, "What amenities? Shopping? Transport? Adequate lighting? Where is it all? Open spaces?" I wonder how much it costs to turn a bit of field into an open space?'

Most of the people who come to Northampton from London do not come primarily for work, but for accommodation. Often they say the work is secondary, and like elsewhere, increasingly arbitrary. Newcomers and native population have this experience in common, that work is seen, not as having a value in itself, but as a means to an end, money. Few talk of creativity or enjoyment in what they do, and many spend their working life resenting the product they make, despising the service they perform. The old boot-and-shoe workers are recording their work experience for the local museum; their skills have been superseded, their past mummified in their own lifetime. Because those skills were acquired at a time when they were inadequately rewarded, they were felt somehow to belong to poverty, and as such, not worth retaining. As the poverty receded, so the skills went also; and it was scarcely noticed that one of a man's fundamental claims to dignity had been forfeited – the right, not just to any work, but to work in which he can express himself, apply his creative and uniquely human power. And now, the reverse of this has been achieved: we believe that our affluence is inseparable from the resentments and frustrations that are so much in evidence everywhere. We are doubly deluded: on the one hand, the market-place cannot provide the happiness it promises; and on the other, our creative skills, which could provide something more modest but more real – a sense of worth – have been taken from us, and locked in the machines that have displaced us. It is these two processes which together assail our humanity – the plundering of our skills, the contamination of our capacity to relate to each other except as rivals for a false and delusive happiness. It is in resistance to these oppressive untruths that people are beginning again to find a common purpose.

While I was at home, we had an impromptu family reunion, which made me feel how these processes affect some of the closest of human ties – those of kinship. The reunion was only

the faintest memory of the gatherings we used to have, because
the family is scattered now, and those of my generation have lost
contact with each other. It was an evening of semi-strangers,
cordial, but overshadowed by the more ample family parties
initiated by our parents forty years ago. There were only six of
us; and it was a random event, unlike those carefully planned
celebrations of the past, which were as inevitable as the calendar
dates on which they fell. If Sheila hadn't run into Reg in town for
the first time in seven years and asked him up for supper; if my
brother and I hadn't chanced to be home at the same time, we
would never have met together.

All our parents had been boot-and-shoe workers; all of them
skilled. Among us there was a coin dealer, a receptionist, a
salesman, a builder and a social worker. Reg is the oldest,
almost sixty now. 'I left school at fourteen and I went to work at
Sears's [shoe factory]. They used to sack you when you'd been
there three years, so they could employ younger kids, cheaper. I
got the sack when I was seventeen because I was whistling "On
the Sunny Side of the Street". Out. Up the Racecourse, there was
about 200 of us, lads like, and we got talking, and we found out
we'd all been sacked for next to nothing, just before we'd turned
seventeen. . . . I had to go to the Board of Guardians. Means test.
The one asking the questions was old man Lewis, boot
manufacturer. He said, "Now tell me, lad, how much exactly
does your father earn?" I looked at him and said, "You'd better
go and look in your books, you employ him." Oh, he didn't like
me. I was red hot in those days, I was the nearest thing to a
Communist.

'When we were lads, we used to go round the pubs on
Saturday night. Amy Jane, she stood six-foot high, stripped to
the waist, she used to challenge people to fights with her bare
fists. None of the men ever took her on. . . . The landlady of the
New York Tavern used to cook a Yorkshire pudding every
Sunday, and offered ten bob to anybody who could eat half of it.
They used to go round the doss-houses, get some poor bugger
who hadn't eaten for a week. Nobody ever finished it. She made
her pudding with duck eggs; a dozen duck eggs. Nobody ever
did finish it, and my God, there was some starved mortals
among them. Unemployment then, that's what it meant – you
didn't eat. Terrible.'

'You need it now, though. It's the only thing that'll make people do their job properly. People need discipline, it's the only thing they understand. Same as a kid. Same as a dog.'

'Trouble is, nobody wants to do a fair day's work any more.'

My brother says, 'I do. I do a fair day's work every day.' He lives in South Africa. He says he is up before dawn, and falls into bed, exhausted, every night at nine o'clock. I say that being up at dawn isn't exactly a justification for being in South Africa. There is a moment's tension, but the disagreement passes without bitterness. They all agree with my brother that Ian Smith is a hero. He paints an idyllic picture of Rhodesia, disturbed in its serenity only by 'outside influences'. He says, 'They're like children, they respond to whoever offers them the most.' I say, 'Don't we all?' My brother is going back to South Africa next week. He says he will be sleeping with a gun by his side.

'You need a gun in England now.'

'I'd use it first, ask questions later. The only thing that matters to me is my wife and kids. I don't care about the rest of the world. It's up to them to look after themselves.'

After the war, Reg had a pub. It was one of the main town-centre pubs, where all the people from the local theatre used to drink. He tells how Shirley Bassey, penniless, once spent a night in the lounge. He remembers Laurel and Hardy, what a wonderful guy Max Bygraves was. The pub was closed down in the '50s, and he took what we called in Northampton 'an outdoor beerhouse'. One day he found a gold sovereign in the till; this intrigued him, and subsequently he became one of the best-known coin dealers in the Midlands. My brother was apprenticed to a carpenter when he left school. He went to Zambia on a Government contract, and thence to South Africa, where he became a builder. The two kinsmen talked about the price of gold, the extent to which the United States could put pressure on South Africa to change her policies, without at the same time endangering the stability of gold. They said what a long way they felt they had come from their origins; how proud they felt that members of an obscure working-class family should now feel themselves personally involved in these important issues.

Reg said that business brings risks and responsibilities. One afternoon, a gang broke into Reg's house. They tied him and his wife up, and took coins valued at about £2,000. 'They tied me up in this chair, and then they tipped me over on the side. I said, "I've got a bad heart you know; if anything happens to me, this'll be murder." They were more scared than I was. They bloody soon put me upright again.'

Talk turns to violence in South Africa. My brother says there will be bloodshed. 'Hasn't there been already?' He means white blood.

Sheila and her husband Ken had been to London for Christmas. They had stayed in a hotel for four days, which had cost £70 each. It wasn't that they particularly relish arranged festivities with strangers, but they are haunted by the memory of the Christmases we all spent together with Sheila's mother, Auntie Cis. We talk about the last Christmas we were together, when Auntie Cis sang 'The Beggar Child and the Maiden' into my tape-recorder. She was already anxious and covered with bruises from the leukaemia which was to kill her the following summer. It is only Christmas that Sheila cannot bear. Then, the ghosts of the extended family that we have failed to renew become too insistent, that seemingly irreducible throng which none the less disappeared so swiftly; it is at these times that we can measure the extent of our loss; and the material consolations seem at their most oppressive and lifeless. Between us all there is a sense of shame that we should all have gone our separate ways in search of individual fulfilment, which still somehow eludes us; but at the same time, we feel helpless. It is as though we are trying to say to each other that we had no choice, no real control over the estrangement that has occurred. The awkwardness between us creates a tension, an over-eagerness to agree. We explore each other's views and feelings tentatively. It is because we are unable to confront our reluctant defection from the family place that the conversation turns to, of all things, the unwillingness to work of car workers; the scroungers on the welfare state; the need for a return to conscription and discipline; a hankering after the kind of authoritarianism that would at least, however it oppressed us, have kept us together.

The only part of the evening when we can be relaxed and secure is when we talk of those who are dead; and we share the sudden shifts between laughter and sadness that come with remembering. Reg has a special affection for my mother, because she nursed his mother through her last illness. He says to me, 'We had some good times with your mum and dad. The night they bombed Coventry, he was over there in his lorry first thing in the morning, to see what was going. He got a load of carpets, slightly singed, God knows where. On the way home, we passed a field of sheep. He stopped the lorry. He said, "They look nice, they'll never miss one of them." He slaughtered it in the back of the lorry, left a trail of blood all the way home. He could've done time for that.'

'Do you remember that time he went to Cis and said, "It's freezing cold outside, can Daisy come in for a bit of a warm?" Cis said, "Who the hell's Daisy?", you know how her mind worked, she probably though it was some fancy-wench. He said, "She's a friend of mine, she's standing out there in the cold." Cis said, "Oh, all right," and the next she knew, he was leading a bloody cow into her kitchen.'

'I know he once sent a ferret up Aunt Maud's leg.'

'What happened to the ferret?'

'I don't know. Aunt Maud survived.'

It is midnight. Reg says, 'Well I have enjoyed myself.' Tess, his wife, says 'He's not kidding. If we go out anywhere, he's generally agitating to get home by nine o'clock.'

We get ready to leave. My brother is going back to Johannesburg in a few days. I am going to London in the morning. We are somehow reluctant to separate, and we stand for a few minutes in the icy wind, looking at each other. We smile, but between us there is an unspoken pain: the scars of kinship.

Tomorrow we shall return to the things we have chosen to do: only they were choices in a context that is not of our making.

We sketch a gesture of goodbye in the cold street. But all we can say is, 'Look after yourself,' 'Don't do anything I wouldn't'. The cheerful admonition to look after ourselves has an edge of sadness, an acknowledgement that there is no one else to do it for us. To Reg Sheila says, 'Don't leave it another seven years before we see you again.'

The SCAREBUNNY

By Dorothy Kunhardt

Illustrated by Kathy Wilburn

A GOLDEN BOOK · NEW YORK
Western Publishing Company, Inc., Racine, Wisconsin 53404

Copyright © 1985 by The Estate of Dorothy M. Kunhardt. Illustrations copyright © 1985 by Kathy Wilburn. All rights reserved. Printed in the U.S.A. by Western Publishing Company, Inc. No part of this book may be reproduced or copied in any form without written permission from the publisher. GOLDEN®, GOLDEN & DESIGN®, A GOLDEN BOOK®, and A LITTLE GOLDEN BOOK® are trademarks of Western Publishing Company, Inc. Library of Congress Catalog Card Number: 84-82599 ISBN 0-307-02164-5 / ISBN 0-307-60635-X (lib. bdg.)   A B C D E F G H I J

Once there was a little boy named Tam, who lived with his mother and father in a nice house that had roses climbing up the porch.

Tam had a little garden of his own. He grew lettuce and carrots and sweet sugar peas. Every day Tam weeded his garden. Every other day he hoed it.

One day when Tam came into his garden, he saw a great big bunny eating a leaf of lettuce.

And the next day the bunny was there again. He had been having a feast. Oh, how he loved lettuce and carrots and peas!

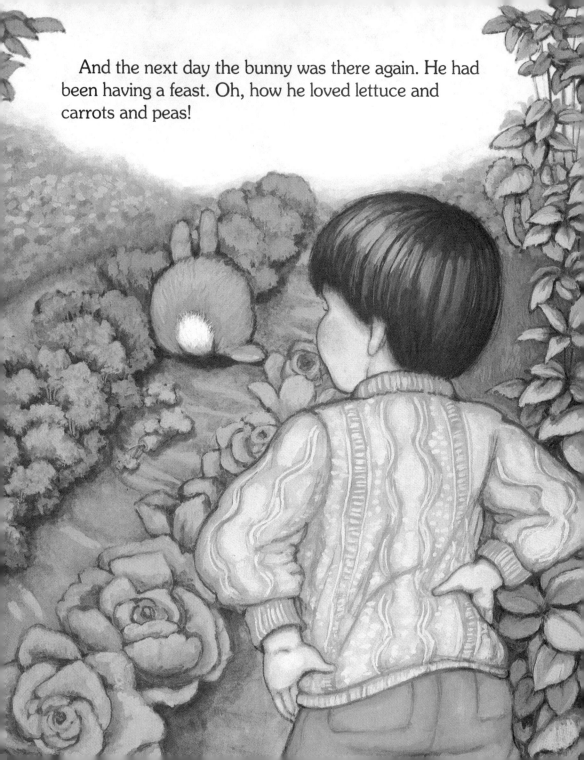

The bunny even came in the rain. Tam thought, "That bad bunny won't be here today, I know." But there he was, wiggling his pink nose and chewing fast.

"Can't you see it's raining? You'll get your fur all wet,"
said Tam. "Go away. You're eating up my whole garden."
The bunny hopped away.

Tam asked his mother, "Do you have some clothes of mine that are too old and got torn by mistake?"

"Yes," said Mother. "I have some old trousers, and a shirt with quite a lot of holes, and your big straw hat that came unbraided."

"Good," said Tam. "I need a scarebunny."

Tam asked his father to build a scarebunny out of two pieces of wood.

"If that bunny sees a scarebunny, he will think it is me, and he will hop away," Tam said.

Tam and his mother dressed the wooden pieces in Tam's old holey clothes. On top of the make-believe head, they put the hat with its straw sticking out.

"This scarebunny will frighten him, won't it?" asked
Tam.
"That's certain," said Father.

The next day when Tam went out to look at the garden, there was the bunny in a corner, eating sweet sugar peas.

And the next day he was much nearer the scarebunny, eating carrots.

And the next day he was close beside the scarebunny, eating lettuce.

Tam chased the bunny, but the bunny hopped away very slowly. He looked at Tam as if he thought Tam was a friend.

"That bad bunny isn't scared by the scarebunny, and he doesn't think it is me, and he isn't even afraid of real me any more," said Tam.

Then Tam had an idea. He divided his garden into two gardens. He drew a line down the middle with his hoe.

"Here are two nice gardens," said Tam. "I didn't need such a big garden."

Tam's father built a little picket fence around one of
the half-gardens. He left the other half-garden without a
fence.

The next day when the bunny saw what Tam had done for him, he hopped quickly to the garden without a fence and began to eat.

"One garden for you and one for me," said Tam.

The bunny wiggled his pink nose and chewed fast to show he was pleased.

Now every day Tam weeds, and every other day he hoes, and the bunny eats in his own garden, and they watch each other. They like to be together.

Now they really are friends.